Ken Hom
Chinese Cookery

Ken Hom
Chinese Cookery

The spellings of Chinese words and place names in this book follow the pinyin system of converting Chinese characters to the Roman alphabet, This system has been officially adopted by the People's Republic of China since 1979 and it closely resembles actual Mandarin pronunciation. We are now more used to seeing Beijing for Peking and Sichuan instead of Szechuan, although other names are perhaps less familiar. I have used the new system throughout except for the spellings of very well-known dishes, such as Peking Duck and *dim sum*, and for a few ingredients which are Cantonese. In the case of the better known places in China the pinyin spelling is followed is followed by the other spelling, as, for example, Guangzhou (Canton).

Acknowledgements:
I am grateful for the assistance of many of the BBC Books staff on the original edition, but especially Heather Holden-Brown, Julian Flanders, Wendy Hobson, Frank Phillips and Doug Young for their editorial and design work, and to Graham Kirk for his beautiful photographs. I must also acknowledge the assistance of Gordon Wing, Megan Jenks, Gerry Cavanaugh, Stephen Tuggle, Chris Farwell, Eva Harris and Erika Maurer. With regard to this new edition, I would be lost at the BBC without my editor Viv Bowler. It is she who has guided this book to its completion, with the able editorial help of both Rhianwen Bailey and Charlotte Lochhead; the wonderful photography of David Munns; the modern arresting design of Janet James and jacket design of John Thompson, as well as Pene Parker, Linda Blakemore and Lisa Pettibone, all at BBC Books. It is their hard work which has helped bring this classic work into the new millennium.

Published by BBC Worldwide Ltd, Woodlands, 80 Wood Lane, London W12 0TT

This edition first published in 2001
Copyright © Promo Group Ltd 2001
The moral right of Ken Hom to be identified as author of this work has been asserted.
The recipes contained in this book first appeared in *Ken Hom's Chinese Cookery*, which was originally published by BBC Books in 1984 and revised and updated in 1993 as *Ken Hom's Illustrated Chinese Cookery*.

ISBN: 0 563 53419 2

Commissioning Editor: Vivien Bowler
Project Editor: Rhianwen Bailey
Designer: Janet James
Art Director for jacket: Pene Parker
New photography for this edition: David Munns © BBC Worldwide 2001
Home Economist: Linda Tubby
Photography re-used from the 1993 edition: © Graham Kirk 1993
Home Economist: Allyson Birch
Illustrator: Kate Simunek

contents

PREFACE 8

INTRODUCTION 10

INGREDIENTS 19

EQUIPMENT 40

TECHNIQUES 44

MENUS AND HOW TO EAT CHINESE FOOD 52
Suggested menus   55

SOUP 56

MEAT 80

CHICKEN, DUCK AND GAME 116

FISH AND SHELLFISH 152
Prawns   174
Crabs   182

VEGETABLES 188

RICE, NOODLES AND DOUGHS 218
Noodles   230
Dumplings, buns and pancakes   243

SNACKS AND SWEETS 250

INDEX 271

notes on the recipes

- Eggs are large
- Wash all fresh produce before preparation
- Spoon measurements are level
- Conversions are approximate and have been rounded up or down. In a few recipes it has been necessary to modify them very slightly. Follow one set of measurements only; do not mix metric and imperial

CONVERSION TABLES

WEIGHTS

½oz	10g
1 oz	25g
1½ oz	40g
2 oz	50g
3 oz	75g
4 oz	110g
5 oz	150g
6 oz	175g
7 oz	200g
8 oz	225g
9 oz	250g
10 oz	275g
12 oz	350g
13 oz	375g
14 oz	400g
15 oz	425g
1 lb	450g
1¼ lb	550g
1½ lb	700g
2 lb	900g
3 lb	1.4kg
4 lb	1.8kg
5 lb	2.3kg

VOLUME

1 fl oz	25 ml
2 fl oz	50 ml
3 fl oz	75 ml
5 fl oz (¼ pint)	150 ml
10 fl oz (½ pint)	300 ml
15 fl oz (¾ pint)	400 ml
1 pint	570 ml
1¼ pints	700 ml
1½ pints	900 ml
1¾ pints	1 litre
2 pints	1.1 litre
2¼ pints	1.3 litre
2½ pints	1.4 litre
2¾ pints	1.6 litre
3 pints	1.7 litre
3¼ pints	1.8 litre
3½ pints	2 litre
3¾ pints	2.1 litre
4 pints	2.3 litre
5 pints	2.8 litre
6 pints	3.4 litre
7 pints	4.0 litre
8 pints (1 gal)	4.5 litre

MEASUREMENTS

¼ inch	0.5 cm
½ inch	1 cm
1 inch	2.5 cm
2 inches	5.0 cm
3 inches	7.5 cm
4 inches	10 cm
6 inches	15 cm
7 inches	18 cm
8 inches	20.5 cm
9 inches	23 cm
11 inches	28 cm
12 inches	30.5 cm

OVEN TEMPERATURES

Mk 1	275°F	140°C
Mk 2	300°F	150°C
Mk 3	325°F	170°C
Mk 4	350°F	180°C
Mk 5	375°F	190°C
Mk 6	400°F	200°C
Mk 7	425°F	220°C
Mk 8	450°F	230°C
Mk 9	475°F	240°C

preface

Chinese food has had enormous impact throughout the world and perhaps the most important influence on Chinese cuisine in modern times has been that of Hong Kong.

In 1997, authority of Hong Kong reverted to the Chinese. There was, and still is, feverish speculation about what this would mean: what the process would entail and how it would affect Hong Kong. A small island dot on the mainland coast of China, Hong Kong is not only a geographic place, it is also a state of mind. Travel writer Jan Morris called it 'the last jewel of the Empire', a 'stupendous epilogue' to imperial history. The People's Republic of China has pledged to allow things to go on much as they have been and for the vast majority of Hong Kong's people – those who must remain and carry on no matter what the future brings – the best and only option is to continue as they have done for decades, working, gambling, building and revelling in the most varied and delectable cuisine.

The opinion of food critics the world over, and I am in full agreement with this consensus, is that Hong Kong offers some of the world's finest Chinese cuisine. The concepts, techniques and recipes of its cuisine are deeply rooted in the rich and ancient traditions of the grand Chinese food culture. There are thousands of restaurants in Hong Kong and from the smallest street food stalls to the most luxurious and elite hotel dining rooms, they all share these elements: quality of ingredients, care in preparation and a serious yet playful attitude toward the necessary recreation (or restoration) we call eating. Work, gambling, shopping and sex are all part of Hong Kong life, and food, in all of its aspects, is a central element to that life. It is a topic of conversation, a serious study and a constant source of anticipation in peoples' lives as they contemplate their next repast.

Hong Kong is open to the world and is literally a crossroad of international trade, commodities, ideas and influences. It is constantly exposed to cultural influences and styles and Hong Kong's cuisine demonstrates the island's ability to receive and absorb what is best in other regional Asian traditions, as it assimilates new foods, ingredients and styles of cooking. As with so many other consumer products,

Hong Kong is one of the richest and most varied food markets and its acceptance of new food products must, I feel, be something like the assimilation into Chinese cooking of tomatoes and corn about a hundred years ago. These were alien foods that rapidly became naturalized and perfectly ordinary components of the cuisine.

It must be understood there has been no real revolution at the eating table: the grander aspects of Chinese cuisine still dominate the Hong Kong culinary scene. But the ever-quickening adoption of new ingredients, and the novel application of old techniques, are reshaping the traditional cuisine. I have noticed, for example, that Hong Kong *dim sum* dishes are lighter, with pastries now fried in oil instead of the traditional lard, and that new spices and flavourings are added, incorporating ingredients such as shrimp paste and Chinese chives. Even the venerable clay pot is now used differently, not only for braising, but also to infuse flavours in a quick and intense blast of heat.

Hong Kong is a vibrant, modern, trend-setting place. Its food trends, in particular, seem to find favour everywhere and even in China its influence is now being felt. Cantonese food, once considered too imperial perhaps, has become chic again as a wealthier and more prosperous China seeks to hurtle itself into the twenty-first century. Many regional Chinese foods are also making a comeback but with a lighter, more modern twist.

Hong Kong has played a huge role in influencing Chinese food, within China and throughout the world. Its fusion of international ingredients, flavours and techniques was what I was so keen to portray in *Chinese Cookery* when it was first published in 1984 and subsequently revised for a new edition in 1993. Chinese cuisine has a rich and wonderful heritage and Hong Kong's contribution and culinary legacy to that cuisine has made it more diverse, more accessible and even richer.

Ken Hom 2001

introduction

Good food has been an important part of my life since my earliest childhood. I well remember my family gathered around the dinner table endlessly discussing what we were to eat, how it would be prepared, what our favourite dishes were, the best methods for cooking various delicacies, and so forth. In fact this is a common experience for most Chinese — food is our favourite topic of conversation. For us food is more than a passion, it is an obsession, and good eating is believed to be essential to good living. We Chinese have an expression: '*Chi fan le mei you?*' which literally means: 'Have you eaten yet?'. It is used universally as a greeting, just as one would ask in English, 'How are you?'. It is also a wish for one's health and happiness. It is an entirely appropriate phrase since food to the Chinese has always meant much more than mere sustenance, and the processes of cultivating, selecting, cooking and consuming it are completely embedded into Chinese culture. Like all Chinese children, I absorbed a great deal of knowledge about Chinese cuisine simply by listening to the dinner table conversations of my relations. My real culinary training, however, took place in my uncle's restaurant in Chicago where I started to work part-time at the age of eleven. In those early days I had all the routine, unpleasant jobs. I remember peeling hundreds of pounds of prawns, a tedious and painful chore. I also have memories of cleaning what seemed like mountains of huge sea snails which were delivered to the kitchen in enormous burlap bags. All the time I was thus employed I was surrounded by the wonderful aromas of the mouth-watering dishes being prepared by the expert chefs. Slowly they taught me why a particular spice went with a certain meat, why this sauce suited that vegetable: in short, the essence of Chinese cooking technique.

Although my family were originally from southern province of Guangdong, my uncle employed chefs from many different parts of China. Many people think that all Chinese cooking is similar, which is understandable since all Chinese cooks share a common technique, and since so many restaurants in the West blur the distinctions between the various regional styles. But China is a vast country with great variations in climate, agricultural tradition and available foodstuffs. It is no wonder then, that there are actually many variations in culinary style within China. They can be separated into four key regional categories:

THE SOUTHERN SCHOOL This is the region of Guangdong (Cantonese) cuisine which is probably the best known in the West because in the nineteenth century many Chinese families emigrated from this area to Europe, Australia and America. Cantonese cooking is regarded by many as the *haute cuisine* of China. Some people attribute this to the influence of the brilliant chefs of the Imperial Court who fled to

Guangzhou (Canton) when the Ming dynasty was overthrown in 1644. The Cantonese are especially interested in exotic delicacies such as dog, snake, frogs' legs and turtle. The area is famous for its sweet and sour dishes, such as Sweet and Sour Pork, for its *dim sum* – a range of delicious snacks which are served as a late breakfast or light lunch – and for its widespread use of soy, hoisin and oyster sauces.

The Cantonese prefer their food slightly undercooked so that the natural flavours and colours are preserved and for this reason stir-frying and steaming are two of the most popular methods of cooking. They also avoid the heavy use of chillies, spices and heavy oils and concentrate instead on achieving a subtle, yet harmonious blend of colours, textures, aromas and flavours. Rice is the staple of the Cantonese diet and the area is known as one of the 'rice-bowls' of China.

THE NORTHERN SCHOOL This area stretches from the Yangzi (Yangtze) River to the Great Wall of China and embraces the culinary styles of Shandong (Shantung), Henan and Beijing. A distinguishing feature of its cuisine is the use of grains, rather than rice, as the staple food, particularly wheat, corn and millet, which the northerners eat in the form of bread, noodles, dumplings and pancakes. Because of the harshness of the climate, fresh vegetables are only available at certain times of the year. To compensate for this, northerners have learned how to preserve foods to see them through their long winters. Vegetables like sweet potatoes, turnips, onions and cabbages which store well are widely used and the region specializes in a range of preserved ingredients such as dried mushrooms, dried and smoked meats, and pickled fruits and vegetables. Unlike all the other regions of China, meat is in much shorter supply, although beef, mutton and goat are available as well as pork. This area contains many of China's four million Moslems who shun pork and their presence has greatly affected its cuisine.

The Imperial Court of China was based in Beijing and its influence on the culinary style of the area is still reflected in some of its more complicated and spectacular dishes such as the celebrated Peking Duck. Of all the elaborate banquet dishes in Chinese cuisine, this is the most glorious. Its subtlety and sophistication offer a distinct contrast to other more strongly-flavoured dishes which characterize northern cooking, depending heavily as it does on garlic, spring onions, leeks, sesame seeds and oil, and sweet bean sauce.

THE EASTERN SCHOOL This region stretches from the eastern coast to central China. It contains the cooking styles of Fujian (Fukien), Jiangxi, Zhejiang and, most important of all, Shanghai, which is the biggest city in China and its greatest port. The region contains some of the most fertile land in all China – which provides a rich variety of fresh fruit and vegetables – and the area is noted for its vegetarian cuisine. The countryside is dominated by the magnificent Yangzi (Yangtze) River and the coastline is very long. Consequently fresh fish and shellfish are also plentiful.

Eastern cooks prefer light and delicate seasonings to maximize the natural flavours of their fresh ingredients. The preferred cooking techniques are stir-frying, steaming, red-cooking (slow simmering in a dark soy sauce) and blanching. Soy sauce from this area is reputed to be the best in China. The region is also famous for some special ingredients: notably black vinegar, which is used both for cooking and as a dipping sauce; Shaoxing rice wine; and Zhejiang ham, which is rather like raw smoked bacon. Sugar is widely used in the cooking of meat and vegetables, as is a great deal of oil, earning this area a reputation for rich food.

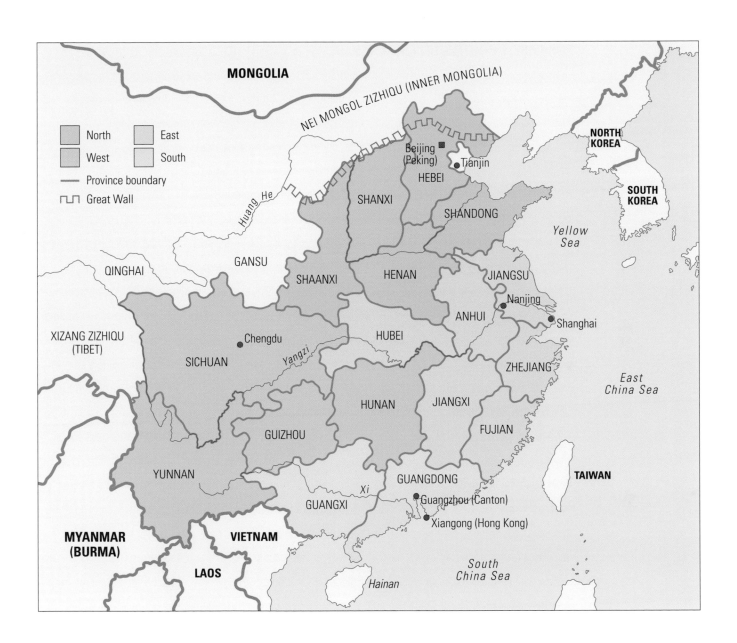

THE WESTERN SCHOOL This area is entirely inland and includes the provinces of Sichuan (Szechuan) and Hunan, the birthplace of the late Chairman Mao. This 'land of abundance', as it is sometimes called, is virtually surrounded by mountains and was almost cut off from the rest of China until this century. Nowadays Sichuan cuisine in particular is popular in the West. In this area summers are hot and sultry and the winters mild. Fruit and vegetables are plentiful as are pork, poultry and river fish. The distinguishing aspect of the culinary style is its reliance on very strong flavourings and hot spices, particularly red chillies, Sichuan peppercorns, ginger, onions and garlic. Outsiders used to suggest that such ingredients were used to mask the taste of the food which had deteriorated in the area's muggy heat. However, regional chefs stand by their cuisine and their command of the art of seasoning. Dishes from this area are usually artful combinations of many flavours and can be hot, sour, sweet and salty all at once.

CHINESE COOKING OUTSIDE CHINA The revolution in China in 1949 and its aftermath had consequences for cooking as well as profound political and social effects. Within China, the great cookery tradition became for quite some time almost moribund. Revolutionaries deemed the art of cooking an elitist and reactionary enterprise, a reminder of Imperial days and therefore best repressed.

However, in the 1980s mainland Chinese leaders decided to allow and encourage the re-emergence of the grand cuisine; an essential part of the booming business of tourism. Since then, there have been dramatic transformations with regard to culinary matters. The material results of economic reforms – especially in agriculture and transportation – and the changed political atmosphere have led to the reopening of traditional cookery schools and of privately-owned restaurants and food stalls. Ingredients that once were exported or otherwise not available are once again in good supply at affordable prices. People once again began to celebrate the seasons, special events and anniversaries with the customary feasts and banquets. In its attempt to create a new Chinese socialist nationalism, the Communist regime had banned many traditional and all regional food specialities; today, all of these favourites have re-emerged. Indeed, with the relatively improved financial circumstances of many urban Chinese, a vibrant restaurant and street food stall economy has revived. Entrepreneurs are offering to their patrons the long-suppressed delights their grandmothers used to prepare in family kitchens.

I have witnessed and experienced these transformations during the last decade through numerous visits. From being a country in which it was next to impossible to find a decent restaurant or obtain a delectable meal, China has made enormous strides towards regaining the glories of its wonderful cuisine. There are now excellent private restaurants in the major cities as well as small villages, wonderful street stall offerings throughout the country and marvellous home-cooked meals everywhere. Much remains to be done and there are still disappointing culinary experiences to be had, but the Chinese people are truly well advanced in the drive to reclaim their glorious cuisine heritage.

The grand tradition of Chinese cookery has not only survived but has been developed to a high degree of excellence in Taiwan and Hong Kong. Many food critics and gourmets now consider Hong Kong to be the greatest centre of Chinese cookery in the world. The best and most traditional ingredients of Chinese cooking flow over the Chinese border into Hong Kong, and China is Hong Kong's chief food supplier. In its eagerness to earn foreign currency, China has fostered a trade which has ensured the maintenance of traditional Chinese cooking in Hong Kong and Hong Kong's economic prosperity has supported the preservation of the best of this cuisine. In this bustling, energetic place there are over 40,000 restaurants and food stalls, all competing for the custom of the inhabitants, many of whom eat most of their meals out. Perhaps no other people in the world are so food-conscious. Even the smallest food stall sells delicious dishes of excellent quality and the top restaurants are regarded as being among the best in the world.

Indeed, I have observed the emergence or crystallization of what I call the 'new Hong Kong cuisine'. This is a new culinary style of a lighter, modern, imaginative Chinese cuisine that combines the best of the ancient Chinese canon with the most compatible influences from the best of the world's cuisines. It is a type of Chinese food that has become the favourite of restaurant-goers throughout the world.

Thanks to the recent dizzying pace of improvements in transportation, communication, marketing and travel facilities, the peoples and cultures of the world have been brought into even greater proximity. This process, to be sure, has not always meant untroubled contacts. But it is safe to say that one of the most positive and benign results of these changes has been to make available to people the world over the foods, ingredients, techniques and culinary styles of what used to be seen as 'exotic cuisines'. So it is with Chinese cookery. Today one may walk into almost any supermarket in Europe, Australia and America and find, for example, fresh ginger, bok choy and a limited spectrum of Chinese sauces and condiments.

This book contains recipes from all the cooking traditions of China as well as some from Hong Kong. It also has a section on techniques (page 44) which covers a range of the cooking methods used such as braising, deep-frying, steaming and stir-frying. If you are new to Chinese cooking, do not feel that you have to prepare a meal which consists entirely of dishes from one particular region. Instead, select dishes which will provide a variety of colours, textures and tastes. On page 55 I have given advice on how to put together a Chinese meal and have suggested menus of varying complexity. Start with some of the simple ones which will give you experience in the basic cooking methods. At first try just one or two Chinese dishes at a time, perhaps incorporating them into a European meal. Chinese snacks, for example, make wonderful starters for any meal and there are many Chinese dishes which can be successfully combined with Western-style meats and salads.

When you prepare your first entirely Chinese meal, select just two or three dishes and serve them with some plain steamed rice. Never select dishes which are all stir-fried or you will have a traumatic time in the kitchen trying to get everything ready at the same time and will arrive at the table hot and flustered. Choose instead to do one braised dish, a cold dish, or something which can be prepared ahead of time then warmed through and limit your stir-frying to just one dish. This way not only will you gain the confidence needed to try more ambitious recipes, but your meal will be all the more authentic for embracing a harmonious blend of cooking techniques.

The Chinese diet is a very healthy one since it depends upon cooking methods which preserve vitamins and use small quantities of meat and no dairy products. Underlying all Chinese cooking is the ancient *yin yang* theory of food science which is closely related to Chinese beliefs about health. In China, all foods are divided into one of three groups: *yin*, for cooling foods; *yang*, for heating foods; and *yin yang* for neutral foods. To the foreigner there is little obvious logic in the way the foodstuffs are assigned to these categories. *Yin* foods include items as diverse as beer, crab, duck and soda water. *Yang* foods include brandy, beef, coffee and smoked fish. Neutral foods include bread, steamed rice, carrots, pigeons and peaches. Not only are all foods sub-divided in this way but people are, too. A *yin* person is quiet and introverted, while a *yang* person is a more active, outgoing type. The effect of different foods on an individual will depend upon the way they conflict with or complement their personality type. The idea is to construct a meal and one's whole diet, to achieve the right balance or harmony. Most Chinese have some knowledge of the *yin yang* food science as the idea is instilled into them from a very young age.

Apart from a sensible mixture of *yin* and *yang* foods, the art of Chinese cookery also lies in achieving a harmonious blend of colour, texture, aroma and flavour. A typical Chinese meal consists of two parts – the *fan* which is the staple grain, be it rice, noodles or dumplings – and the *cai* which covers the rest of the dishes: meat, poultry, fish and vegetables. The average meal comprises three to four *cai* dishes, one *fan* dish and a soup. The *cai* dishes should each have a different main ingredient: for example, one meat, one fish and one vegetable. A variety of techniques will be used to cook these dishes. A fish may be steamed, a meat braised, while the vegetables may be stir-fried. The meal will also be designed so that each dish varies and yet complements the others in terms of appearance, texture and flavour. One dish will be spicy and another mild; one may be chewy and another crisp. The total effect should appeal to all the senses. All these dishes will be placed in the centre of the table and shared between the diners who help themselves and each other to a little of this and then a little of that. Eating for the Chinese is a communal experience and a shared meal is regarded as the visible manifestation of the harmony which should exist between family and friends.

I have made a feature of vegetarian recipes in this book, putting non-meat recipe titles in tinted boxes. Vegetarian food and restaurants are very much in evidence in China today, a tradition in the first six centuries AD from the Buddhist reverence for all forms of animal life. While non-animal foods existed before the rise of Buddhism, it did add prestige to such foods as soy, mung beans and beancurd on which much of Chinese cuisine depends.

Below:
Buddhist Casserole
(*page 214*)

The subtle and distinctive taste of Chinese food depends in part on this use of special Chinese ingredients. Of the recipes I have given here, some use ingredients which are more complicated than others. Where possible I have suggested suitable Western alternatives, but I'm afraid that if you want to cook authentic Chinese food there is ultimately no alternative but to track down a reliable source of the key ingredients. Fortunately, it is becoming easier to find some of these in supermarkets, and Chinese grocers are proliferating in many parts of the world. The section on ingredients (page 19) lists all the specialist items which I have used in the recipes and it will help you to know what to look and ask for. You may find it useful to refer to this before embarking on a shopping trip to your nearest Chinese grocer.

Your Chinese grocer may also be a good place to buy a wok. Although it is perfectly possible to cook Chinese food successfully using ordinary Western kitchen utensils, you will probably want to invest in a wok eventually to use for stir-frying at least. The beauty of the wok is that its shape ensures that heat is evenly distributed all over the pan, making for fast cooking, and its depth allows you to stir and toss foods rapidly. Equally important, you need to use far less oil for deep-frying than you would with a deep-fat fryer. Woks usually work better on gas, although it is possible to get a flat-bottomed variety which is more suitable for electric cookers. I have given some advice on choosing and seasoning a wok on pages 40-1.

There is an old Chinese proverb which says, 'To the ruler, the people are heaven; to the people, food is heaven'. Once you have embarked on the exciting road to discovering the mysteries and pleasures of Chinese cooking you will soon find how sublime Chinese food can be. The time and the conditions are both propitious for the universal enjoyment of Chinese cookery. It can be done and should be, as a part of our daily lives, both East and West. I wish you happy cooking and delicious eating.

Ken Hom

Below:
Hot Bean Thread
Noodles (*page 241*)

ingredients

China's vast size and different climatic settings have led to a profusion of edibles. Joined to a 4000-year-long culinary tradition, these factors have produced a cuisine unmatched in range, depth, ingenuity and technique. No other civilization has so delightfully exploited the food resources available to it.

Despite the size of the country and the spectrum of climates within its borders, a shared philosophical approach to food and its significances and common affinities and techniques do exist, making Chinese cooking a discernible, definable whole. Variations there certainly are, but in both theory and practice Chinese cooking clearly shares the same identity from the cold north to the subtropical south. What chiefly constitutes that identity are the special ingredients, the common techniques, and the traditional implements of Chinese cuisine.

Techniques can be learned, implements can be obtained, but authentic ingredients can quite often be elusive. Fortunately, events of the past decades have opened up the world to China's products. Today, even in the West, many of the most exotic foods are readily available. The recipes in this book were all tested with easily obtainable ingredients. You too can enjoy authentic Chinese cuisine.

The following is a list of the authentic ingredients which I have used in this book. It also includes some which were not used, but you may find on many Chinese restaurant menus. There are also some notes on vegetables and information on rice, noodles and flour. One ingredient commonly used in China which you will *not* find mentioned here is monosodium glutamate (also known as MSG, Ve Tsin, Accent, seasoning or taste powder). This is a white crystalline extract of grains and vegetables widely used to tenderize and enhance the natural flavour of certain foods, particularly meat, in Japan and China and in Western food processing. Some people have an adverse reaction to it, experiencing symptoms such as headaches, excessive thirst and palpitations. This allergic response is sometimes known as 'Chinese restaurant syndrome'. I believe that the freshest and finest ingredients need no enhancing and I therefore never use MSG.

AUBERGINE These pleasing purple-skinned vegetables, also known as eggplants, range in size from the larger plump ones, easy to find in supermarkets, to the small, thin variety which the Chinese prefer for their more delicate flavour. Look for those with smooth, unblemished skin.

Chinese people normally do not peel aubergines since the skin preserves texture, taste and shape. Large aubergines should be cut according to the recipe, sprinkled with a little salt and left to sit for twenty minutes. They should then be rinsed and any liquid blotted dry with kitchen paper. This process extracts bitter juices and excess moisture from the vegetable before it is cooked, giving a truer taste

Left:
Green beans

to a dish. The aubergines also absorb less moisture after this process. I often skip this procedure if I am using Chinese aubergines.

BAMBOO SHOOTS Bamboo shoots are the young edible shoots of some kinds of bamboo: only about 10 per cent of all types of bamboo shoots are commonly available. Fresh bamboo shoots are the best, although unfortunately they are only available tinned in Britain. These are an acceptable substitute for the fresh and are reasonably priced. Pale yellow with a crunchy texture, they come peeled and either whole or thickly sliced. They can be bought at Chinese grocers as well as in most supermarkets and delicatessens. Rinse them thoroughly before use and transfer any remaining shoots to a jar, cover them with fresh water and keep in the refrigerator. If the water is changed daily, they will keep for up to a week.

BEAN SPROUTS Now widely available, these are the sprouts of the green mung bean, although some Chinese markets also stock yellow soya bean sprouts which are much larger. Bean sprouts should always be very fresh and crunchy. They will keep for several days when loosely wrapped in kitchen paper inside a plastic bag in the vegetable drawer of a refrigerator.

BEANCURD Beancurd (opposite, left) is also known by its Chinese name *doufu* or, in Japanese, *tofu*. It has played a crucial role in Chinese cookery for over 1000 years since it is highly nutritious and rich in protein. Beancurd has a distinctive texture but a bland taste. It is made from yellow soya beans, which are soaked, ground, mixed with water and then cooked briefly before being solidified. In Britain it is usually sold in two forms: as firm cakes or as a thickish junket; however, it is also available in several dried forms and in its fermented version. The soft junket-like variety (sometimes called *silken tofu*) is used for soups, while the solid type is used for stir-frying, braising and poaching. Solid beancurd 'cakes' are white in colour and are sold in supermarkets and Chinese grocers as well as in many health food shops. They are packed in water in plastic containers and may be kept in this state in the refrigerator for up to five days, providing the water is changed daily.

To use solid beancurd, cut the amount required into cubes or shreds using a sharp knife. Do this with care as it is delicate. It also needs to be cooked carefully as too much stirring can cause it to crumble. Whatever its shape or texture, it remains highly nutritious.

BIRDS' NEST This is one of the most sought-after of Chinese delicacies. There are shops in Hong Kong and Taiwan specializing in birds' nest, which comes in all grades. It is sold dried and must be soaked before using, as instructed in recipes calling for it. The result, like sharks' fin, is a flavourless, soft, crunchy jelly that relies for flavour on the sauce or broth in which it is cooked.

Above, left:
Beancurd
Above, right:
Black beans

BITTER MELON This unusual vegetable is also an acquired taste that has as many detractors as it has fans. Even the Chinese must learn to love it. Bitter melon has a bumpy, dark to pale green skin and has a slightly bitter quinine flavour that has a cooling effect in one's mouth. The greener the melon, the more bitter its taste and many cooks look for the milder yellow-green varieties.

To use bitter melon, cut it in half, de-seed it and discard the interior membrane. Then, to lessen its bitter taste, either blanch or salt it, according to the recipe's instructions. You can store it in a loose plastic or paper bag in the bottom of your refrigerator for three to five days, depending on its condition.

BLACK BEANS These small black soya beans (above, right), also known as salted black beans, are preserved by being fermented with salt and spices. They have a distinctive, slightly salty taste and a pleasant, rich smell. Thus prepared they are a tasty seasoning, especially when used in conjunction with garlic or fresh ginger. They are inexpensive and can be obtained from Chinese grocers, usually in tins labelled 'Black Beans in Salted Sauce', but you may also see them packed in plastic bags. Rinse them before use; I prefer to chop them slightly, too, as it helps to release their pungent flavour. Transfer any unused beans and liquid to a sealed jar and the beans will keep indefinitely if stored in the refrigerator.

CAUL FAT Caul fat is a lacy membrane often used by European and Chinese cooks to encase stuffings and to keep food moist while cooking. Actually the lower stomach of a pig or cow, caul fat melts during cooking and keeps meats and fillings moist and delicious. It is highly perishable so buy it in small quantities and use it quickly. For longer storage, wrap the caul fat carefully and freeze it. To defrost, rinse in cold water. I find that soaking caul fat in cold water helps to separate the fat without tearing its lacy and fragile webs. You can order caul fat from your local butcher.

CHILLIES Chillies are used extensively in western China and somewhat less frequently in the south. They are the seed pods of the capsicum plant and can be obtained fresh, dried or ground. One must differentiate between and among the various types because, for one thing, they vary greatly in taste and spiritedness.

FRESH CHILLIES: these can be distinguished by their small size and elongated shape. They should look fresh and bright with no brown patches or black spots. There are several varieties. Red chillies are generally milder than green ones because they sweeten as they ripen.

To prepare fresh chillies, first rinse them in cold water. Then, using a small sharp knife, slit them lengthways. Remove and discard the seeds. Rinse the chillies well under cold running water and then prepare them according to the recipe's instructions. Wash your hands, knife and chopping board before preparing other foods and be careful not to touch your eyes until you have washed your hands thoroughly with soap and water. The seeds are especially pungent and 'hot' to a fault.

DRIED RED CHILLIES: these are small, thin and about 1 cm (½ inch) long. They are commonly employed to season oil used in stir-fried dishes, in sauces and in braising. They are normally left whole or cut in half lengthways with the seeds being left in. The Chinese like to blacken them and leave them in the dish during cooking but, as they are extremely hot and spicy, you may choose to remove them immediately after using them to flavour the cooking oil. They can be found in Chinese and Asian grocers as well as in most supermarkets and will keep indefinitely in a tightly covered jar. When eating out, most diners carefully move the blackened chillies to one side of their plates.

CHILLI POWDER: this is made from dried red chillies and is also known as cayenne pepper. It is pungent, aromatic and ranges from hot to very hot; it is used to enhance the spiciness of dishes. You will be able to buy it in any supermarket. As with chillies in general, your own palate will determine the acceptable degree of 'hotness' to be provided to each dish by this spice.

CHILLI BEAN SAUCE: (see Sauces and Pastes, page 32)

CHILLI OIL/CHILLI DIPPING SAUCE: this is sometimes used as a dipping condiment as well as a seasoning in China. Of course, as chillies vary, so do the oils vary in strength and flavour. You can purchase chilli oil from Chinese markets. The Thai and Malaysian versions are especially hot; the Taiwanese and Chinese versions are more subtle. Such commercial products are quite acceptable, but I include this recipe because the home-made version is the best. Remember that chilli oil is too dramatic to be used directly as the sole cooking oil; it is best used as part of a dipping sauce or as a condiment, or combined with other milder oils. I include black beans in this recipe for additional flavours so that I can also use it as a dipping sauce.

Once made, put the chilli oil in a tightly-sealed glass jar and store in a cool, dark place where it will keep for months.

TO MAKE CHILLI OIL/CHILLI OIL DIPPING SAUCE

300 ml (10 fl oz) groundnut oil
2 tablespoons dried red chillies, including seeds, coarsely chopped
1 tablespoon whole unroasted Sichuan peppercorns
2 tablespoons whole black beans, rinsed and dried

Heat a wok or large frying pan until it is very hot. Add the oil and when it is very hot and slightly smoking, turn the heat to low. Add the chillies, peppercorns and black beans and cook gently for about 15 minutes. Allow the mixture to cool undisturbed and then pour it into a jar. Leave it to stand for two days then strain the oil. It will keep indefinitely.

CHINESE BROCCOLI Chinese broccoli is very crunchy, slightly bitter and resembles Swiss chard in flavour. It is quite delicious with an earthy, 'green' taste. It has deep olive green leaves and is sometimes sprinkled with white flowers. When selecting it, look for stems which are firm and leaves which look fresh and green. It is prepared in exactly the same way as broccoli and should be stored in a plastic bag in the vegetable crisper of the refrigerator where it will keep for several days. Where Chinese broccoli is not to be found, substitute ordinary broccoli.

CHINESE FLOWERING CABBAGE

Chinese flowering cabbage, or choi sum (right), is part of the wide mustard green cabbage family and is fortunately now available in some supermarkets. This cabbage has green leaves and may have small yellow flowers which are eaten along with the leaves and stems. In China this is one of the most common and popular leafy vegetables and is delicious as a stir-fry dish.

**Above:
Chinese leaves**

CHINESE WHITE CABBAGE (BOK CHOY) Although there are many varieties, the most common bok choy is the one with a long, smooth, milky-white stem and large, crinkly, dark green leaves. The size of the plant indicates how tender it is, the smaller the better. Bok choy has a light, fresh, slightly mustardy taste and requires little cooking. It is now widely available in supermarkets. Look for firm crisp stalks and unblemished leaves. Store bok choy in the vegetable crisper of your refrigerator.

CHINESE LEAVES (PEKING CABBAGE) Chinese leaves (left) come in various sizes from long, compact barrel-shaped cabbages to short, squat-looking types. They are also tightly packed with firm, pale green (or in some cases slightly yellow), crinkled leaves. This versatile vegetable is used for soups and added to stir-fried meat dishes. Its sponge-like ability to absorb flavours and its sweet, pleasant taste and texture make it a favourite for chefs who match it with rich foods. This is a delicious crunchy vegetable with a mild but distinctive taste. Store it as you would ordinary cabbage.

CHINESE LONG BEANS These beans are also known as yard-long beans and can grow to almost a metre in length. They are not related to green beans, the long beans having originated in Asia. There are two varieties: the pale green ones and the dark green, thinner ones. Buy beans that are fresh and bright green, with no dark marks. You will usually find beans sold in looped bunches and there is no need to string them before cooking – simply cut off the hard end tip. They have a crunchy taste and texture like string beans but cook faster. Store the fresh beans in a plastic bag in the refrigerator and use within four days.

CHINESE WHITE RADISH (MOOLI) Chinese white radish (opposite, left) is also known as Chinese icicle radish, as mooli, or by its Japanese name, daikon. It is long and white and rather like a carrot in shape but usually much larger. It is a winter radish or root and can withstand long cooking without disintegrating. It thus absorbs the flavours of the food it is cooked with and yet retains its distinctive radish taste and texture. They are always peeled before use. Look for firm, heavy, solid unblemished ones. They should be slightly translucent inside, solid and not fibrous. You can find them in supermarkets and at Chinese or Asian markets. Store them in a plastic bag in the vegetable drawer of your refrigerator where they will keep for over a week.

CINNAMON STICKS OR BARK Cinnamon sticks (opposite, centre) are curled, paper-thin pieces of the bark of the cinnamon tree. Chinese cinnamon comes as thicker sticks of this bark. The latter is highly aromatic and more pungent than the cinnamon sticks found in the West, so try to obtain the Chinese version if you can. If you cannot find them, the Western sticks are an adequate substitute. They add a refreshing taste to braised dishes and are an important ingredient of five-spice powder. Store them in a tightly-sealed jar to preserve their aroma and flavour. Ground cinnamon is not a satisfactory substitute.

Above, left:
Chinese white radishes
Above, centre:
Cinnamon sticks
Above, right:
Coriander

CITRUS PEEL Dried citrus peel made from tangerines or oranges is used extensively in Chinese cookery to flavour braised and smoked dishes. The peel also adds an intense aroma and taste to stir-fried dishes. Drying the peel concentrates the flavour, but you can use the same quantity of fresh peel if necessary. Chinese dried citrus peel can be found in Chinese grocers, usually in cellophane or plastic packets. However, it is simple to make your own dried peel.

TO MAKE DRIED CITRUS PEEL

Peel the skin off a tangerine or orange, scraping away as much of the white pith as possible or coarsely grate the peel. Lay the peel on kitchen paper and dry it in the sun, in an airing cupboard or in a warm but turned-off oven until it is dry and very hard. Store in a tightly-sealed container in a cool dry place.

TO USE DRIED CITRUS PEEL

Soak the required amount of peel in warm water until it softens, then chop or slice it according to the recipe.Add grated peel without soaking it first.

CORIANDER (CHINESE PARSLEY) Fresh coriander, (above, right) Chinese parsley or cilantro, is one of the relatively few herbs used in Chinese cookery. It looks like flat parsley but its pungent, musky, citrus-like flavour gives it a distinctive character which is unmistakable. Its feathery leaves are often used as a garnish, or they can be chopped and mixed into sauces and stuffings. Common parsley cannot be used as a substitute. Many supermarkets, Asian and Chinese grocers stock it as do a few greengrocers. When buying fresh coriander, look for deep green, fresh-looking leaves. Yellow and limp leaves indicate age and should be avoided.

To store coriander, wash it in cold water, drain it thoroughly, and dry it in a salad spinner, then wrap it in kitchen paper. Store it in the vegetable drawer of your refrigerator where it should keep for several days.

CORNFLOUR In China there are many flours and types of starch, such as water chestnut powder, taro starch and arrowroot. They are primarily used to bind and thicken sauces and to make batter. These exotic starches and flours are not as commonly available outside China, but I have found cornflour works just as well in my recipes. As part of a marinade, it helps to coat the food properly and it gives dishes a velvety texture. It also protects food during deep-frying by helping to seal in the juices and it can be used as a binder for minced stuffings. Cornflour is blended with cold water until it forms a smooth paste before it is used in sauces. During the cooking process, the cornflour turns clear and shiny.

EGG WHITE Egg whites are often used in Chinese recipes as a key ingredient for coating that is used to seal in a food's flavour and juices when the food is plunged into hot oil. It is especially important in velveting. One egg white from a large egg generally equals about 2 tablespoons. You can easily freeze the egg whites in tablespoon-size cubes in an ice-cube tray.

FIVE-SPICE POWDER Five-spice powder is less commonly known as five-flavoured powder or five-fragrance spice powder and it is becoming a staple in the spice section of supermarkets. Chinese grocers always keep it in stock. This brown powder is a mixture of star anise, Sichuan peppercorns, fennel, cloves and cinnamon. A good blend is pungent, fragrant, spicy and slightly sweet at the same time. The exotic fragrance it gives to a dish makes the search for a good mixture well worth the effort. It keeps indefinitely in a well-sealed jar.

FLOUR

GLUTINOUS RICE FLOUR: this flour, made from glutinous rice, gives a chewy texture to dough. It is widely used in China as an ingredient in the rich dim sum pastries. However, it is not an acceptable substitute in recipes that call for ordinary rice flour.
RICE FLOUR: this flour is made from raw rice and is used to make fresh rice noodles. Store it as you would wheat flour.

FUNGUS (See Chinese Mushrooms)

GARLIC Garlic has been an essential seasoning in Chinese cookery for thousands of years. Indeed, Chinese food would be unrecognizable without the highly aromatic smell and distinctive taste of garlic. The Chinese use it in numerous ways: whole, finely chopped, crushed and pickled. It is used to flavour oils as well as spicy sauces and it is often paired with other equally pungent ingredients such as spring onions, black beans and fresh ginger.

Select fresh garlic which is firm and preferably pinkish in colour. It should be stored in a cool, dry place but not in the refrigerator where it can easily become mildewy or begin sprouting.

GINGER Fresh root ginger (below, left) is an indispensable ingredient in authentic Chinese cookery. Its pungent, spicy and fresh taste adds a subtle but distinctive flavour to soups, meats and vegetables. It is also an important seasoning for fish and seafood since it neutralizes fishy smells. Root ginger looks rather like a gnarled Jerusalem artichoke and can range in size from 7.5 cm (3 inches) to 15 cm (6 inches) long. It has pale brown, dry skin which is usually peeled away before use. Select fresh ginger which is firm with no signs of shrivelling. It will keep in the refrigerator, wrapped in cling film, for up to two weeks. Fresh ginger is available in most supermarkets and greengrocers as well as all Chinese and Asian markets. Dried powdered ginger has a quite different flavour and should not be substituted for fresh ginger.

GINGER JUICE: made from fresh ginger, this is used in marinades to give a subtle ginger taste without the bite of fresh chopped pieces. Here is a simple method of extracting ginger juice: cut unpeeled fresh ginger into 2.5 cm (1 inch) chunks and drop them into a running food processor. When the ginger is finely chopped, transfer it to a cotton or linen towel and squeeze out the juice by hand. Alternatively, mash some fresh ginger with a kitchen mallet or the side of a cleaver or knife until most of the fibres are exposed. Then simply squeeze out the juice by hand through a cotton or linen towel.

HAM Chinese ham has a rich, salty flavour and is used primarily as a garnish or seasoning to flavour soups, sauces, stir-fried dishes, noodles and rice. Chinese hams are not available outside Asia, but a good substitute is either Parma ham, which can be found in good supermarkets or delicatessens, or lean smoked bacon (with any rind or fat cut away).

LEEKS Leeks (below, right) found in China are large and cylindrical and resemble a giant spring onion with a white garlic-like husk. Leeks found in the West are a good substitute with their mild, slightly sweet, onion flavour. To prepare them, cut off and discard the green tops and roots and slice the leek in half lengthways. Wash them well to make absolutely sure you have got rid of any bits of grit and store them in a plastic bag in the vegetable drawer of your refrigerator.

Right:
Ginger
Far right:
Leeks

LILY BUDS Also known as tiger lily buds, golden needles or lily stems, dried lily buds are an ingredient in muxi (mu shu) dishes and hot and sour soups. They provide texture as well as an earthy taste to any dish. Soak the buds in hot water for about 30 minutes or until they are soft. Cut off the hard ends and shred or cut in half according to the recipe directions. They are quite inexpensive and can be found in Chinese markets. Store them in a jar in a dry place.

MALTOSE SUGAR (See also Sugar.) This type of malt sugar is a liquid syrup that adds a wonderful richness to stews and sauces without a cloying sweetness. It can be stored at room temperature and is found only in Chinese markets. Honey can be used as a substitute.

MANGETOUT (SNOW PEAS) This familiar vegetable combines a tender, crunchy texture and a sweet, fresh flavour. Look for pods that are firm with very small peas, which means they are tender and young. Mangetout are readily available at supermarkets and they keep for at least a week in the vegetable crisper of the refrigerator.

MUSHROOMS Mushrooms are a popular ingredient in Chinese cookery. There are many varieties and they are used both fresh and dried. The most common are:

CHINESE DRIED MUSHROOMS: there are many varieties of these which add a particular flavour and aroma to Chinese dishes. They can be black or dark brown in colour. The very large ones with a lighter colour and a cracked surface are the best. They are usually the most expensive so use them with a light touch. They can be bought in boxes or plastic bags from Chinese grocers. Store them in an air-tight jar.

TO USE CHINESE DRIED MUSHROOMS

Soak the mushrooms in a bowl of warm water for about 20 minutes or until they are soft and pliable. Squeeze out the excess water and cut off and discard the woody stems. Only the caps are used.

The soaking water can be saved and used in soups and as rice water. Strain the liquid through a fine sieve to discard any sand or residue from the dried mushrooms before use.

CHINESE TREE FUNGUS: these tiny, black, dried leaves are also known as cloud ears; when soaked, they puff up to look like little clouds. Soak the dried fungus in hot water for 20 to 30 minutes until soft. Rinse well, cutting away any hard portions. Fungi are valued for their crunchy texture and slightly smoky flavour. You can find them at Chinese markets, usually wrapped in plastic or cellophane bags. They keep indefinitely in a jar stored in a cool dry place.

CHINESE WOOD EAR FUNGUS: these fungi are the larger variety of the Chinese tree fungi described above. Prepare, soak and trim them in the same manner. In soaking, they will swell up to four or five times their size. Sold in Chinese markets, they keep indefinitely when stored in a jar in a cool dry place.

STRAW MUSHROOMS: these are among the tastiest mushrooms found in China. When fresh, they have deep brown caps which are moulded around the stem. In the West, they are only available in tins. They can be bought in Chinese grocers and in some supermarkets and delicatessens. Drain and rinse in cold water before use.

NOODLES AND PASTA In China, people eat noodles (pasta) of all kinds, day and night. They provide a nutritious, quick, light snack. Several styles of Chinese noodle dishes have now made their way to the West, including the fresh, thin egg noodles which are browned on both sides and the popular thin rice noodles. Both kinds can be bought in Chinese markets fresh and dried. Here is a listing of the major types of noodles:

WHEAT NOODLES AND EGG NOODLES: these are made from hard or soft wheat flour and water but some are also made with egg. Supermarkets and delicatessens also stock both the dried and fresh variety. Flat noodles are usually used in soups and rounded noodles are best for stir-frying or pan-frying. The fresh ones freeze nicely if they are well wrapped. Thaw them thoroughly before cooking.

TO COOK WHEAT AND EGG NOODLES

Noodles are very good blanched and served with main dishes instead of plain rice.

225 g (8 oz) fresh or dried Chinese egg or wheat noodles

If you are using fresh noodles (over page), immerse them in a pan of boiling water and cook them for 3 to 5 minutes or until you find their texture done to your taste. If you are using dried noodles, either cook them according to the instructions on the packet, or cook them in boiling water for 4 to 5 minutes. Drain and serve.

If you are cooking noodles in advance or before stir-frying them, toss the cooked and drained noodles in 2 teaspoons of sesame oil and put them into a bowl. Cover this with cling film and refrigerate. They remain usable for about two hours.

Above:
Fresh egg noodles

RICE NOODLES: these dried noodles are opaque white and come in a variety of shapes. One of the most common examples is rice stick noodles which are flat and about the length of a chopstick. They can also vary in thickness. Use the type called for in each recipe. Rice noodles are very easy to prepare. Simply soak them in warm water for 20 minutes until they are soft. Drain them in a colander or a sieve and then they are ready to be used in soups or to be stir-fried.

FEN RICE NOODLES (SHA HE RICE NOODLES): the Chinese make large sheets of *fen*, which means rice noodles, from a basic mixture of rice flour, wheat starch and water. This is steamed in sheets and then, when cooked, cut into noodles to be eaten immediately. These fresh noodles are most often served with a sauce.

BEAN THREAD (TRANSPARENT) NOODLES: these noodles, also called cellophane noodles, are made from ground mung beans and not from a grain flour. They are available dried and are very fine and white. Easy to recognize, packed in their neat, plastic-wrapped bundles, they are stocked by Chinese markets and supermarkets. They are never served on their own, instead being added to soups or braised dishes or being deep-fried and used as a garnish. They must be soaked in warm water for about 5 minutes before use. As they are rather long, you might find it easier to cut them into shorter lengths after soaking. If you are frying them, they do not need soaking beforehand, but they do need to be separated. A good technique for separating the strands is to pull them apart in a large paper bag which stops them from flying all over the place.

OILS Oil is the most commonly used cooking medium in China. The favourite is vegetable or groundnut or peanut oil (see below). Animal fats, usually lard and chicken fat, are also used in some areas, particularly in northern China. I always use groundnut (peanut) oil since I find animal fats too heavy.

Throughout this book I have indicated where oils can be re-used. Where this is possible, simply cool the oil after use and filter it through muslin or a fine strainer into a jar. Cover it tightly and keep in a cool, dry place. If you keep it in the refrigerator, it will become cloudy, but it will clarify again when the oil returns to room temperature. I find oils are best re-used just once and this is healthier since constantly re-used oils increase in saturated fat content.

GROUNDNUT (PEANUT) OIL: this is also known as arachide oil. I prefer to use this for Chinese cookery because it has a pleasant, unobtrusive taste. Although it has a higher saturated fat content than some oils, its ability to be heated to a high temperature without burning makes it perfect for stir-frying and deep-frying. Most supermarkets stock it, but if you cannot find it, use corn oil instead.

CORN OIL: corn or maize oil is also quite suitable for Chinese cooking. It has a high heating point although I find it to be rather bland and slightly disagreeable to smell. It is high in polyunsaturates and is therefore one of the healthier oils.

OTHER VEGETABLE OILS: some of the cheaper vegetable oils available include soya bean, safflower and sunflower oils. They are light in colour and taste and can also be used in Chinese cooking, but they smoke and burn at lower temperatures than groundnut oil and therefore care must be used when cooking with them.

SESAME OIL: this thick, rich, golden-brown oil made from sesame seeds has a distinctive, nutty flavour and aroma. It is widely used in Chinese cookery as a seasoning but is not normally used as a cooking oil because it heats rapidly and burns easily. Therefore, think of it more as a flavouring than as a cooking oil. It is often added at the last moment to finish a dish. Sold in bottles, you can obtain it in many supermarkets and all Chinese grocers.

PEANUTS

PEANUTS Raw peanuts are widely used in Chinese cooking to add flavour and a crunchy texture; they are especially good when marinated or added to stir-fry dishes. They can be bought in good supermarkets, health food shops and Chinese grocers. The thin red skins need to be removed before you use the nuts. To do this, simply immerse them in a pan of boiling water for about two minutes. Drain them and let them cool, then the skins will come off easily.

RICE

LONG-GRAIN RICE: this is the most popular rice for cooking in China and there are many different varieties. Although the Chinese go through the ritual of washing it, rice purchased at supermarkets doesn't require this step. It's nice to see so many new varieties of rice appearing on supermarket shelves.

SHORT-GRAIN RICE: short-grain rice is most frequently found in northern China and is used for making rice porridge; a popular morning meal. It is starchier than long-grain white rice.

GLUTINOUS RICE: this is also known as sweet rice or sticky rice. It is short, round and pearl-like and has a higher gluten content than other rices. The Chinese use it in stuffings, rice pudding and pastries. It is used for rice dishes, sometimes wrapped in lotus leaves and served after Chinese banquets. It is also used for making Chinese rice wine and vinegar. Most Chinese markets and supermarkets stock it. Glutinous rice must be soaked for at least two hours (preferably overnight) before cooking. You may cook it in the same way as long-grain rice (see page 220).

TO WASH RICE

You may do this optional step if you wish to do as the Chinese do. Put the required amount of rice into a large bowl. Fill the bowl with cold water and swish the rice around with your hands. Carefully pour off the cloudy water, keeping the rice in the bowl. Repeat this process several times until the water is clear.

SHAOXING RICE WINE An important component in Chinese cookery, this wine is used extensively for cooking and drinking throughout China. I believe the finest to be from Shaoxing in Zhejiang Province in eastern China. It is made from glutinous rice, yeast and spring water. Chefs use it for cooking as well as in marinades and sauces; its taste and aroma is incomparable. Now available in Chinese markets and in some wine shops in the West, it should be kept tightly corked at room temperature. A good quality, dry pale sherry can be substituted but cannot equal the rich, mellow taste of rice wine. Do not confuse this wine with sake, which is the Japanese version of rice wine and quite different. Western grape wines are not an adequate substitute either.

SALT Table salt is the finest grind of salt. But many chefs feel that Maldon sea salt has a richer flavour. Sea salt is frequently found in bins at Chinese markets. Rock salt with its larger crystals makes an excellent medium for heat conduction and is often used in regional southern Chinese dishes, especially with chicken or pigeon.

SAUCES AND PASTES Chinese cookery involves a number of thick, tasty sauces and pastes. They are essential to the authentic taste of Chinese cooking and it is well worth making the effort to obtain them. Most are sold in bottles or tins by good supermarkets and Chinese grocers. Tinned sauces, once opened, should be transferred to screw-topped glass jars and kept in the refrigerator where they will last indefinitely.

CHILLI BEAN SAUCE: this thick, dark sauce or paste which is made from soya beans, chillies and other seasonings varies from mildly hot to very hot and spicy, depending on the brand you buy. It is available in jars in large supermarkets or Chinese grocers. I like the brands from Hong Kong, China or Taiwan. I tend to avoid the Singapore brands which often tend to include MSG and additives. Be sure to seal the jar tightly after use and store in the refrigerator or in a cool place. Do not confuse it with chilli sauce (see below) which is a hotter, redder, thinner sauce made without beans and used mainly as a dipping sauce for cooked dishes.

CHILLI SAUCE: this is a bright red, hot sauce made from chillies, vinegar, sugar and salt. It is sometimes used for cooking, but it is mainly used as a dipping sauce. There are various brands and you should experiment until you find the one you like best. If you find it too strong, dilute it with a little hot water. Do not confuse it with chilli bean sauce (see above) which is a thick, dark sauce used for cooking.

HOISIN SAUCE: this is a thick, dark, brownish-red sauce which is made from soya beans, vinegar, sugar, spices and other flavourings. It is sweet and spicy. Hoisin sauce is sold in tins and jars (it is sometimes also called barbecue sauce) and is available in supermarkets and Chinese grocers. If refrigerated, it can keep indefinitely.

OYSTER SAUCE: this thick, brown sauce is made from a concentrate of oysters cooked in soy sauce and brine. Despite its name, oyster sauce does not taste fishy. It has a rich flavour and is used not only in cooking but also as a condiment, diluted with a little oil, for vegetables, poultry and meats. It is usually sold in bottles and can be bought in supermarkets and Chinese grocers. The higher-priced brands tend to be the best. I find it keeps best in the refrigerator.

SESAME PASTE: this rich, thick, creamy brown paste is made from sesame seeds. It is used in both hot and cold dishes. It is sold in jars at large supermarkets or Chinese grocers. You can use smooth peanut butter instead which resembles it in texture.

SOY SAUCES: soy sauce is an essential ingredient in Chinese cooking. It is made from a mixture of soya beans, flour and water, which is then fermented naturally and aged for some months. The liquid which is finally distilled is soy sauce. There are two main types:

Light soy sauce: as the name implies, this is light in colour, but it is full of flavour and is the better one to use for cooking. It is saltier than dark soy sauce. It is known in Chinese grocers as Superior Soy.

Dark soy sauce: this sauce is aged for much longer than light soy sauce, hence its darker, almost black, colour. It is slightly thicker and stronger than light soy sauce and is more suitable for stews. I prefer it to light soy as a dipping sauce. It is known in Chinese grocers as Soy Superior Sauce.

Most soy sauces sold in supermarkets in the past were dark soy. However, both of the main soy sauces are now widely available. Chinese grocers sell both types and the quality is excellent. Be sure you buy the correct one as the names are very similar.

WHOLE YELLOW BEAN SAUCE: this thick, spicy, aromatic sauce is made of yellow beans, flour and salt which are fermented together. It is quite salty, but it adds a distinctive flavour to Chinese sauces. There are two forms: whole beans in a thick sauce and mashed or puréed beans (sold as Crushed Yellow Bean Sauce). I prefer the whole bean variety because it is slightly less salty and has a better texture.

(CHINESE) SAUSAGES Chinese sausages (left) look exactly like thin salami and are about 15 cm (6 inches) long. They are made from duck liver, pork liver or pork meat and are cured. They are dark red in colour with white flecks of fat. Their tasty flavour varies according to type, but they are sweet rather than spicy. They must be steamed for 10 minutes before they can be eaten and are most commonly used to season chicken and rice dishes. They are obtainable from Chinese grocers.

SESAME SEEDS These are dried seeds of the sesame herb. Unhulled, the seeds range from greyish white to black in colour, but once the hull is removed, the sesame seeds are found to be tiny, somewhat flattened, cream coloured and pointed on one end. Keep them in a glass jar in a cool dry place and they will last for several weeks.

TO MAKE TOASTED SESAME SEEDS

Heat a wok or heavy frying pan until hot. Add the sesame seeds and stir occasionally. Watch them closely and when they begin to lightly brown, about 3 to 5 minutes, stir them again and pour them on to a plate.

Alternatively, you could pre-heat the oven to gas mark 3, 160°C (325°F).

Spread the sesame seeds on a baking sheet and roast them in the oven for about 10 to 15 minutes until they are nicely toasted and lightly browned.

When they are toasted, allow them to cool thoroughly and store in a glass jar in a cool, dark place.

SHALLOTS Shallots are mild-flavoured members of the onion family. They are small – about the size of pickling onions – with copper-red skins. They have a distinctive onion taste without being as strong or as overpowering as ordinary onions. They are readily available in supermarkets and greengrocers. In China, you will find them fresh or pickled and they are paired with preserved eggs as a snack. They are expensive, but their sweet flavour permeates food; a few go a long way. Keep them in a cool, dry place (not the refrigerator) and peel, slice or chop them as you would an onion.

SHARKS' FIN Along with birds' nest, this is the other main exotic delicacy of China. Southern Chinese restaurants and expensive restaurants in other areas of China sometimes offer a long list of sharks' fin dishes. Extremely expensive, it is a blatant symbol of extravagance. The fin is the dorsal 'comb fin' or the two ventral fins of any of a variety of sharks. Preparation usually involves an elaborate process of soaking and boiling in several changes of water and stocks. Like birds' nest, it has little flavour but is prized for its texture. It is usually served with a rich stock, as in the Sharks' Fin Soup, or stuffed in poultry or scrambled with eggs and crab.

SHERRY If you cannot get Shaoxing rice wine, you can use a good quality, dry, pale sherry instead. Do not use sweet or cream sherries.

SHRIMP PASTE Used in the south of China, this ingredient adds an exotic flavour and fragrance to dishes. Made from shrimps (left) which are ground and fermented, it has an odour before cooking much stronger than its actual taste. It is like anchovy paste in texture. It can be found in major supermarkets and Chinese markets, usually in glass jars. Refrigerated, it will keep indefinitely.

SICHUAN PEPPERCORNS Sichuan peppercorns are known throughout China as 'flower peppers' because they look like flower buds opening. They are reddish-brown in colour and have a strong, pungent odour which distinguishes them from the hotter black peppercorns. They are actually not from peppers at all; they are the dried berries of a shrub which is a member of the citrus family. Their smell reminds me of lavender while their taste is sharp and mildly spicy. They can be ground in a conventional pepper mill and are very often roasted before they are ground to bring out their full flavour. They are inexpensive and sold wrapped in cellophane or plastic bags in Chinese grocers. They will keep indefinitely if stored in a well-sealed container.

TO ROAST SICHUAN PEPPERCORNS

Heat a wok or heavy frying pan to a medium heat. Add the peppercorns (you can cook about 150 g (5 oz) at a time) and stir-fry them for about 5 minutes until they brown slightly and start to smoke. Remove from the heat and let them cool.

Grind the peppercorns in a pepper mill or with a mortar and pestle. Seal the mixture tightly in a screw-top jar until required. Alternatively keep the whole roasted peppercorns in a well-sealed container and grind them when required.

SICHUAN PRESERVED VEGETABLES There are many types of Chinese pickled vegetables. One of the most popular is Sichuan preserved vegetable, a speciality of Sichuan province. This is the root of the mustard green, pickled in salt and hot chillies. Sold in tins in Chinese grocers, it gives a pleasantly crunchy texture and spicy taste to dishes. Before using it, rinse in cold water and then slice or chop as required. Any unused vegetable should be transferred to a covered jar and stored in the refrigerator where it will keep indefinitely.

SILK SQUASH (CHINESE OKRA) This is a long, thin, cylindrical squash with deep narrow ridges and one tapered end. Choose firm, unblemished, dark green ones. Peel the ridges. If the vegetable is young, you can leave on some of the green; if older, it is best to peel away all the skin. The inside flesh turns soft and tender as it cooks, tasting like a cross between a cucumber and courgette. Absorbent, it readily picks up flavours of the sauce or food with which it is cooked.

SPINACH Western varieties of spinach are quite different from those used in China. Nevertheless, they make satisfactory substitutes for the Chinese variety. Spinach is most commonly stir-fried, so frozen spinach is obviously unsuitable since it is so moist. Chinese water spinach is the type most frequently cooked in China and is available in Chinese grocers. It has hollow stems and delicate, green, pointed leaves; it is also lighter in colour than common spinach and has a milder taste. It should be cooked when it is very fresh, preferably on the day it is bought.

SPRING ROLL SKINS These are the paper-thin pastry wrappers which are filled with bean sprouts and other vegetables to make spring rolls. They are about 15 cm (6 inches) square, are white and are made from a soft flour and water dough. Since they are easily available and quite inexpensive, it is not worth the time to make them at home. I suggest you buy them frozen in packets of 20 to 30 from Chinese grocers or your local supermarket. They keep well in the freezer when wrapped in cling film.

STAR ANISE The star anise is a hard, star-shaped spice and is the seed pod of the anise bush. It is similar in flavour and fragrance to common anise, but it is more robust and liquorice-like. Star anise is an essential ingredient of five-spice powder and is widely used in braised dishes to which it imparts a rich taste and fragrance. It is sold in plastic packs by Chinese grocers and should be stored in a tightly-covered jar in a cool, dry place.

Below:
Yellow lump sugar

SUGAR Sugar has been used – sparingly – in the cooking of savoury dishes in China for a thousand years. Properly employed, it helps balance the various flavours of sauces and other dishes. Chinese sugar comes in several forms: as rock or yellow lump sugar (left), as brown sugar slabs and as maltose or malt sugar. I particularly like to use rock sugar which is rich and has a more subtle flavour than that of refined granulated sugar. It also gives a good lustre or glaze to braised dishes and sauces. You can buy it in Chinese grocers where it is usually sold in packets. You may need to break the lumps into smaller pieces with a wooden mallet or rolling pin. If you cannot find it, use white sugar or coffee sugar crystals (the amber, chunky kind) instead.

CHINESE BLACK TEA Chinese black tea is a full-bodied, fragrant and smooth tea with a rich aroma and a superb bouquet. There are various kinds of which Keemun is one of the most well known. Tea is used in smoked dishes or for simmering, as in the Marbled Tea Eggs (page 258). You can purchase Chinese black teas in many supermarkets, delicatessens and all Chinese grocers. I prefer to store tea in tins since these keep the tea in the freshest possible condition.

VINEGAR Vinegars are widely used in Chinese cooking. Unlike Western vinegars, Chinese vinegars are usually made from rice. There are many varieties, ranging in flavour from the spicy and slightly tart to the sweet and pungent.

WHITE RICE VINEGAR: this is clear and mild in flavour. It has a faint taste of glutinous rice and is used for sweet and sour dishes.

BLACK RICE VINEGAR: this is very dark in colour and rich, though mild, in taste. It is used for braised dishes, sauces, and sometimes as a dipping sauce for crab.

RED RICE VINEGAR: this is sweet and spicy in taste and is usually used as a dipping sauce for seafood.

All of these vinegars, which are quite inexpensive, can be bought in major supermarkets or Chinese grocers. They are sold in bottles and will keep indefinitely. If you cannot get Chinese vinegars, I suggest you use a cider vinegar, not a European wine vinegar. Malt vinegar can be used, but its taste is stronger and more acidic.

WATER CHESTNUTS Water chestnuts are a sweet root vegetable or bulb about the size of a walnut. They are white and crunchy. In China they are eaten as a snack, having first been boiled in their skins, or peeled and then simmered in rock sugar. They are also used in cooked dishes, especially in southern China.

In this country, fresh water chestnuts can sometimes be obtained from Chinese grocers or good supermarkets. They are tastier than canned ones and will keep, unpeeled, in a paper bag in the refrigerator for up to two weeks. Peel them before use and, if you have any left over, put them back in the refrigerator covered with cold water. Canned water chestnuts are sold in many supermarkets and Chinese grocers. They have a good texture but little taste. Rinse them well in cold water before you use them and store any unused ones in a jar of cold water. They will keep for several weeks in the refrigerator if you change the water daily.

WONTON SKINS Wonton skins are made from egg and flour and can be bought fresh or frozen from Chinese grocers. They are thin pastry-like wrappings which can be stuffed with minced meat and fried, steamed or used in soups. They are sold in little piles of 8 cm (3¼ inch) yellowish squares, wrapped in plastic. The number of squares or skins in a packet varies from about 30 to 36, depending upon the supplier. Fresh wonton skins will keep for about 5 days if stored in cling film or a plastic bag in the refrigerator. If you are using fresh wonton skins, just peel off the number you require and thaw them thoroughly before you use them.

extra hot chilli oil

Regions: All

150 ml (5 fl oz) oil, preferably groundnut (peanut)
4 tablespoons dried red chillies, including seeds, coarsely chopped
2 teaspoons whole unroasted Sichuan peppercorns

For those who like hot and spicy food, chilli oil is a must. It can be purchased ready-made from Chinese grocers, but it is also easy to make yourself. Chilli oil can be added as a final spicy touch to dishes during cooking or it can be used as a dipping sauce either on its own or combined with vinegar and soy sauce, as for the Potsticker Dumplings (pages 244-5). For a milder chilli oil see the recipe on page 23.

Heat a wok or large frying pan until it is very hot. Add the oil and when it is very hot and slightly smoking turn the heat to very low. Add the chillies and pepper-corns and allow to cook gently for 15 minutes. Allow the mixture to cool undisturbed and then pour it into a jar. Leave to stand for 2 days, then strain the oil. It will keep indefinitely.

five-spice salt

Regions: Beijing and Sichuan

3 tablespoons salt
1 teaspoon five-spice powder

This dipping mixture is similar to the Sichuan peppercorn and salt mixture but has the distinctive fragrance of five-spice powder. It is best served with fried meat like chicken and pigeon, or fried fish.

Heat a wok or heavy frying pan until it is very hot. Then add the salt and stir-fry for a minute or so until it is quite hot. Remove the pan from the heat and stir in the five-spice powder. Mix well and allow to cool, then put the mixture in a jar and seal until needed.

ginger sherry or rice wine

Regions: All

3 tablespoons finely chopped fresh ginger
85 ml (3 fl oz) Shaoxing rice wine or dry sherry

This is simply sherry or rice wine flavoured with fresh ginger. The mixture works well as a variation in recipes which call for sherry or rice wine. Putting fresh ginger in sherry or rice wine is also a good method of preserving it and it can then be eaten as a snack.

Combine the ginger and the Shaoxing rice wine or dry sherry and put the mixture into a jar in the refrigerator until you are ready to use it. It will keep for at least 2 months.

ginger and spring onion sauce

Region: Canton

3 tablespoons finely chopped spring onions

2 teaspoons finely chopped fresh ginger

2 teaspoons salt

3 tablespoons groundnut (peanut) oil

In this simple sauce, the oil is heated and then poured over the seasonings to bring out their full taste and fragrance. It is a dipping sauce best used with poultry and meat dishes like Braised Chicken with Leeks (page 134) and Twice-Cooked Chicken (page 135).

Put all the ingredients except the oil in a small heatproof bowl and mix them well. Heat a wok or frying pan until it is very hot. Add the oil and when it is very hot and slightly smoking, remove the pan from the heat. Pour the hot oil into the bowl with the other ingredients. The sauce should sizzle for a few seconds and is ready to use.

roasted salt and pepper

Regions: All

50 g (2 oz) whole unroasted Sichuan peppercorns

75 g (3 oz) coarse sea salt or table salt

This roasted salt and pepper mixture which is made with Sichuan peppercorns is used throughout China as a dip for deep-fried foods. The dry-roasting method releases all the flavours of the peppercorns.

Heat a wok or heavy frying pan over a medium heat. Add the peppercorns and the salt and stir-fry them until the mixture is slightly smoking and lightly browned.
Then grind it using a grinder, clean coffee mill or mortar and pestle. Seal the mixture tightly in a jar until you are ready to use it.

sweet and sour sauce

Regions: Canton and Fujian

2 tablespoons ginger marmalade

2 tablespoons orange marmalade

1 teaspoon salt

3 tablespoons Chinese white rice vinegar or cider vinegar

2 tablespoons tomato ketchup

This is my version of a subtle and tasty sweet and sour sauce which can be used for any deep-fried foods such as the Fried Wonton (page 260). It keeps well in a tightly-sealed jar in the refrigerator.

Combine all the ingredients together in a small bowl and mix them thoroughly. Transfer the mixture to a small dish if it is to be used at once or put it into a jar and refrigerate until needed.

equipment

Traditional Chinese cooking equipment is not essential for the preparation of Chinese food, but there are some tools which will make it very much easier. Moreover, there is a gain when one relies upon implements that have been use-tested over many centuries. Once you become familiar with woks and clay pots, for example, you will have entered the Chinese culinary world. Most of the items listed below can be bought at cookware shops, department stores, even some supermarkets.

WOK All your faith in Chinese cookery and your own skills will come to naught without good woks. A most useful and versatile piece of equipment, the wok may be used for stir-frying, blanching, deep-frying and steaming foods. Its shape, with deep sides and either a tapered or a slightly flattened bottom, allows for fuel efficient, quick and even heating and cooking. In the stir-frying technique, the deep sides prevent the food and oils from spilling over; in deep-frying, much less oil is required because of the shape and the concentration of the heat and ingredients at the wok's base.

There are two basic wok types, the traditional Cantonese version, with short, rounded handles on either side of the edge or lip of the wok; and the pau wok (above), which has one long handle from 30 to 35 cm (12 to 14 inches) long. The two-handled model is easier to move when it is full of liquid. It is thus best for steaming and deep-frying. The pau wok is best for stir-frying because it is easier to hold over the heat with one hand while your free hand is stirring the foods with a long spoon or spatula. The long handle also keeps you more safely distanced from splashing hot oils.

You should know that the round-bottomed wok can only be used on gas hobs. Woks are now available with flatter bottoms designed for use on electric hobs, as well as for the popular ceramic hob. Although this shape really defeats the purpose of the traditional design, it does help to concentrate intense heat at the centre and it also has the advantage over ordinary frying pans that it has deeper sides.

CHOOSING A WOK: choose a wok preferably about 30 to 35 cm (12 to 14 inches) in diameter, with deep sides. It is easier, and safer, to cook a small batch of food in a large wok than a large quantity in a small one. Be aware that some modernized woks are too shallow or too flat-bottomed and thus no better than a frying pan. A heavier wok, preferably made of carbon steel, is superior to the lighter stainless steel or aluminium type, which cannot take very high heat and tend to scorch themselves and food.

SEASONING A WOK: all woks (except non-stick ones) need to be seasoned. Many need to be scrubbed first as well to remove the machine oil which is applied to the surface by the manufacturer to protect it in transit. This is the *only* time you will ever scrub your wok – unless you let it rust up. Scrub it with a cream cleanser and water to remove as much of the machine oil as possible. Then dry it and put it on the hob on a low heat. Add 2 tablespoons of vegetable oil (do not use olive oil to season a wok) and, using kitchen paper, rub it over the inside of the wok until the entire surface is lightly coated with oil. Heat the wok slowly for about 20 minutes and then wipe it thoroughly with more kitchen paper. The paper will become blackened. Repeat this process of coating, heating and wiping until the kitchen paper wipes clean. Your wok will darken and become well seasoned with use, which is a good sign.

CLEANING A WOK: once your wok has been seasoned, it should never be scrubbed with soap or water, clean water is all that is needed. The wok should be thoroughly dried after each use. Putting the cleaned wok over a low heat for a minute or so should do the trick. If, perchance, it does rust a bit, then it must be scrubbed with a cream cleanser and re-seasoned.

WOK ACCESSORIES

Wok stand: this is a metal ring or frame designed to keep a conventionally-shaped wok steady on the hob and it is essential if you want to use your wok for steaming, deep-frying or braising. Stands come in two designs. One is a solid metal ring punched with about six ventilation holes. The other is like a circular thin wire frame. If you have a gas cooker use *only the latter type* as the more solid design does not allow for sufficient ventilation and may lead to a build-up of gas which could put the flame out completely.

Wok lid: this light and inexpensive domed cover, usually made from aluminium, is used for steaming. The lid normally comes with the wok, but if not, it may be purchased at a Chinese or Asian market, or you may use any domed pot lid that fits snugly.

Spatula: a long-handled metal spatula shaped rather like a small shovel is ideal for scooping and tossing food in a wok. Alternatively any good long-handled spoon can be used.

Rack: when steaming foods in your wok, you will need a wooden or metal rack or trivet to raise the food to be cooked above the water level. Wok sets usually include a rack but, if not, Asian and Chinese grocers sell them separately. Department stores and hardware shops also sell wooden and metal stands which can serve the same purpose. Any rack, improvised or not, that keeps the food above the water so that it is steamed and not boiled will suffice.

Bamboo brush: this bundle of stiff, split bamboo is used for cleaning a wok without scrubbing off the seasoned surface. It is an attractive, inexpensive implement but not essential. A soft washing-up brush will do just as well.

DEEP-FAT FRYERS These are very useful and you may find them safer and easier to use for deep-frying than a wok. The quantities of oil given in the recipes are based on the amount required for deep-frying in a wok. If you are using a deep-fat fryer instead, you will need about double that amount, but never fill it more than half-full with oil.

CLEAVERS To Chinese cooks the cleaver is an all-purpose cutting instrument that makes all other knives unnecessary. Once you become proficient with a cleaver, you will see how it can be used on all types of food to slice, dice, chop, fillet, shred, crush or whatever. In practice, most Chinese chefs rely upon three different sizes of cleaver – light, medium and heavy — to be used appropriately. Of course, you may use your own familiar kitchen knives, but if you decide to invest in a cleaver, choose a good quality stainless steel model and keep it sharpened.

CHOPPING BOARD One decided improvement over the traditional implements of Chinese cooking is the modern chopping board made of hardwood or white acrylic. The typical Chinese chopping board is of soft wood which is both difficult to maintain and, being soft, provides a fertile surface for bacteria. The hardwood or white acrylic boards are easy to clean, resist bacterial accumulation and last much longer. Chinese cookery entails much chopping, slicing and dicing so it is essential to have a dependable and large, steady, chopping board. For reasons of hygiene, never place cooked meat on a board on which raw meat or poultry has been prepared. For raw meats always use a separate board and clean it thoroughly after each use.

STEAMERS Steaming is not a very popular cooking method in the West. This is unfortunate because it is the best method for preparing many foods of delicate taste and texture, such as fish and vegetables. Steaming is a method well worth learning. In China, bamboo steamers have been in use for thousands of years. Bamboo steamers come in several sizes of which the 25 cm (10 inch) is the most suitable for home use. The food is placed in the steamer and that in turn is placed above boiling water in a wok or pot. To prevent the food from sticking to the steamer as it cooks, clean damp muslin can be placed under the food itself. A tight-fitting bamboo lid prevents the steam escaping; several steamers, stacked one above the other, may be utilized at once. Of course, any kind of wide, metal steamer can be used if you prefer. Before using a bamboo steamer for the first time, wash it and then steam it empty for about 5 minutes.

RICE COOKERS Electric rice cookers are increasing in popularity. They cook rice perfectly and keep it warm throughout a meal. A rice cooker also has the advantage of freeing a burner or element, making for a less cluttered hob. They are relatively expensive, however, so unless you eat rice frequently I do not think they are worth the expense.

SAND OR CLAY POTS For braised dishes, soups and rice cooking, the Chinese rely upon these lightweight clay pots (left), whose design allows for the infusion of aromas and tastes into foods. Their unglazed exteriors have a sandy texture, hence their other name. Clay pots are available in many sizes, with matching lids, and, being quite fragile, they are often encased in a wire frame. They are to be used directly on the hob (most Chinese do not have home ovens) but never put an empty sand pot on to a heated element or place a hot sand pot on a cold surface: the shock will crack it. Clay pots should always have at least some liquid in them and, when filled with food, they can take very high heat. If you use an electric hob, use an asbestos pad to insulate the pot from direct contact with the hot coils. You can, of course, use a saucepan instead. Note: because of the release of hot steam when you lift the lid, always lift the lid away from you.

CHOPSTICKS Many Western diners are challenged by chopsticks, but I always encourage their use. It is an interesting experience to attempt any new technique and chopsticks do indeed offer the novice a physical entrée into Chinese cuisine. Chopsticks are used as a combination spoon and fork, for stirring, beating, whipping and mixing. But, of course, one may get along nicely with our own spoons, forks, ladles, spatulas and whisks.

Chopsticks are readily and cheaply available. I prefer the wooden version, but in China plastic ones are more commonly used (and re-used) for reasons of hygiene and economy.

MISCELLANEOUS Stainless steel bowls of different sizes, along with strainers and colanders, round out the list of basic implements. They will be very useful because you will often have to drain or strain oils and juices and because you will be doing much mixing of wonderful foods. It is better to have one too many tools than one too few.

techniques

All human constructions that aspire to greatness require deep and solid foundations. So it is with Chinese cuisine. The preparation of foods and ingredients before cooking is more important and time-consuming in Chinese cookery than in any other cuisine. As with other constructions, however, once the foundation has been prepared, the rest is comparatively quick and easy.

Chinese cookery presupposes that every ingredient has been properly prepared for the cooking process. This means that meats and vegetables have been cut into appropriate shapes and sizes so as to cook quickly and evenly while retaining their natural tastes and textures. As an important by-product, such preparation enhances the visual appeal of whatever is being served. Chinese cooks, therefore, are quite specific about cutting techniques, especially where vegetables are concerned. While the cleaver is the traditional cutting implement, you may use any appropriate sharp knife.

Chinese cookery is a sophisticated cuisine which involves a number of methods uncommon in the West. Several different techniques may be used in the preparation of a single dish. There is nothing mysterious about such techniques and mastery of them comes quickly in almost every case. When you plan your meals be sure to select dishes that involve a range of techniques. Limit yourself to one stir-fried dish per meal until you have become used to the techniques that this crucial style of cooking employs.

SLICING

HORZONTAL OR FLAT SLICING

SLICING This is the conventional method of slicing food. Hold the food firmly on the chopping board with one hand and slice the food straight down into very thin slices. Meat is always sliced across the grain to break up the fibres and to make it more tender when it is cooked. If you use a cleaver rather than a knife for this, hold the cleaver with your index finger over the far side of the top of the cleaver and your thumb on the side nearest you to guide the cutting edge firmly. Hold the food with your other hand, turning your fingers under for safety. Your knuckles should act as a guide for the blade.

HORIZONTAL OR FLAT SLICING This is a technique for splitting food into two thinner pieces while retaining its overall shape, as in slicing kidneys. The cleaver with its wide blade is particularly suitable for this. Hold the blade of the cleaver or knife parallel to the chopping board. Place your free hand on top of the piece of food to keep it steady. Using a gentle cutting motion slice sideways into the food. Depending on the recipe you may need to repeat this process, cutting the two halves into even thinner, flat pieces.

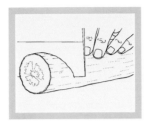

DIAGONAL SLICING

DIAGONAL SLICING This technique is used for cutting vegetables such as asparagus, carrots or spring onions. The purpose is to expose more of the surface of the vegetable to the heat for quicker cooking. Angle the knife or cleaver at a slant and cut evenly.

ROLL CUTTING

ROLL CUTTING This is rather like diagonal slicing but is used for larger vegetables such as courgettes, aubergines and Chinese white radish (mooli). Begin by making one diagonal slice at one end of the vegetable. Then turn it 180 degrees and make the next diagonal slice. Continue until you have chopped the entire vegetable into evenly-sized, diamond-shaped chunks.

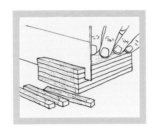

SHREDDING

SHREDDING This is a process like the French julienne technique by which food is cut into fine matchstick-like shreds. First cut the food into slices and then pile several slices on top of each other and cut them *lengthways* into fine strips. Some foods, particularly meat and chicken breasts, are easier to shred if they are first stiffened slightly in the freezer for about 20 minutes.

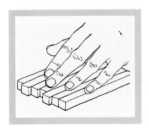

DICING

DICING This is a simple technique of cutting food into small cubes or dice. The food should first be cut into slices. Stack the slices and cut them again *lengthways* into sticks just as you would for shredding (above). Stack the strips or sticks and cut crossways into evenly-sized cubes or dice.

MINCING

MINCING This is a fine-chopping technique. Chefs use two cleavers to mince, rapidly chopping with them in unison for fast results. One cleaver or knife is easier for the less expert, although the process will, of course, take a little longer! First slice the food and then, using a sharp knife or cleaver, rapidly chop the food until it is rather spread out over the chopping board. Scrape it into a pile, chop again and continue chopping until the food reaches the desired state. You may find it easier to hold the knife or cleaver by the top of the blade (rather than by the handle) with two hands, as though you were chopping parsley. A food processor may also be used for this but be careful not to over-mince the food or you will lose texture and taste.

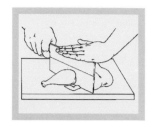

CHOPPING

SCORING

CHOPPING This is a term which is used for any technique which requires food to be completely cut through. Usually this applies to whole birds or to cooked food with bones which need to be cut into smaller pieces. The food to be cooked should be placed on a firm cutting surface. Use a straight, sharp, downward motion with the cleaver or knife. To chop through bones, hit down with the blade and then finish off the blow with the flat of your other hand on the top edge of the cleaver or knife. A heavy-duty cleaver or knife is best for these tasks.

SCORING This is a technique used to pierce the surface of foods to help them cook faster and more evenly. It also gives them an attractive appearance. Use a cleaver or a sharp knife and make cuts into the food at a slight angle to a depth of about 3 mm (1/8 inch). Take care not to cut all the way through. Make cuts all over the surface of the food, cutting criss-cross to give a wide, diamond-shaped pattern.

MARINATING Keeping raw meat or poultry for a time in a liquid such as soy sauce, rice wine and cornflour improves its flavour and tenderizes it. Other spices or seasonings such as sugar, chillies, five-spice powder or Sichuan peppercorns may be added. The marinating time is usually at least 20 minutes in order to infuse the meat or poultry properly with the flavours of the marinade. Once the infusion is complete the food is usually lifted out of the marinade with a slotted spoon before it is cooked.

THICKENING Cornflour blended with an equal quantity of water is frequently used in Chinese cookery to thicken sauces and glaze dishes. Always make sure the mixture is smooth and well blended before adding it. You do not want a lumpy glaze.

VELVETING Velveting is used to prevent delicate foods like chicken breasts or prawns from overcooking. The food is coated with a mixture of unbeaten egg white, cornflour and sometimes salt. It is then put into the refrigerator for about 20 to 30 minutes to ensure that the coating adheres to the food. The velvet cloak protects the flavour and texture of the food when it is put into oil or hot water.

BLANCHING Putting food into hot water or into moderately hot oil for a few minutes will cook it briefly but not entirely. It is a sort of softening-up process to prepare the food for final cooking. Chicken is often blanched in oil or water after being velveted (see above). Meat is sometimes blanched to rid it of unwanted gristle and fat and in order to ensure a clean taste and appearance. Blanching in water is common with hard vegetables such as broccoli or carrots. The vegetable is plunged into boiling water for several minutes. It is then drained and plunged into cold water to arrest the cooking process. In such cases blanching usually precedes stir-frying to finish the cooking. You must always avoid overcooking your foods at the blanching stage.

POACHING This is a method of simmering food gently until it is partially cooked. It is then put into soup or combined with a sauce and the cooking process continued. Delicately-flavoured and textured foods such as eggs and chicken are often poached.

STIR-FRYING This is the most famous of all Chinese cooking techniques and it is possibly the trickiest since success with it depends upon having all the required ingredients prepared, measured out and immediately at hand and on having a good source of fierce heat. Its advantage is that, properly executed, stir-fried foods can be cooked in minutes in very little oil so they retain their natural flavours and textures. It is very important that stir-fried foods are not overcooked or made greasy – and it is surprising how easy it is to do this. But keep trying because once you have mastered this technique you will find that it becomes your favourite technique. Using a wok is definitely an advantage when stir-frying as its shape not only conducts the heat well but its high sides enable you to toss the stir-fry ingredients rapidly, keeping them constantly moving while cooking.

Having prepared all the ingredients for stir-frying, this is how you proceed:

Heat the wok or frying pan until it is very hot before adding the oil. This prevents food sticking and will ensure an even heat. Groundnut (peanut) oil is my favourite precisely because it can take this heat without burning. Add the oil and swirl the hot oil evenly over the surface of the wok. The wok and oil should be very hot indeed – slightly smoking – before you add the next ingredient unless you are going on to flavour the oil (see next point).

If you are flavouring the oil it should be hot and slightly smoking before you add the garlic, spring onions, ginger, dried red chilli or salt. Toss them quickly in the oil for a few seconds. Continue to the next step of the recipe. In some recipes these flavourings will then be removed and discarded before cooking proceeds.

When you add the series of ingredients as described in the recipe, proceed to stir-fry by tossing them over the surface of the wok or pan with the metal spatula or long-handled spoon. If you are stir-frying meat, let each side rest for just a few seconds before continuing to stir. Keep moving the food from the centre of the wok to the sides. Stir-frying is a noisy business and is usually accompanied by quite a lot of splattering because of the high temperature at which the food must be cooked, hence my preference for the long-handled wok.

Some stir-fried dishes are thickened with a mixture of cornflour and cold water. To avoid getting a lumpy sauce be sure to remove the wok or pan from the heat for a minute before you add the mixture, which must be thoroughly blended before it is added. The sauces can then be returned to the heat and thickened.

DEEP-FRYING This is one of the most important techniques in Chinese cooking. The trick is to regulate the heat so that the surface of the food is sealed but does not brown so fast that the food is uncooked inside. As with any technique, mastery comes with practice. Although deep-fried food must not be greasy the process does require a lot of oil. The Chinese use a wok for deep-frying which requires rather less oil than the more stable deep-fat fryer. If you use a wok for deep-frying, be certain that it is fully secure on its stand before adding the oil and on no account leave the wok unsupervised. Most people will find a deep-fat fryer easier and safer to use. Be careful not to fill this more than half-full with oil.

Some points to bear in mind when deep-frying:

Wait for the oil to get hot enough before adding the food to be fried. The oil should give off a haze and almost produce little wisps of smoke when it is the right temperature, but you can test it by dropping in a small piece of food. If it bubbles all over then the oil is sufficiently hot. Adjust the heat as necessary to prevent the oil from actually smoking or overheating.

To prevent splattering, use kitchen paper to dry the food thoroughly. If the food is in a marinade, remove it with a slotted spoon and let it drain before putting it into the oil. If you are using batter make sure all the excess batter drips off before adding the food to the hot oil.

Oil used for deep-frying can be re-used. Cool it and then strain it into a jar through several layers of muslin or through a fine mesh to remove any particles of food which might otherwise burn if re-heated and give the oil a bitter taste. Label the jar according to the food you have cooked in the oil and only re-use it for the same thing. Oil can be used only twice before it begins to lose its effectiveness.

SHALLOW-FRYING This technique is similar to sautéeing. It involves more oil than stir-frying but less than for deep-frying. Food is fried first on one side and then on the other. Sometimes the excess oil is then drained off and a sauce added to complete the dish. A frying pan is ideal for shallow-frying.

SLOW-SIMMERING AND STEEPING These processes are similar. In slow-simmering, food is immersed in liquid which is brought almost to the boil and then the temperature is reduced so that it simmers, cooking the food to the desired degree. This technique is used for making stock. In steeping, food is similarly immersed in liquid (usually stock) and simmered for a time. The heat is turned off and the heat of the liquid finishes off the cooking processes.

BRAISING AND RED-BRAISING This technique is most often applied to tougher cuts of meat and certain vegetables. The food is usually browned and then put into stock which has been flavoured with seasonings and spices. The stock is brought to the boil, the heat reduced and the food simmered gently until it is cooked.

Red-braising is simply the technique by which food is braised in a dark liquid such a soy sauce. This gives food a reddish-brown colour, hence the name. This type of braising sauce can be saved and frozen for re-use. It can be re-used many times and becomes richer in flavour.

STEAMING Steaming has been used by the Chinese for thousands of years. Along with stir-frying and deep-frying, it is the most widely used technique. Steamed foods are cooked by a gentle moist heat which must circulate freely in order to cook the food. It is an excellent method for bringing out subtle flavours and so is particularly appropriate for fish. Bamboo steamers are used by the Chinese but you could use any one of several utensils.

Using a bamboo steamer in a wok: for this you need a large bamboo steamer about 25 cm (10 inches) wide. Put about 5 cm (2 inches) of water in a wok and bring it to a simmer. Put the bamboo steamer containing the food into the wok where it should rest safely perched on the sloping sides. Cover the steamer with its matching lid and steam the food until it is cooked. Top up with boiling water as required.

Using a wok as a steamer: put about 5 cm (2 inches) of water into a wok. Then put a metal or wooden rack into the wok. Bring the water to a simmer and put the food to be steamed on to a heatproof plate. Lower the plate on to the rack and cover the wok tightly with a wok lid. Check the water level from time to time and replenish it with hot water when necessary. The water should never make direct contact with the food.

Using a large roasting pan or pot as a steamer: put a metal or wooden rack into the pan or pot and pour in about 5 cm (2 inches) of water. Bring it to a simmer and put the food to be steamed on to a plate. Lower the plate on to the rack and cover the pan or pot with a lid or with aluminium foil. Replenish the water as necessary.

Using a European steamer: if you have a metal steamer which is wide enough to take a plate of food then this will give you very satisfactory results. Make sure of the level of the water in the base: it must not all evaporate nor should it be so high as to touch the food.

If you do not have a metal or wooden rack you could use a small empty tin can to support the plate of food. Remember that the food needs to remain above the water level and must not get wet. The water level should always be at least 2.5 cm (1 inch) below the edge of the food plate. (Be sure to use a heatproof plate.)

ROASTING In China roasting is only done in commercial establishments since most homes do not have ovens. The Chinese roast food in large metal, drum-shaped ovens which stand about 1.5 metres (5 feet) high and are fuelled by charcoal. The food is hung on hooks inside the oven over intense heat. The idea is to expose all the surface of the food to the heat to give it a crisp outer surface and a moist interior. You can approximate the Chinese method of putting food on to a rack in a roasting pan so that the hot air of the oven can circulate round it.

BARBECUING This is a variation on roasting and it is common in parts of northern and southern China. Marinated meat is placed over a charcoal fire and the meat constantly basted to keep it moist. Today modern grills and barbecues produce much the same result.

TWICE-COOKING As the name implies, this is a two-step process involving two quite different techniques, such as simmering and stir-frying. It is used to change the texture of food, to infuse it with flavour, and to render foods which are difficult to cook into a more manageable state. It is useful for removing fat from meat before final cooking.

RE-HEATING FOODS Steaming is one of the best methods of re-heating food since it warms it without cooking it further and without drying it out. To re-heat soups and braised dishes, bring the liquid slowly to a simmer, but do not boil. Remove it from the heat as soon as it is hot to prevent overcooking. The microwave oven is also useful for re-heating foods.

GARNISHES The Chinese pay much attention to the presentation of their cuisine. This is why cutting techniques are so important since the size and shape of individual ingredients should harmonize with each other. We also like to decorate dishes with various kinds of garnish ranging from the simple spring onion brush to the elaborate tomato rose. Here are some instructions for making some simple, attractive garnishes.

SPRING ONION BRUSHES

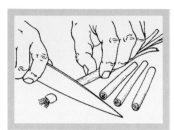 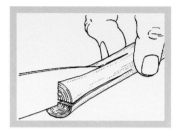 

1 Cut off the green part of the spring onion and trim off the base of the bulb. You should have a 7.5 cm (3 inch) white segment left.

2 Make a lengthways cut about 2.5 cm (1 inch) long at one end of the spring onion. Roll the spring onion 90 degrees and cut again. Repeat this process at the other end.

3 Soak the spring onions in iced water and they will curl into flower brushes. Spin or pat them dry before use.

RADISH ROSES

 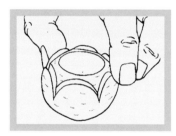 

1 Remove any leaves, trim the top and the root end of the radish.

2 Make thick, rounded cuts to form petals.

3 Soak the radishes in iced water for about an hour.

CARROT FLOWERS

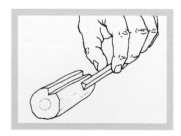 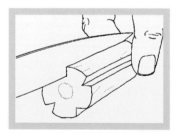 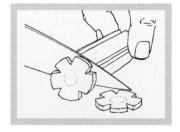

1 Peel the carrots and cut them into 7.5 cm (3 inch) chunks.

2 Cut a V-shaped slice down the length of each chunk. Repeat, making 3 or 4 more lengthways cuts around each.

3 Slice the carrots crossways to form thin flower shapes. Soak them in cold water until required.

FRESH CHILLI FLOWERS

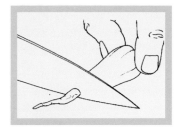

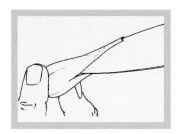

1 Trim the tip of the chilli but do not remove the stem.

2 Make 4 cuts lengthways from the stem of the chilli to the tip to form 4 sections. Remove and discard any seeds.

3 Soak the chillies in cold water. They will 'flower' in the water.

TOMATO ROSES

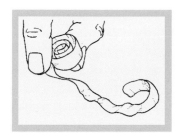

1 Select firm tomatoes and, using a very sharp knife, peel off the skin from the top in one piece as though you were peeling an apple. Do not break the strip.

2 Roll the strip of tomato skin into a tight coil.

3 Turn the coil over and you should have a tomato rose.

CUCUMBER FANS

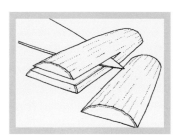

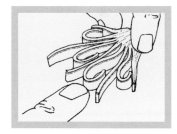

1 Using a sharp knife, cut the rounded end off half a cucumber. Then cut the cucumber in half lengthways.

2 Turn each cucumber piece so that the skin side is upper most. Make a horizontal slice to reduce the thickness of each cucumber piece, so that you end up with a slice which is mainly skin with just a little flesh.

3 Make parallel cuts down the length of the slice, as shown in the diagram. The cuts will have to curve slightly so that you will be able to splay the slices out like a fan.

4 Starting with the second slice, bend every alternate slice in towards the base of the cucumber piece, tucking them in so that they stay securely in place.

5 Keep the cucumber fans in cold water until you are ready to use them.

menus
AND HOW TO EAT CHINESE FOOD

Traditionally, Chinese meals always consist of a soup, a rice, noodle or bread dish, a vegetable dish and at least two other dishes which may be mainly meat, fish or chicken. The meal may be preceded and concluded with tea, but during the meal itself soup – really a broth – will be the only beverage. That is, soup is drunk not as a first course as in the West but throughout the meal. The exception to this is a banquet when soup, if it is served at all, comes at the end of the meal or as a palate-cleanser at several points during the dinner. On such occasions, wine, spirits, beer or even fruit juice will be drunk with the food. At banquets (which are really elaborate dinner parties) dishes are served one at a time so that the individual qualities of each dish can be properly savoured. There may be as many as eight to twelve courses. Rice will not be served except at the end of the meal when fried rice might be offered to anyone who has any appetite left.

At ordinary family meals all the dishes comprising the meal are served together, including the soup. The food is placed in the centre of the table. Each person has their own rice bowl into which they put a generous amount of steamed rice. Then, using chopsticks (above), they help themselves to a little of one dish, transferring this to their rice bowl. Once this has been eaten together with some rice, they will have a chopstick-full of another dish. No Chinese would dream of heaping their rice bowl with what they regarded as their full share of any dish before proceeding to eat. Eating is a communal affair and each diner will take care to see that everyone else at the table is receiving a fair share of everything. You may perceive what a civilizing and socializing practice this is.

Of course you can eat Chinese food any way you like. I think it blends deliciously with many European dishes and when you are new to Chinese cooking you may find it easier to try out just one or two dishes at a time, incorporating them into a non-Chinese menu. Chinese soups, for example, make excellent starters and stir-fried vegetables are delicious with grills and roasts.

When you do devise an all-Chinese meal, try to see that you have a good mix of textures, flavours, colours and shapes. Apart from a staple dish, such as steamed rice, you should opt for a variety of meat, poultry and fish. It is better to serve one meat and one fish dish rather than two meat dishes, even if the meats are different. It will also be a better-balanced meal (and easier to prepare) if you use a variety of cooking methods. Serve a stir-fried dish with a braised, steamed or cold dish. It's important to try to select one or two things which can be prepared in advance. Avoid doing more than two stir-fried dishes as you will thus obviate frantic activity at the last minute.

TABLE SETTING You don't need any special crockery or cutlery for serving Chinese food, although I think it tastes decidedly better when it is eaten with chopsticks rather than a fork. Knives are unnecessary since Chinese food is always cut into bite-sized pieces before it is served. Each person will need a rice bowl, a soup bowl, a teacup if you are serving tea and a small plate for any bones and such. A small dish or saucer each will also be needed if you are serving any dipping sauces. Soup or cereal bowls will do for the rice and soup. Chopsticks are usually set to the right of the rice bowl where a knife would normally be put. A spoon, metal or china, will be needed for soup and as an adjunct to chopsticks for noodles.

The Chinese always help themselves (and others) to the food using their own chopsticks though some people provide separate serving chopsticks.

USING CHOPSTICKS

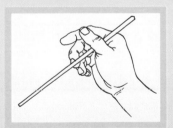

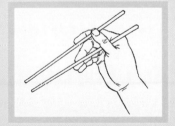

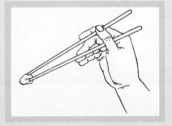

1 Put one chopstick between your thumb and first finger, holding the chopstick about two-thirds the way up from the thinner end. Let it rest on your third finger.

2 Put the second chopstick between your thumb and forefinger so that its tip is level with the first chopstick below.

3 Keep the lower chopstick steady and move the top one to pick up food.

It is perfectly acceptable to lift your rice bowl under your chin and 'shovel' rice into your mouth with your chopsticks.

WHAT TO DRINK If you want to be authentic, serve an appropriate soup with your Chinese meals. If you prefer, you could serve tea, preferably Chinese tea which is drunk without milk and sugar. There are several different types of Chinese tea. Green or unfermented tea is made from green leaves which, when

infused, result in a pale yellowish tea with a refreshing, astringent taste. Black tea is made from fermented black leaves and is red when infused. It has a hearty, robust flavour. Oolong tea is made from partially fermented leaves and is strong and dark. But of all Chinese teas I think green Jasmine tea is the nicest with food. (Do not confuse any of these teas with 'China tea' which is a tea blended for the British market.)

Chinese wines are usually made from fermented rice, the most famous being Shaoxing which is also used for cooking. It has a very different flavour from wine made from grapes and is rather an acquired taste. Many European wines go very well with Chinese food, particularly dry whites and light reds. In recent years whisky and cognac have become very popular with the more affluent Hong Kong Chinese who drink these neat with their meals.

MENUS AND SERVINGS Throughout this book I have given some suggestions about what accompanying dishes would go with a particular recipe. There is, of course, no need to stick rigidly to these ideas. Although most Chinese meals consist of at least three dishes, plus rice and soup, I recommend that you concentrate on achieving success with relatively few dishes until you become more familiar with Chinese cooking techniques and with the recipes themselves. Chefs apart, the Chinese themselves would not expect to be proficient in cooking the real delicacies of their cuisine. These they would order in a restaurant and would not attempt at home. (The Chinese who live in towns and cities eat out a great deal, although many restaurants are very humble, simple places.)

Chinese cooking can be very time-consuming. The recipes in this book are based on the expectation that you will cook two meat, chicken or fish dishes per meal. (This is in addition to a vegetable dish, rice or noodles and, probably, a soup.) This way the total meat, chicken and fish allowance per person will be about 175–225 g (6–8 oz). If you prefer to cook just one such dish then you will probably have to double the quantities given in the recipe. Doing this at least means that you will have a chance to try the authentic taste of Chinese food without quite so much work. Once you gain confidence you will be able to cope with preparing more dishes.

Suggested menus

Here are some suggestions for a variety of well-balanced and delicious menus.

Everyday family meals

SERVES 4

Tomato Eggflower Soup (page 62)
Steamed Fish with Garlic, Spring Onions and Ginger (page 160)
Stir-Fried Beef with Orange (page 104)
Lettuce with Oyster Sauce (page 210)
Steamed Rice (page 221)

Kidney and Beancurd Soup (page 70)
Stir-Fried Minced Pork (page 84)
Cold Marinated Bean Sprouts (page 198)
Stir-Fried Ginger Broccoli (page 199)
Steamed Rice (page 221)

Beef Noodle Soup (page 234)
Fried Wonton (page 260)
Stir-Fried Cucumbers with Hot Spices (page 208)
Peaches in Honey Syrup (page 266)
(This menu is for a light lunch or supper.)

Curried Sweetcorn Soup with Chicken (page 64)
Five-Spice Spareribs (page 95)
Fried Fish with Ginger (page 155)
Cold Spicy Noodles (page 231)
Stir-Fried Mangetout with Water Chestnuts (page 210)

Summer dinner parties

SERVES 6

Sesame Prawn Toast (page 255)
Chinese Chicken Salad (page 141)
Stir-Fried Pork with Spring Onions (page 85)
Stir-Fried Spinach with Garlic (page 216)
Steamed Rice (page 221)
Fruit Compote (page 266)

SERVES 4

Cold Spicy Noodles (page 231)
Chicken Pieces in Black Bean Sauce (page 119)
Stir-Fried Scallops with Pigs' Kidneys (page 172)
Cold Sweet and Sour Chinese Leaves (page 202)
Fresh Fruit (page 264)

Special dinner or banquet

This menu should be attempted when you feel reasonably competent at Chinese cooking. It takes quite a lot of preparation and you will find it easier to manage the whole meal if you have already experimented with the individual dishes. It is designed so that each dish is served as a separate course.

SERVES 6 TO 8

Caramel Walnuts (page 263)
Sweetcorn Soup with Crabmeat (page 75)
Rainbow Beef in Lettuce Leaves (page 100-1) or
Peking Duck with Chinese Pancakes (pages 142-3 and 248)
Stir-Fried Mangetout with Water Chestnuts (page 210)
Braised Pork with Beancurd (page 94)
Fresh Fruit (page 264)

Winter dinner parties

SERVES 4

Hot and Sour Soup (page 76)
Sichuan-Style Scallops (page 173)
Five-Spice Red-Braised Pigeons (page 148)
Braised Cauliflower with Oyster Sauce (page 201)
Steamed Rice (page 221)

SERVES 4–6

Wonton Soup (page 66)
Curried Chicken with Peppers (page 121)
Peking Braised Lamb (page 112)
Braised Spicy Aubergines (page 191)
Steamed Rice (page 221)
Prawn Crackers (page 253)
Mongolian Hot Pot (page 110-11)
Stir-Fried Pork with Spring Onions (page 85) (optional)

Soups are rarely served as a separate course in China, except at banquets. During some formal banquets, light soups are served at various stages of dining. They signal the end of a course and are used to cleanse the palate in preparation for the next one. Most commonly a clear broth will be served at the end of the dinner but before the dessert. At family meals soup is served at the same time as all the other dishes. In this case it complements the various tastes and textures of the meal and also serves as a beverage.

There are two basic types of soup in Chinese cookery: light and heavy. Light soups are clear broths garnished with a little meat, fish, seafood or vegetable. Such soups are a liquid accompaniment to other dishes. (Drinks such as water, wine and tea are rarely served with a family meal in China.) I remember family gatherings when a large tureen of clear soup with bits of delicious meats and seasonal vegetables would dominate the centre of the table, with all of the other dishes arranged round it. It was considered good form always to drink a good helping of it during the meal.

The heavy soups are more like separate courses or meals in their own right. They are substantial in texture, more like stews than soups, and are made from a rich stock with the addition of meat, fish or seafood, chopped vegetables and seasonings. These soups are generally thickened with a starch such as cornflour or water chestnut flour. Some are made in a heatproof casserole and simmered slowly until all the flavours marry. Sharks' fin is one of the most famous Chinese thick soups. It is a classic, gourmet soup. Its essential ingredient (sharks' fin) is expensive to obtain and the soup is time-consuming to make, so it is not really suitable for the domestic kitchen and is best enjoyed in a restaurant.

The key to a good Chinese soup, as to any soup, is good stock. I learned about Chinese stock first by watching my mother making it with meticulous care in her kitchen. These lessons were reinforced for me in my uncle's restaurant where a large pot of stock was the heart of the kitchen. All the world's great cuisines emphasize the importance of stock. The French call it the fonds de cuisine, the basis or foundation of cooking. In China, stock is essential in many recipes and it is indispensable in soup. In Chinese cuisine, stock is generally made from chicken, with pork bones sometimes being added to enrich the broth. Beef is used more in northern China; however, many Chinese from other regions consider its flavour too strong for their palate.

All the soups in the following chapter are easy to make, particularly if you have already made stock in advance. They can be served, Chinese-style, with other dishes, or as a separate course, or on their own as a light meal. You need not limit your enjoyment of these soups to an all-Chinese meal as Chinese soups blend deliciously with European food.

soup

CHICKEN STOCK

Chicken stock is an all-purpose base for soups and sauces. Its chief ingredient is inexpensive; it is light and delicious; and it marries well with other foods, enhancing and sustaining them. Small wonder it is an almost universally present ingredient in Chinese cookery. Thus, from the Imperial kitchens to the most humble food stalls, good stock is the basic ingredient. The usual Chinese chicken stock is precisely that: the essence of chicken, with complements of ginger and spring onions often added. Combined with the condiments that give Chinese food its distinctive flavour, good stock captures the essential taste of China. Many of the most famous recipes in the repertoire require such stock. There are two basic types. One is a clear stock made from chicken bones and meat; the other is a richer stock that uses ham and pork bones. The different recipes call for different stocks but both types make a solid base for soups and sauces.

During the Qing dynasty, the last Imperial dynasty (1644–1911), Chinese cuisine reached its peak of classical perfection. One of the most highly-prized dishes featured in the Imperial banquets was a bowl of clear soup, a consommé of chicken stock, much appreciated for its subtle, light, flavourful elegance.

This serves as a reminder that stock so prepared can also be used as a clear soup. I find that the richer stocks made with ham or pork bones are heavier and not quite fitting for my eating preferences. This simple recipe for stock reflects what I believe works best for any Chinese dish.

There are commercially prepared canned or cubed (dried) stocks but many of them are of inferior quality, being either too salty or containing additives and colourings that adversely affect your health as well as the natural taste of good foods. Stock does take time to prepare but it is easy to make your own – and when homemade, it is the best. You can make a big batch and freeze it for your own use when needed. Your first step on the path to success with Chinese cooking must be to prepare and maintain an ample supply of good chicken stock. I prefer to make large quantities of it at a time and freeze it. Once you have a supply of stock available you will be able to prepare any number of soups or sauces very quickly. Here are several important points to keep in mind when making stock.

Good stock requires meat to give it richness and flavour. It is therefore necessary to use at least some chicken meat, if not a whole bird.

The stock should never boil. If it does it will turn cloudy as the fat will be incorporated into the liquid. The best flavours come with a clear stock.

Use a tall, heavy pan so the liquid covers all the solids and evaporation is slow.

Simmer slowly and skim the stock regularly. Be patient, you will reap the rewards each time you prepare a Chinese dish.

Strain the finished stock well, through layers of muslin or a fine strainer.

Let the stock cool thoroughly, refrigerate and remove any fat before freezing it.

The classic Chinese method to ensure a clear stock is to blanch the meat and bones before simmering. I find this unnecessary. My method of careful skimming achieves the same result with less work. Remember to save all your fresh uncooked chicken bones and carcasses for stock. They can be frozen until you are ready to make it. (If you find the portions of this recipe too large for your needs, cut the quantities in half.)

Makes about 3.4 litres (6 pints)

2 kg (4½ lb) uncooked chicken bones, such as backs, feet, wings, etc.
750 g (1½ lb) chicken pieces, such as wings, thighs, drumsticks, etc.
3.4 litres (6 pints) cold water
3 slices fresh ginger
6 spring onions
6 cloves garlic, unpeeled
1 teaspoon salt

Put the chicken bones and chicken pieces into a very large pan. (The bones can be put in either frozen or defrosted.) Cover with the cold water and bring to a simmer. Meanwhile cut the ginger into diagonal slices, 5 x 1 cm (2 x ½ inch). Remove the green tops of the spring onions. Lightly crush the garlic, leaving the skins on.

Using a large, flat spoon, skim off the scum as it rises from the bones. Watch the heat as the stock should never boil. Keep skimming until the stock looks clear. This can take from 20 to 40 minutes. Do not stir or disturb the stock.

Turn the heat down to a low simmer.

Add the ginger, spring onions, garlic and salt. Simmer the stock on a very low heat for between 2 and 4 hours, skimming any fat off the top at least twice during this time. (The stock should be rich and full-bodied which is why it needs to be simmered for such a long time. This way the stock – and any soup you make with it – will have plenty of flavour.)

Strain the stock through several layers of dampened muslin or through a very fine mesh strainer, and then let it cool completely. Remove any fat which has risen to the top. It is now ready to be used or transferred to containers and frozen for future use.

pork and chicken stock

Pork is used extensively in Chinese cookery and pork bones, when added to chicken stock, make for a richer, tastier and sweeter soup. It was a favourite in our house not only as a beverage but as a 'rinse' for our rice bowls between courses. I also loved chewing on the cooked bones and looking for morsels of pork to dip in soy sauce. Use this stock as a light flavourful soup with your Chinese meals.

Regions: All

Makes about 2.25 litres (4 pints)

1 slice fresh ginger

2 spring onions

750 g (1½ lb) uncooked pork bones

2.25 litres (4 pints) Chicken Stock (page 59)

½ teaspoon salt

Cut the ginger into slices 5 x 1 cm (2 x ½ inch). Trim the green tops off the spring onions leaving the white part. Put the pork bones into a large pan together with the chicken stock. (Thaw the pork bones beforehand if they are frozen otherwise you will get a cloudy stock.) Bring the liquid to a simmer and skim off any scum that rises to the surface. Then add the ginger, spring onion whites and salt. Simmer on a very low heat for 1½ hours.

Strain the stock through dampened muslin or through a fine mesh strainer, and then leave it to cool. When the stock is cold remove any fat which has risen to the surface. It is now ready to be used as soup or as a stock for other soups such as Ham and Marrow Soup (page 72). You can also freeze it for future use.

chicken and spinach soup

Spinach, with its distinctive taste and deep green colour, is a favourite of the Chinese. This soup is light and very attractive. Its ingredients are blanched separately before they are combined with the stock so each retains its own taste. This is easy to make and many of the steps can be done in advance.

Region: Shanghai

Serves 4

450g (1 lb) fresh spinach
175 g (6 oz) chicken breasts
1 egg white
½ teaspoon salt
1 teaspoon cornflour
1.2 litres (2 pints) Chicken Stock (page 59)
2 tablespoons light soy sauce
2 teaspoons sugar
1 tablespoon Shaoxing rice wine or dry sherry
2 teaspoons sesame oil
2 tablespoons finely chopped spring onions

Remove the stems of the spinach and wash the leaves well. Blanch the leaves for a few seconds in a pan of boiling water until they are just wilted. Rinse them in cold water to prevent further cooking.

Cut the chicken into thin slices about 5 cm (2 inches) long and combine it with the egg white, salt and cornflour. Let it sit in the refrigerator for about 20 minutes.

In a separate pan of boiling water, blanch the chicken slices for 2 minutes until they are slightly firm and white; drain. The soup can be prepared up to this point several hours ahead.

Just before you are ready to eat, bring the chicken stock to a simmer and season it with the soy sauce, sugar and Shaoxing rice wine or dry sherry. Add the blanched spinach and chicken slices. Bring the soup back to simmering point, stir in the sesame oil and then add the spring onions. Serve at once.

tomato eggflower soup

Tomatoes were introduced into China less than 200 years ago, probably brought to China by the Portuguese. They were gradually adopted into southern Chinese cuisine and have become one of its most popular ingredients. Their intense, sweet flavour, brilliant colour and versatility make them perfect for Chinese cookery. Here they are used to enhance my adaptation of lightly beaten eggs which lie flat on the surface of the soup like lilies on a pond. This effect is created by gently guiding the eggs over the soup in strands instead of dropping the mixture in all at once which would cause the egg to lump together. The egg mixture slightly thickens the soup, which nevertheless remains very light.

This is an impressive-looking soup but it is very easy to make. It is especially delightful in summer when fresh tomatoes are at their most plentiful. Although canned tomatoes are acceptable, fresh ones are always preferable.

Serves 4

1.2 litres (2 pints) Chicken Stock (page 59)
225 g (8 oz) fresh or canned tomatoes
2 eggs
2 teaspoons sesame oil
1 teaspoon sugar
1 teaspoon salt
1 tablespoon light soy sauce
3 tablespoons finely chopped spring onions, white part only

FOR THE GARNISH
3 tablespoons finely chopped spring onion, green tops only

Put the chicken stock into a pan and bring it to a simmer. If you are using fresh tomatoes, peel, seed and cut them into 2.5 cm (1 inch) cubes. If you are using canned tomatoes, chop them into small chunks. Lightly beat the eggs with the sesame oil in a small bowl.

Add the sugar, salt and soy sauce to the stock and stir to mix them in well. Then add the tomatoes and simmer for 2 minutes. Next stir in the spring onions and then add the egg mixture in a very slow, thin stream. Using a chopstick or fork, pull the egg slowly into strands. (I have found that stirring the egg in a figure of eight works quite well.) Garnish with the finely chopped spring onion tops. Serve at once.

watercress soup

Here is a soup from my childhood. My mother used to make it with pork pieces and its delightful fragrance emanating from the kitchen signified good things to come. I would remove the pork pieces from the soup and dip them in soy sauce before eating them. Then I would pour some of the soup into my rice bowl to flavour the rice. In our family restaurant, this soup was a favourite at staff meals because of its wonderfully delicate flavour and because it is so easy to make. Nowadays I prefer it plain, without any meat added. Use only the leaves of the watercress for a delicate taste.

Regions: Canton and Fujian

Serves 4

1.2 litres (2 pints) Chicken Stock (page 59)
2 tablespoons light soy sauce
1 teaspoon sugar
½ teaspoon salt
¼ teaspoon freshly ground white pepper
150 g (5 oz) watercress, stems removed
2 teaspoons finely chopped fresh ginger
3 tablespoons finely chopped spring onions

Bring the stock to a simmer in a large pan. Add the soy sauce, sugar, salt and pepper and simmer for 3 minutes. Then add the watercress leaves, ginger and spring onions and continue to simmer the soup for a further 4 minutes. Serve at once.

curried sweetcorn soup with chicken

Regions: Canton and Fujian

Curry is especially popular in southern and eastern China where returning emigrants have brought the influence of curry from south-east Asia. The Chinese favour curry powder or paste which comes from Madras but, unlike Indians, Chinese cooks use curry only as a light addition to the usual Chinese seasonings, a subtle touch rather than a dominant tone.

This is not a traditional Chinese soup but is my version of sweetcorn soup which has become popular in the West. It is easy to make and is delicious. If you use canned creamed corn which is already quite thick, you could leave out the cornflour mixture. The rich golden sheen of the curried soup makes it an appealing, bright dish for a dinner which might include Stir-Fried Pork with Spring Onions (page 85), a green vegetable such as spinach and plain steamed rice. as spinach and plain steamed rice.

Serves 4

450 g (1 lb) fresh sweetcorn on a cob, or 275 g (10 oz) canned sweetcorn

225 g (8 oz) boneless chicken breasts, skinned

1 egg white

1 teaspoon salt

1 teaspoon sesame oil

1 teaspoon cornflour

1 egg

1 teaspoon sesame oil

1.2 litres (2 pints) Chicken Stock (page 59)

1 tablespoon Shaoxing rice wine or dry sherry

1 tablespoon curry powder or paste

1 teaspoon salt

1 teaspoon sugar

2 teaspoons cornflour blended with 2 teaspoons water

FOR THE GARNISH

2 tablespoons finely chopped spring onions

If using fresh corn, wash the cobs and remove the kernels with a sharp knife or cleaver. You should end up with about 275 g (10 oz). If you are using canned corn, empty the contents into a bowl and set it aside. Using a cleaver or a sharp knife, thinly slice the chicken breasts into fine shreds about 7.5 cm (3 inches) long. Mix the chicken shreds with the egg white, salt, sesame oil and cornflour in a small bowl and refrigerate for 15 minutes. Beat the whole egg and sesame oil together in another small bowl and set it aside.

Bring a small pan of water to the boil. Turn off the heat, quickly blanch the chicken shreds until they just turn white. (This should take about 20 seconds.) Remove them with a slotted spoon and drain them well. Bring the stock to a simmer in a large pan, add the sweetcorn and simmer for 10 minutes, uncovered. Add the Shaoxing rice wine or dry sherry, curry powder, salt, sugar and, if you are using it, the cornflour mixture. Bring it back to the boil, then lower the heat and simmer for another 5 minutes. Add the blanched chicken shreds, then add the egg and sesame oil mixture in a very slow, thin stream. Using a chopstick or fork, pull the egg slowly into strands. Ladle into a large soup tureen, garnish with the spring onions and serve at once.

chicken and mushroom soup

Region: Canton

This soup combines two classic southern Chinese ingredients: chicken and dried mushrooms. Dark chicken meat from the legs and thighs is most often used for this soup to give it a rich, strong flavour and a good texture. Use the dried Chinese mushrooms as their smoky flavour enhances the total effect of the soup.

There are two techniques involved here. The chicken is first stir-fried to give it a rich flavour. Then all the other ingredients are simmered together with the cooked chicken. The result is a good hearty soup which would go well with French bread and butter for a non-Chinese meal. It also re-heats nicely, tasting even better next day.

Serves 4

225 g (8 oz) boneless chicken thighs or legs, skinned

2 tablespoons Shaoxing rice wine or dry sherry

2½ tablespoons light soy sauce

1 teaspoon sesame oil

1 teaspoon cornflour

25 g (1 oz) Chinese dried mushrooms

1.2 litres (2 pints) Chicken Stock (page 59)

1 tablespoon finely chopped spring onions

1 teaspoon salt

½ teaspoon freshly ground white pepper

25 g (1 oz) Parma ham or lean smoked bacon, shredded

2 teaspoons groundnut (peanut) oil

Cut the chicken into 1 cm (½ inch) cubes, retaining any bones. Put them into a bowl with 1 tablespoon of Shaoxing rice wine or dry sherry, 1½ tablespoons of soy sauce, the sesame oil and cornflour. Let the mixture stand for 20 minutes.

Soak the mushrooms in warm water for 20 minutes. Drain them and squeeze out excess liquid. Remove and discard the stems and shred the caps into thin strips.

Bring the stock to a simmer in a large pan. Drain any marinade from the chicken into the stock. Add the mushrooms, spring onions, salt, pepper, ham or bacon and the remaining rice wine or sherry and soy sauce. Leave to simmer.

Meanwhile heat a wok or large frying pan until it is very hot. Add the oil and when it is very hot and slightly smoking, add the chicken. Stir-fry the chicken pieces over a high heat for about 5 minutes until they are nicely brown. Drain them in a colander. Add them to the soup and simmer together for 5 minutes and serve at once.

wonton soup

This is one of the most popular soups in street food stalls throughout southern China and it is equally popular in Chinese restaurants in the West. Ideally, soup wonton should be stuffed savoury dumplings poached in clear water and then served in a rich broth. This recipe makes a simple but authentic wonton soup, perfect for any family meal. Wonton skins can be obtained from Chinese grocers, as well as supermarkets. They are yellowish in colour, square, and packaged in small stacks. They can be found on the shop's cool shelf or in the freezer. (Thaw them thoroughly if they are frozen.)

Region: Canton

Serves 4 to 6

FOR THE FILLING

250g (9 oz) peeled uncooked prawns, de-veined and coarsely chopped

250 g (9 oz) minced pork

1 teaspoon salt

1/2 teaspoon freshly ground white-pepper

1 1/2 tablespoons light soy sauce

2 tablespoons finely chopped spring onions

1 tablespoon Shaoxing rice wine or dry sherry

1 teaspoon sugar

2 teaspoons sesame oil

1 egg white, lightly beaten

250 g (9 oz) wonton skins

1.2 litres (2 pints) Chicken Stock (page 59)

1 tablespoon light soy sauce

1 teaspoon sesame oil

FOR THE GARNISH

Chopped spring onions

Put the prawns and pork in a large bowl; add the salt and pepper and mix well, either by kneading with your hands or by stirring with a wooden spoon. Then add all the other filling ingredients and stir them well into the prawn and pork mixture. Cover the bowl with cling film and chill for at least 20 minutes.

Put 1 tablespoon of the filling in the centre of the first wonton skin. Dampen the edges with a little water and bring up the sides of the skin around the filling. Pinch the edges together at the top to seal; it should look like a small filled bag. Fill the remaining wontons.

When the wontons are ready, bring the stock, soy sauce and sesame oil to a simmer in a large pan. In another large pan, bring salted water to a boil and poach the wontons for 1 minute or until they float to the top. Remove them immediately and transfer them to the pan with the stock. Continue to simmer them in the stock for 2 minutes. Ladle into a large soup tureen or individual bowls. Garnish with the spring onions and serve at once.

ham and bean sprout soup

This is a simple soup which typifies the fresh, light cooking of the south. Like many good soups, it takes a little effort to prepare, but it is worth it. It is best to use bean sprouts which are really fresh to give your soup a good crunchy texture. Chinese ham is traditionally used to produce the distinctive smoky flavour, but since it cannot be obtained in Europe, lean smoked bacon or Parma ham are satisfactory substitutes.

Regions: Canton and Fujian

Serves 4

50 g (2 oz) bean thread (transparent) noodles
75 g (3 oz) fresh bean sprouts
1.2 litres (2 pints) Chicken Stock (page 59)
1 tablespoon light soy sauce
75 g (3 oz) Parma ham or lean smoked bacon, shredded
2 tablespoons finely chopped fresh coriander
2 tablespoons finely chopped spring onions

Soak the noodles in a bowl of warm water for about 20 minutes or until they are soft. Drain them thoroughly in a colander and cut them into 5 cm (2 inch) pieces. Remove both ends of the bean sprouts. This will give the soup a cleaner look.

Bring the chicken stock to a simmer in a large pan. Add the drained noodles and soy sauce and simmer for 2 minutes. Then add the ham or bacon, coriander and spring onions and simmer for 30 seconds. Finally, add the bean sprouts and simmer for another 30 seconds. Serve at once.

ham and pigeon steamed in soup

Region: Shanghai

The unusual technique for making this soup is not difficult to master. It is called double-steamed, where rich ingredients are steamed for hours in a covered casserole filled with soup. This extracts all the flavours from the ingredients and is often used for making the classic Sharks' Fin and Birds' Nest Soups. The result is a distinctive soup; clear and rich but also light. Game birds other than pigeon, such as partridge, snipe or quail, would work equally well. This elegant rich, clear consommé is ideal for a dinner party. I would make it in advance and freeze it, as it re-heats well.

Serves 4

2 x 350–450 g (12–16 oz) pigeons
25 g (1 oz) Parma ham or lean smoked bacon
4 slices fresh ginger
1.2 litres (2 pints) Chicken Stock (page 59)
4 spring onions
2 tablespoons Shaoxing rice wine or dry sherry
½ teaspoon salt

Using a sharp, heavy knife or cleaver, cut the pigeons into quarters. Bring a pan of water to the boil, turn the heat down and add the pigeons. Simmer them for 10 minutes. (This blanching rids the pigeons of some of their fat and impurities.) Remove them with a slotted spoon and discard the water. Cut the Parma ham or bacon into very fine shreds and cut the ginger into slices 5 x 0.5 cm (2 x ¼ inch).

Next set up a steamer or put a rack into a wok or deep pan and add 5 cm (2 inches) of water. Bring to the boil.

Meanwhile, bring the stock to the boil in another large pan and then pour it into a heatproof glass or china casserole. Add the pigeon, ham, spring onions, ginger, Shaoxing rice wine or dry sherry and salt and cover it with a lid or foil. Put the casserole on the rack and cover the wok or pan tightly with a lid or foil. (You now have a casserole within a steamer, hence the name 'double steaming'.) Turn the heat down and steam gently for 2 to 3 hours or until the pigeon is tender. Top up with boiling water occasionally.

You can also simmer the soup very slowly in a conventional pan, but the resulting taste will be quite different.

When the soup is cooked, remove all the ingredients with a slotted spoon and discard the spring onions, ginger and ham. Serve the soup together with the pigeon pieces. The soup can be served immediately or cooled and stored in the refrigerator or freezer to be re-heated.

kidney and beancurd soup

My mother often made kidney soup for our family dinner because it was tasty and inexpensive. Sometimes she added watercress or spinach to it. In this recipe the kidneys are cleaned in bicarbonate of soda and quickly blanched before being added to the stock. This prevents the kidney juices from clouding the soup. It is a light and nutritious soup which re-heats well. Serve it with Cashew Chicken (page 130) and Spicy Stir-Fried Mushrooms (page 211).

Serves 4 to 6

450 g (1 lb) pigs' kidneys

1 teaspoon bicarbonate of soda

2 teaspoons Chinese white rice vinegar or cider vinegar

1 teaspoon salt

400 g (14 oz) fresh beancurd

1.2 litres (2 pints) Chicken or Pork and Chicken Stock (page 59 or page 60)

1 tablespoon finely chopped fresh ginger

2 teaspoons finely chopped spring onions

2 tablespoons light soy sauce

2 teaspoons sugar

1 teaspoon salt

Using a sharp knife, remove the thin outer membrane of the kidneys. Then, with a sharp cleaver or knife, cut each kidney in half, cutting horizontally to keep the shape of the kidney. Cut away the small knobs of fat and any tough membrane which surrounds them. Put the kidney halves flat on the cutting surface and score the top of each half, making light cuts in a criss-cross pattern all over the surface (see page 113). Then cut the halved kidneys into thin slices. Toss the kidney slices with the bicarbonate of soda and let them sit for about 20 minutes. Then rinse them thoroughly with cold water and toss them in the vinegar and salt. Put them into a colander and let them drain for at least 30 minutes or more.

Bring a pan of water to the boil. Blot the kidney slices dry with kitchen paper and blanch them in the water for about 2 minutes. Drain them in a colander or sieve and set aside. Cut the beancurd into 1 cm (½ inch) cubes.

In a separate pan, bring the stock to a simmer and add the rest of the ingredients. Simmer for about 5 minutes and then add the kidney slices to the soup. Give the soup several stirs and simmer another 2 minutes. Serve at once or allow to cool and re-heat gently when required.

beancurd spinach soup

Colourful and light, this soup contrasts bright green spinach with white beancurd. **Regions: Canton and Fujian**
A good, home-made chicken stock is vital here as the ingredients are subtly flavoured
and textured. It is easy to make. This dish is a perfect starter for any meal.

Serves 4

450 g (1 lb) fresh spinach, stems removed

450 g (1 lb) beancurd

1.2 litres (2 pints) Chicken Stock (page 59)

1 tablespoon Shaoxing rice wine or
dry sherry

1 tablespoon light soy sauce

1 teaspoon salt

1 teaspoon sugar

1 teaspoon sesame oil

1 teaspoon dark soy sauce

Salt and freshly ground black pepper
to taste

FOR THE GARNISH

Chopped spring onions

Wash the spinach well and leave to drain.

Gently cut the beancurd into 1 cm (½ inch) cubes; drain on kitchen paper.

Put the chicken stock into a pan and bring it to a simmer. Add the beancurd and simmer for 2 minutes. Add the rest of the ingredients except the spinach and simmer for another 10 minutes. Add the spinach and cook for 2 minutes. Add the spring onions and serve.

ham and marrow soup

Region: Sichuan

Although courgettes and marrows, as we know them, are not available in China, there are many similar members of the same family which are used in Chinese cookery. This is an adaptation of a traditional recipe which calls for 'hairy melon' or Chinese marrow, which is much more appetizing than it sounds. The exterior of Chinese marrow is fuzzy and hairy, rather like a peach – hence its name. I think that marrow tastes very similar and makes an excellent alternative. This is basically a clear soup. It goes well with Sweet and Sour Pork (page 88-9) and Stir-Fried Spinach with Garlic (page 216).

Serves 4

225 g (8 oz) marrow or courgettes

1.2 litres (2 pints) Chicken or Pork and Chicken Stock (page 59 or page 60)

50 g (2 oz) Parma ham or lean smoked bacon, finely shredded

1½ teaspoons chilli bean sauce

1½ tablespoons light soy sauce

2 teaspoons dark soy sauce

1 teaspoon Shaoxing rice wine or dry sherry

½ teaspoon salt

¼ teaspoon freshly ground white pepper

FOR THE GARNISH

2 teaspoons sesame oil

Trim the ends of the marrow or courgettes and, if you are using marrow, remove the seeds. Cut into 1 cm (½ inch) cubes. Bring the stock to the boil in a large pan. Add the marrow or courgettes, ham or bacon and all the other ingredients. Simmer the soup, uncovered, for 15 minutes. Add the sesame oil and give it a good stir. Ladle into a large soup tureen or individual bowls and serve at once.

cabbage and pork soup

Simple combinations of basic foods make tasty soups and soups such as this one are typical fare in northern Chinese homes, especially in autumn and winter when cabbage is abundant. This version is easy to make and very tasty; the sweetness of the cabbage blending nicely with the pork-flavoured broth.

Region: Beijing

Serves 4

1.2 litres (2 pints) Chicken Stock (page 59)

175 g (6 oz) lean pork, shredded

1 teaspoon Shaoxing rice wine or dry sherry

2 teaspoons light soy sauce

½ teaspoon cornflour

½ teaspoon sesame oil

1 tablespoon groundnut (peanut) oil

350 g (12 oz) Chinese leaves, shredded crossways

1 teaspoon Shaoxing rice wine or dry sherry

2 teaspoons light soy sauce

1 teaspoon dark soy sauce

Salt and freshly ground black pepper to taste

FOR THE GARNISH

Spring onions, finely chopped

Put the chicken stock into a medium-sized pan and bring it to a simmer.

Combine the pork with the Shaoxing rice wine or sherry, soy sauce, cornflour and sesame oil. Heat a wok or frying pan until it is very hot. Add the groundnut oil and when it is hot and slightly smoking, add the pork and stir-fry for 1 minute. Remove from the heat and set aside.

Add the Chinese leaves, Shaoxing rice wine or dry sherry and soy sauces to the simmering stock and simmer for 5 minutes. Add the pork to the stock and simmer for a further 1 minute. Season to taste with salt and pepper. Ladle into a large soup tureen or individual soup bowls. Garnish with spring onions and serve at once.

sweetcorn soup with crabmeat

My mother often made this soup using fresh sweetcorn. For convenience, tinned or frozen corn may be substituted but I think my mother's recipe is quite superior. It reheats well and has a rich, thick texture which goes well with Beef in Oyster Sauce (page 103) and Stir-Fried Ginger Broccoli (page 199).

Region: Canton

Serves 4

450 g (1 lb) fresh sweetcorn on the cob, or 275 g (10 oz) canned or frozen sweet corn

1 egg white

1 teaspoon sesame oil

1.2 litres (2 pints) Chicken Stock (page 59)

1 tablespoon Shaoxing rice wine or dry sherry

1 tablespoon light soy sauce

2 teaspoons finely chopped fresh ginger

1 teaspoon salt

¼ teaspoon freshly ground white pepper

1 teaspoon sugar

2 teaspoons cornflour blended with 2 teaspoons water

225 g (8 oz) freshly cooked or frozen crabmeat

FOR THE GARNISH

2 tablespoons finely chopped spring onions

If using fresh corn, wash the cobs and remove the kernels with a knife or cleaver. (You should end up with about 275 g (10 oz) of corn.) Mix the egg white and sesame oil in a bowl and set it aside.

Bring the stock to a boil in a large pan and add the corn. Simmer for 15 minutes, uncovered and then add the Shaoxing rice wine or dry sherry, soy sauce, ginger, salt, pepper, sugar and cornflour mixture. Bring it back to the boil, then lower the heat to a simmer. Add the crabmeat and then slowly pour in the egg white mixture in a steady stream, stirring all the time. Ladle into a large soup tureen and garnish with the spring onions. Serve at once.

hot and sour soup

This Chinese soup has become quite popular in the Western world because it is heavy and suited to cold climates. It combines sour and spicy elements in a rich, tasty stock, and re-heats very well. The list of ingredients may be daunting but the recipe is, in fact, quite easy to make. It is delicious, replete with different textures and contrasting flavours. It originated in northern China, but I know that it is also renowned in the western parts of China where spicy foods are a speciality.

Regions: Beijing and Sichuan

Serves 4

100 g (4 oz) lean boneless pork,
finely shredded

FOR THE MARINADE
1 teaspoon light soy sauce
1 teaspoon Shaoxing rice wine or
dry sherry
½ teaspoon sesame oil
½ teaspoon cornflour
a pinch of salt
a pinch of sugar
25 g (1 oz) dried Chinese mushrooms
15 g (½ oz) dried 'tree ear' mushrooms
2 eggs, beaten with a pinch of salt
2 teaspoons sesame oil
1.2 litres (2 pints) Chicken Stock (page 62)
2 teaspoons salt
250 g (9 oz) fresh bean curd, drained
and shredded
1½ tablespoons light soy sauce
1 tablespoon dark soy sauce
1 teaspoon freshly ground white pepper
6 tablespoons Chinese white rice vinegar
or eider vinegar
2 teaspoons sesame oil
1 tablespoon chilli oil
2 tablespoons finely chopped
fresh coriander

Combine the pork with the soy sauce, Shaoxing rice wine or dry sherry, sesame oil, cornflour, salt and sugar. Mix well and set aside. Soak the mushrooms and tree ear mushrooms in warm water for 20 minutes. Drain and squeeze out any excess liquid. Discard the stems and finely shred the caps. In a small bowl, combine the eggs and salt with the sesame oil and set aside.

Bring the stock to a simmer in a large pan and add the salt. Stir in the pork and simmer for 1 minute. Then add the mushrooms and beancurd and continue to simmer for 2 minutes.

Add the egg mixture in a very slow, thin stream. Using a chopstick or fork, pull the egg slowly into strands.

Remove the soup from the heat, and stir in the soy sauces, pepper and vinegar. Give the soup a good stir, then finally add the sesame oil, chilli oil and fresh coriander and stir. Ladle into a large soup tureen or individual bowls and serve.

chinese cabbage soup

Classically simple clear soups such as this one are served in many Chinese homes. The soup is consumed as a beverage throughout the meal. It must therefore be light and refreshing. The Chinese leaves add a touch of sweetness while the preserved vegetables add a nice bite. If you want it to be completely vegetarian, you can substitute water or vegetable stock for the chicken stock.

Regions: Beijing and Sichuan

Serves 4

1.2 litres (2 pints) Chicken Stock (page 59)

450 g (1 lb) Chinese leaves, shredded crossways

100 g (4 oz) Sichuan preserved vegetables, thoroughly rinsed and finely chopped

1 tablespoon light soy sauce

2 teaspoons dark soy sauce

2 tablespoons Shaoxing rice wine or dry sherry

2 teaspoons sugar

Salt and freshly ground black pepper to taste

2 teaspoons sesame oil

FOR THE GARNISH

Spring onions, chopped

Put the chicken stock into a medium-sized pan and bring it to a simmer. Add the Chinese leaves and preserved vegetables and simmer for 3 minutes. Add the soy sauces, Shaoxing rice wine or dry sherry and sugar and simmer for 5 minutes. Season with salt and pepper and stir in the sesame oil. Ladle into a large soup tureen or individual bowls. Garnish with the spring onions and serve at once.

Left, opposite:
Chinese Mushroom
(*page 28*)

asparagus and minced chicken soup

Although asparagus is a relatively new vegetable in the repertoire of Chinese vegetables, **Regions: Hong Kong and Canton** it has become quite popular in Hong Kong and southern China. In this light, flavourful soup it is paired with chicken, which has been chopped and mixed with egg white. The result is a light soup of delicate flavours and contrasting colours: perfect as a starter.

Serves 4

1.2 litres (2 pints) Chicken Stock (page 59)

225 g (8 oz) fresh asparagus

225 g (8 oz) boneless chicken breasts, skinned

1 egg white

1 teaspoon sesame oil

½ teaspoon salt

2 teaspoons Shaoxing rice wine or dry sherry

2 teaspoons light soy sauce

1 teaspoon salt

Freshly ground black pepper to taste

FOR THE GARNISH

Chopped spring onions

Put the chicken stock into a medium-sized pan and bring it to a simmer. Cut the asparagus into 2.5 cm (1 inch) pieces.

Cut the chicken breasts into small pieces. Put them with the egg white, sesame oil and salt in a food processor or blender and blend until smooth. Put the mixture in a small bowl and cover with cling film. Put it in the refrigerator for 5 minutes.

Add the asparagus, Shaoxing rice wine or dry sherry, soy sauce, salt and pepper to the simmering stock. Cook for 3 minutes or until the asparagus is cooked. Remove the pan from the heat. Add the chicken mixture, stirring vigorously to break up any large lumps. Return the pan to the stove and simmer for another 1 minute. Garnish with spring onions and serve at once.

Whenever my family talked about meat we invariably referred to pork. On rare occasions we ate beef and even less frequently lamb. This was probably because although I was brought up in America, my family came from southern China where beef and lamb are not common. Beef, mutton and goat are more popular in northern China, a reflection of the Moslem and Mongolian influences in this area. In the main, however, most Chinese think of meat as being pork. So, as you might expect, there are innumerable pork dishes in Chinese cuisine. Pork is an extremely versatile meat which can be prepared in many different ways and its subtle flavour lends itself to many complementary ingredients, seasonings and sauces. Pork fat is also highly prized and it is cooked in various ways which render it not only edible but delicious.

This chapter contains some recipes for beef and lamb since Chinese cuisine does utilize all edible meats. If you like, you can also substitute beef for pork in some of the recipes. Stir-fried Pork with Spring Onions (page 85) and Stir-Fried Minced Pork (page 84) will work just as well with beef.

Sheep and goat share the same Chinese written character. Goat is more widely available in northern China, but it is also eaten in other areas. I prefer to use lamb instead. A Chinese poet once wrote 'There are seventy-two ways of cooking lamb; of these only eighteen or nineteen are palatable.' These recipes here are within the latter category!

I prefer to use meat which has not been frozen since freezing breaks down the cell structure and makes the meat watery when it is thawed; besides I think the fresh meat has a better flavour. This is particularly important when selecting meat for stir-frying. Meat should be as dry as possible so that it will fry rather than steam in its own juices. Although the Chinese are very fond of meat they eat it in small quantities. This is one reason why Chinese food is so healthy.

meat

CUTS OF MEAT

The following European cuts of meat are most suitable for Chinese cooking.

Pork For stir-frying use loin chops with the bones and all the fat removed, or pork steaks or fillet. Pork belly is best for braising. The best minced pork comes from the blade which is a reasonably-priced cut.

Beef I prefer fillet steak for stir-frying since it is lean and tender and full of flavour. Although it is expensive, a little goes a long way. Sirloin, rump and T-bone steak are also suitable. My favourite cut for braising is brisket. Although it is fatty, its taste and ability to absorb the flavours of a sauce are unbeatable. The Chinese love the texture of braised brisket. Shin and chuck steak are also suitable for slow-cooking.

Lamb Loin chops with the bones and all the fat removed are perfect for stir-frying, as are lamb fillets (which come from the neck) and lamb steaks. The best cuts for braising are breast, scrag end of neck or shoulder.

Dried and cured meats Lack of refrigeration means that various meats which are preserved by drying or curing are also popular in Chinese cuisine. Dried beef is often eaten as a snack while cured ham is used in cooking. The regions of Zhejiang and Yunnan are famous for their hams which unfortunately are unobtainable in the West, although Parma ham or smoked bacon are acceptable substitutes for Zhejiang or Yunnan ham.

Offal In Chinese cookery nothing is ever wasted. Every part of a beast is utilized. Even what Westerners deride as 'offal' is extremely popular. It is usually braised, except for liver which is commonly stir-fried.

pork with black bean sauce

Pork goes particularly well with black beans, the salty and pungent flavour of which is so distinctively southern Chinese. This simple, homely stir-fried dish is one which I often ate as a child. Sometimes my mother would vary the taste by adding an extra spicy touch of chilli bean sauce. It is very quick to cook and goes well with plain rice and any stir-fried vegetable.

Region: Canton
Method: Stir-frying

Serves 4

450g (1 lb) lean pork
1 tablespoon Shaoxing rice wine or dry sherry
1 tablespoon light soy sauce
2 teaspoons sesame oil
1 teaspoon cornflour
1½ tablespoons groundnut (peanut) oil
1½ tablespoons black beans, rinsed and coarsely chopped
1 tablespoon finely chopped garlic
3 tablespoons finely chopped spring onions
1 tablespoon chopped shallots
1½ tablespoons light soy sauce
1 teaspoon sugar
1 tablespoon Chicken Stock (page 59) or water
1 tablespoon sesame oil

Cut the pork into thin slices 5 cm (2 inches) long. Put the slices into a bowl and mix them well with the Shaoxing rice wine or dry sherry, soy sauce, sesame oil and cornflour. Leave to marinate for about 20 minutes.

Heat a wok or large frying pan until it is very hot. Add half the oil and when it is very hot and slightly smoking, lift the pork out of the marinade with a slotted spoon, put it in the wok and quickly stir-fry it for about 2 to 3 minutes. Transfer it to a bowl at once.

Wipe the wok or pan clean, re-heat it and add the rest of the oil. Quickly add the black beans, garlic, spring onions and shallots. A few seconds later add the rest of the ingredients. Bring the mixture to a boil and then return the pork to the wok or pan. Stir-fry the entire mixture for another 5 minutes. Turn it on to a warm serving platter and serve at once.

stir-fried minced pork

The secret of this delicious, easy to prepare and inexpensive dish lies in the use of preserved vegetables which are typical of northern Chinese cuisine. In the north, people must preserve vegetables by salting or pickling since the winters are long and cold. You can use the Cold Sweet and Sour Chinese Leaves (page 202) instead of the Sichuan or Tianjin preserved vegetable, but it is worth the effort of buying the latter from a Chinese grocer. I like to serve this as a stuffing for fresh lettuce leaves or Chinese Pancakes (page 248). Plain steamed rice and a simple, stir-fried vegetable dish such as Stir-Fried Spinach with Garlic (page 216) would also go well with this dish.

Region: Beijing
Method: Stir-frying

Serves 4

100 g (4 oz) Sichuan or Tianjin preserved vegetable or Cold Sweet and Sour Chinese Leaves (page 202)

1½ tablespoons groundnut (peanut) oil

450 g (1 lb) minced pork

2 tablespoons dark soy sauce

1 tablespoon Shaoxing rice wine or dry sherry

2 teaspoons sesame oil

2 teaspoons sugar

FOR THE GARNISH

3 tablespoons finely chopped spring onions

Rinse the preserved vegetable or Cold Sweet and Sour Chinese Leaves well in cold water. Drain them in a colander and then blot them dry with kitchen paper. Chop them finely and set them aside.

Heat a wok or large frying pan until it is very hot. Add the oil and when it is very hot and slightly smoking, add the pork and stir-fry it for 2 minutes. Stir constantly to break up any lumps. Then add the Chinese leaves or preserved vegetable and the rest of the ingredients. Continue to stir-fry for another 5 minutes or until the pork is cooked. Turn it on to a warm serving platter and serve at once.

If you are serving it with Chinese pancakes or lettuce leaves, each person piles a little of the meat mixture into a pancake or lettuce leaf, wraps it up well and eats it with their fingers.

stir-fried pork with spring onions

This dish is in the southern Chinese tradition. The key to success when cooking this recipe is not to overcook the pork.

Region: Canton
Method: Stir-frying

Serves 3 to 4

450 g (1 lb) lean boneless pork

1 tablespoon Shaoxing rice wine or dry sherry

1 tablespoon light soy sauce

2 teaspoons sesame oil

1 teaspoon cornflour

8 spring onions

1 tablespoon groundnut (peanut) oil

2 teaspoons salt

1 teaspoon freshly ground black pepper

1 teaspoon sugar

Cut the pork into thin slices 5 cm (2 inches) long. Mix with the Shaoxing rice wine or dry sherry, soy sauce, sesame oil and cornflour. Leave to marinate for about 20 minutes. Slice the spring onions diagonally into 5 cm (2 inch) lengths. **Heat a wok** or frying pan until it is very hot. Add the oil and when it is very hot and slightly smoking, add the pork slices and stir-fry them until they are brown. Add the spring onions, salt, pepper and sugar. Continue to stir-fry until the pork is cooked and slightly firm – about 5 minutes. Remove and arrange on a warm serving platter. Pour any remaining juices in the wok over the pork and serve.

lionhead pork meatball casserole

This dish has a fanciful name and is very popular in eastern as well as other parts of China. The meatballs are said to resemble a lion's head and the cabbage leaves its mane. It is a hearty and delicious dish. The secret of its distinctive texture may be found in the combination of cold water and egg white with fatty minced pork, the result being a light and fluffy meatball. In China, the mixing is done by hand with the cook throwing the meat against the side of a bowl to tenderize and fluff the meat. This dish can be prepared in advance and re-heated.

Region: Shanghai
Methods: Pan-frying and braising

Serves 4

450 g (1 lb) Chinese leaves, stalks separated and cut into 5 cm (2 inch) strips

175 g (6 oz) water chestnuts, peeled if fresh, rinsed if canned (page 37)

450 g (1 lb) fatty minced pork

1 egg white

4 tablespoons cold water

2 tablespoons light soy sauce

1 tablespoon dark soy sauce

2 tablespoons Shaoxing rice wine or dry sherry

1½ tablespoons sugar

2 teaspoons salt

½ teaspoon freshly ground black pepper

Cornflour, for dusting

3–4 tablespoons groundnut (peanut) oil

2 teaspoons groundnut (peanut) oil

4 cloves garlic, peeled and crushed

450 ml (15 fl oz) Chicken Stock (page 59)

Prepare the Chinese leaves and coarsely chop the water chestnuts. Mix pork with the egg white and cold water by hand. The mixture should be light and fluffy. Do not use a blender as it would make the mixture too dense. Then add the water chestnuts, soy sauces, Shaoxing rice wine or dry sherry, sugar, salt and pepper and mix for another 30 seconds.

Divide the mixture into six equal parts and roll each into a meatball. Dust each meatball with cornflour. Heat a wok or large frying pan until it is very hot. Add the oil and when it is very hot and slightly smoking, add the meatballs. Turn the heat down and slowly brown the meatballs. Remove the meatballs from the pan and drain on kitchen paper.

Clean the wok or pan and re-heat it until it is hot. Then add the 2 teaspoons oil and when it is very hot and slightly smoking, add the garlic and stir-fry for 10 seconds. Then add the Chinese leaves and stir-fry for 20 seconds. Then add the chicken stock and continue to cook for 2 minutes until the leaves are soft. Transfer the mixture to a heavy flameproof casserole or saucepan. Lay the meatballs on top of the leaves, bring the mixture to a boil, then turn the heat to very low, cover and simmer for 1½ hours.

Arrange the leaves on a warm serving platter, lay the meatballs on top, pour the sauce over the dish and serve at once.

twice-cooked pork

This recipe captures many of the elements of authentic, ancient Chinese cuisine. Most of the flavour of pork is concentrated in the fat, but the problem with fatty meat is its chewy, greasy texture. Twice-cooking is the age-old Chinese solution to this problem. First the meat is simmered slowly to make it tender and to render some of the fat; then it is stir-fried to rid it of most of the remaining fat. Despite the loss of so much of the fat, the meat retains its authentic pork flavour. Here the pork is finished off in a spicy mixture that makes it delicious and mouth-watering. The original Chinese recipe calls for pork belly; if this is unavailable, meaty spareribs can be substituted. This dish goes well with plain rice and re-heats well.

Region: Sichuan
Methods: Stir-frying and braising

Serves 4

1 kg (2 lb) pork belly or meaty spareribs

4 slices fresh ginger

6 spring onions

2 tablespoons groundnut (peanut) oil

3 tablespoons finely chopped garlic

1 small onion, thinly sliced

1 red pepper, de-seeded and thinly sliced

1 green pepper, de-seeded and thinly sliced

225 g (8 oz) leeks, green part removed and shredded

3 tablespoons Chicken Stock (page 59)

3 tablespoons hoisin sauce

1½ tablespoons chilli bean sauce

2 tablespoons Shaoxing rice wine or dry sherry

1 tablespoon dark soy sauce

1 teaspoon salt

1 teaspoon sugar

Bring a pan of salted water to the boil, add the belly or spareribs and simmer for 10 minutes, skimming all the while. Add the ginger and spring onions, turn the heat to low, cover tightly and simmer for 1 hour. Drain the pork in a colander. Discard the liquid, ginger and spring onions. When the pork is cool enough, cut it into 5 x 1 cm (2 x ½ inch) pieces.

Heat a wok or large frying pan until it is very hot. Add the oil, and when it is very hot and slightly smoking, add the pork and use the wok cover or pan lid to keep the fat from splattering. Stir-fry for 20 minutes until brown or, if you are using belly, until the fat is rendered. Drain carefully in a colander, keeping 1 tablespoon of oil in the wok or pan. Re-heat the wok or pan and when it is hot, add the garlic, onion, peppers and leeks and stir-fry for 4 minutes or until the vegetables are tender. Add the rest of the ingredients, return the pork to the mixture, turn the heat down, cover and braise for 15 minutes until tender. Turn on to a platter and serve at once.

sweet and sour pork

Of all Chinese dishes, Sweet and Sour Pork is probably one of the best known in the West. Unfortunately for Westerners, it is rarely properly made, often consisting of heavy, doughy balls containing a scrap of pork drenched in a hideously sweet, red sauce. Properly prepared, sweet and sour Chinese dishes are so delicately balanced that one is hard pressed to describe them as either strictly sweet or sour. In my version of this classic dish, you will find that balance. It is best served with plain steamed rice and a simple blanched vegetable such as cabbage or Chinese Leaves in Soy Sauce (page 206).

Regions: Canton and Fujian
Methods: Deep-frying and braising

Right:
Chinese leaves
(*page 24*)

Serves 4

450 g (1 lb) lean pork

1 tablespoon Shaoxing rice wine or
dry sherry

1 tablespoon light soy sauce

2 teaspoons sesame oil

½ teaspoon salt

100 g (4 oz) green pepper (about 1)

100g (4 oz) red pepper (about 1)

100 g (4 oz) carrots

50 g (2 oz) spring onions

1 egg, beaten

2 tablespoons cornflour

Cornflour, for dusting

450 ml (15 fl oz) groundnut (peanut) oil
(see Deep-Fat Fryers, page 42)

75 g (3 oz) canned lychees, drained, or
fresh orange segments

FOR THE SAUCE

150 ml (5 fl oz) Chicken Stock (page 59)

1 tablespoon light soy sauce

2 teaspoons dark soy sauce

2 teaspoons sesame oil

½ teaspoon salt

1 teaspoon freshly ground white pepper

1½ tablespoons Chinese white rice
vinegar or cider vinegar

1 tablespoon sugar

2 tablespoons tomato purée or ketchup

2 teaspoons cornflour

1 tablespoon water

Cut the pork into 2.5 cm (1 inch) cubes. Put the cubes into a bowl together with the Shaoxing rice wine or dry sherry, 1 tablespoon of light soy sauce, sesame oil and ½ teaspoon salt, and leave to marinate for 20 minutes. Meanwhile, cut the green and red peppers into 2.5 cm (1 inch) squares. Peel and cut the carrots and spring onions into 2.5 cm (1 inch) pieces. (The uniform size of meat and vegetables adds to the visual appeal of the dish.) Bring a pan of water to the boil and blanch the carrots for 4 minutes; drain and set aside.

Mix the egg and cornflour in a bowl until they are well blended into a batter. Lift the pork cubes out of the marinade, dust them with cornflour, put them into the batter and coat each piece well. Heat the oil in a deep-fat fryer or large wok until it is slightly smoking. Remove the pork pieces from the batter with a slotted spoon and deep-fry them until golden. Drain the deep-fried pork cubes on kitchen paper.

Combine the chicken stock, soy sauces, sesame oil, salt and pepper, vinegar, sugar and tomato puree or ketchup in a large saucepan. Bring it to a boil. Add the peppers, carrots and spring onions and stir well. In a small bowl, blend together the cornflour and water. Stir this mixture into the sauce and bring it back to the boil. Turn the heat down so that the mixture is simmering. Add the lychees or oranges and pork cubes. Mix well, and then turn the mixture on to a deep platter and serve at once.

roast crispy pork

Whole roast adult pigs as well as suckling pigs are often found throughout southern China in shops specializing in roast meats. Their meats are delicious with rice or in stir-fried dishes. The secret to getting crispy skin is to blanch the skin and to let it dry with a technique similar to the one used for Peking Duck. Then the skin is slowly roasted so that most of the fat cooks off, leaving soft tender pork flesh marbled with velvety fat. Much of the work can be done ahead of time. Left-overs make a wonderful sandwich filling.

Serves 4 to 6

1.5 kg (3 lb) boneless pork belly, with rind

FOR THE MARINADE
4 tablespoons coarse sea salt
2 tablespoons Sichuan peppercorns roasted and freshly ground (page 35)
2 teaspoons freshly ground five-spice powder
1 tablespoon sugar

Pierce the rind side of pork with a sharp fork or knife until the skin is covered with fine holes. Insert a meat hook into the meat to secure it. Bring a pot of water to a boil and using a large ladle, pour the hot water over the rind side of the pork several times. Set the pork belly aside.

Heat a wok or large frying pan until it is very hot. Add the salt, peppercorns, five-spice and sugar and stir-fry for 3 minutes until it is hot and well mixed. Allow the mixture to cool slightly. When it is warm enough to handle, rub this mixture on the flesh side of the pork. Hang the meat to dry for 8 hours or overnight in a cool place or in front of a fan.

Pre-heat the oven to gas mark 6, 200°C (400°F). Place the pork on a rack, rind side up, over a tray of water. Roast for 15 minutes then reduce the heat to gas mark 4, 180°C (350°F) and continue to roast for 2 hours. Increase the heat to gas mark 8, 230°C (450°F) for 15 minutes. Remove the pork from the oven and leave it to cool. Carve it into bite-size pieces, arrange on a serving platter and serve.

cold peking pork

Cold platters are commonly served at banquets in the north of China. It should be prepared a day in advance, making menu-planning easier. The pork is first blanched for a few minutes to rid it of any impurities, and is then slowly simmered in a rich liquid infused with Chinese spices. The cooked meat is removed and the braising liquid reduced. This is poured over the pork which is left to marinate overnight. This is ideal for summertime and would make a tasty cold dish for a picnic.

Serves 4 to 6

750 g (11/2 lb) pork leg, fillet end or shoulder, in one piece

FOR THE BRAISING LIQUID
1.2 litres (2 pints) Chicken Stock (page 59)
3 slices fresh ginger
3 spring onions
5 whole star anise
3 tablespoons Shaoxing rice wine or dry sherry
2 tablespoons five-spice powder
5 tablespoons Chinese rock sugar or ordinary sugar
5 tablespoons dark soy sauce
1 tablespoon salt
1 tablespoon whole Sichuan peppercorns, roasted (page 35) (optional)

Bring a pan of water to the boil and blanch the pork in it for about 3 to 5 minutes. Remove it with a slotted spoon, discard the liquid and chop the rind into small pieces. Rinse the pan clean and return the pork to it. Add all the braising liquid ingredients and the pieces of rind. Bring the mixture to the boil, then turn the heat down to a very low simmer. Cover the pan and simmer for about 2 hours.

Remove the cooked pork from the pot with a slotted spoon and skim off as much fat as possible. Turn the heat back to high and reduce the liquid to about half. Put the pork into a bowl or deep dish. Strain the reduced liquid and pour it over the meat. Allow it to cool and put it into the refrigerator. Let it sit in the refrigerator for at least 8 hours before serving.

Just before serving, remove the pork and slice it as thinly as possible. If the juice has jellied, cut it into cubes and arrange it as a garnish around the sliced pork, simply pour some of the cooled liquid over the pork slices and serve.

honey glazed pork

This is my adaptation of a famous Chinese dish called Honey Ham with Lotus Seed. Chinese ham is braised in a sugar, Shaoxing rice wine and lotus seed mixture that has been reduced to a syrup which glazes the ham like honey. This process usually takes about 4 hours, but I have found that the method can be applied to thick pork chops, taking considerably less time while maintaining the excellent results. Serve this with plain steamed rice and a simple green vegetable dish.

Regions: Hunan and Sichuan
Method: Braising

Serves 4 to 6

450 g (1 lb) boned pork chops, at least 3.5 cm (1½ inches) thick

½ teaspoon salt

2 spring onions

2 slices fresh ginger

1½ tablespoons groundnut (peanut) oil

FOR THE BRAISING SAUCE

450 ml (15 fl oz) Shaoxing rice wine or dry sherry or 150 ml (5 fl oz) Shaoxing rice wine or dry sherry mixed with 300 ml (10 fl oz) Chicken Stock (page 59)

2 tablespoons light soy sauce

100 g (4 oz) Chinese rock sugar or ordinary sugar

3 tablespoons whole Sichuan peppercorns, roasted (page 39)

Lightly salt the chops and set them aside. Cut the spring onions into 7.5 cm (3 inch) lengths and cut the ginger into slices 7.5 cm x 5 mm (3 x 1/4 inch).

Heat a wok or large frying pan over high heat until it is hot. Add the oil, and when it is very hot and slightly smoking, reduce the heat and add the spring onions and ginger. After a few seconds add the chops and cook until browned.

Meanwhile, bring the braising sauce ingredients to the boil in a large pan or casserole and then turn the heat down to a simmer. Add the browned chops, spring onions and ginger mixture. Turn the heat as low as possible, cover and simmer for about 20 minutes or until the pork is tender.

When the chops are cooked, remove them from the liquid and let them cool slightly before you slice them, cutting them diagonally. Remove any surface fat from the braising liquid and then spoon some of the braising liquid over the pork slices. Serve immediately. The rest of the braising liquid can be cooled and frozen for future use. (Remove any surface fat before transferring it to the freezer.)

braised pork with beancurd

Region: Sichuan
Method: Braising

This is one of the most famous family dishes in China. It is sometimes known as 'Ma Po's' beancurd. My mother used to make a wonderful version of this simple peasant dish using a range of spices to transform fresh but rather bland beancurd into truly delicious fare. This recipe is typical of the Chinese flair for stretching scarce meat and it makes an economical, tasty and nutritious dish. Make it in advance and reheat.

Serves 4

450 g (1 lb) fresh firm beancurd

1½ tablespoons groundnut (peanut) oil

1 tablespoon finely chopped garlic

1 tablespoon finely chopped fresh ginger

350 g (12 oz) minced pork

3 tablespoons finely chopped spring onions

1 tablespoon chilli bean sauce or chilli powder

1 teaspoon sugar

1½ tablespoons Shaoxing rice wine or dry sherry

1 tablespoon dark soy sauce

1 tablespoon light soy sauce

1½ tablespoons whole yellow bean sauce

1 teaspoon whole Sichuan peppercorns, roasted and freshly ground (page 35) (optional)

65 ml (2½ fl oz) Chicken Stock (page 59)

FOR THE GARNISH

2 tablespoons finely chopped spring onions

Cut the beancurd into 1 cm (½ inch) cubes and put them into a sieve to drain. Lay them on kitchen paper to drain for another 10 minutes.

Heat a wok or large frying pan until it is very hot. Add the oil and when it is very hot and slightly smoking, add the garlic and ginger. A few seconds later add the minced pork and stir-fry it for 2 minutes. Then add all the other ingredients except the beancurd. Bring the mixture to the boil and then turn the heat down low. Add the beancurd and mix it in well but gently, taking care not to break the chunks. Let the mixture simmer, uncovered, for about 15 minutes. (If necessary add a little more stock.) Garnish with the chopped spring onions.

five-spice spareribs

This is a delightful meat dish which engages the palate with many contrasting tastes. The spareribs are first marinated, next deep-fried in oil, and then slowly braised in an unusual, piquant sauce. It can be easily re-heated and the taste improves if it is cooked the day before it is eaten.

Region: Beijing
Methods: Deep-frying and braising

Serves 4

750 g (1½ lb) pork spareribs
600 ml (1 pint) groundnut (peanut) oil (see Deep-Fat Fryers, page 42)

FOR THE MARINADE

1 tablespoon Shaoxing rice wine or dry sherry
1 tablespoon light soy sauce
1 tablespoon Chinese black rice vinegar or cider vinegar
2 teaspoons sesame oil
1 tablespoon cornflour

FOR THE SAUCE

2 tablespoons finely chopped garlic
2 teaspoons five-spice powder
3 tablespoons finely chopped spring onions
3 tablespoons Chinese rock sugar
3 tablespoons Shaoxing rice wine or dry sherry
150 ml (5 fl oz) Chicken Stock (page 59)
1½ tablespoons light soy sauce
2 tablespoons dried grated orange peel (page 25)
85 ml (3 fl oz) Chinese black rice vinegar or cider vinegar

Have your butcher separate the spareribs into individual ribs and then into chunks which are approximately 7.5 cm (3 inches) long. Alternatively do this yourself using a heavy, sharp cleaver that can cut through the bones. Mix the marinade ingredients together in a bowl and steep the spareribs in the marinade for about 25 minutes at room temperature. Remove the spareribs from the marinade with a slotted spoon.

Heat the oil in a deep-fat fryer or large wok. When the oil is very hot and slightly smoking, slowly brown the marinated spareribs in several batches until they are brown. Drain each cooked batch on kitchen paper. (Leave the cooking oil to cool. Strain it through a filter if you want to re-use it when cooking pork.)

Put the sauce ingredients into a clean wok or frying pan. Bring the sauce to the boil and then reduce the heat. Add the spareribs, cover and simmer gently for about 40 minutes, stirring occasionally. If necessary, add a little water to the sauce to prevent the spareribs from drying up. Skim off any surface fat, turn on to a warm serving plate and serve at once.

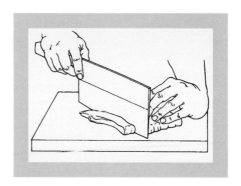

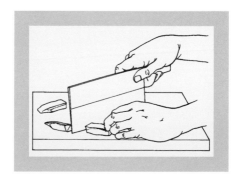

chilli pork spareribs

Although this recipe involves a series of techniques, much of the work can be done in advance and the dish can be quickly completed at the last moment. The combination of spices and sauces are the hallmark of dishes from western China. The spareribs can be finished in the oven, under a grill or on a barbecue.

Region: Sichuan
Methods: Deep-frying and braising

Serves 4

600 ml (1 pint) groundnut (peanut) oil (see Deep-Fat Fryers, page 42)

750 g (1½ lb) pork spareribs, separated into individual ribs

FOR THE BRAISING SAUCE

900 ml (1½ pints) Chicken Stock (page 59)

2 tablespoons chilli bean sauce

1 tablespoon rock sugar or ordinary sugar

85 ml (3 fl oz) Shaoxing rice wine or dry sherry

1½ tablespoons dark soy sauce

2 tablespoons light soy sauce

2 tablespoons finely chopped garlic

3 tablespoons finely chopped spring onions

2 tablespoons whole yellow bean sauce

3 tablespoons hoisin sauce

2 tablespoons cornflour blended with 3 tablespoons water

Heat the oil in a deep-fat fryer or large wok, and deep-fry the spareribs until they are brown and crisp. Do this in several batches, draining each cooked batch well on kitchen paper.

Combine all the sauce ingredients in a large pan and bring to the boil. Add the deep-fried spareribs, cover and simmer for about 1 hour or until they are tender. Drain off the sauce and remove any remaining fat. (This sauce can now be frozen and re-used the next time you want to make this dish. The dish may be prepared up to this point the day before.)

Pre-heat the oven to gas mark 4, 180°C (350°F). Put the spareribs on to a rack in a roasting tin and bake them in the oven for 15 to 20 minutes until they are nice and brown. Baste them from time to time with the braising sauce if you like. You can also cook the spareribs under a grill or on a barbecue until they are brown. Using a cleaver or a sharp, heavy knife, chop the spareribs into pieces 6 cm (2½ inches) long. Turn on to a warm serving platter and serve at once.

steamed pork with spicy vegetables

Preserved vegetables are often used to flavour meats in China. Their addition to recipes is used as a method of stretching and flavouring meats. This dish can be made with Cold Sweet and Sour Chinese Leaves (page 202) or with Sichuan preserved vegetable which can be bought tinned from Chinese grocers and which has a pleasant crunchy texture. This recipe employs the technique of steaming which keeps the dish moist and hot without any risk of overcooking the pork. It is a tasty family dish that re-heats well. It goes nicely with Stir-Fried Rice Noodles with Vegetables (page 237).

Region: Sichuan
Method: Steaming

Serves 4

75 g (3 oz) Sichuan preserved vegetable
450 g (1 lb) minced pork
1 egg white
1 tablespoon Shaoxing rice wine or dry sherry
1 tablespoon chilli bean sauce
2 teaspoons dark soy sauce
1 teaspoon light soy sauce
2 teaspoons sugar
3 tablespoons finely chopped spring onions
1 tablespoon finely chopped fresh ginger

Rinse the preserved vegetable or Cold Sweet and Sour Chinese Leaves thoroughly under running water and drain them in a sieve or colander. Then chop them finely and put them into a bowl. Add the pork and all the other ingredients and mix everything together very well. Put the mixture on to a deep plate and make a well in the centre where the juices can collect during cooking.

Next set up a steamer or put a rack into a wok or deep pan and fill it with 5 cm (2 inches) of water. Bring the water to the boil over a high heat. Put the pork on to a heatproof plate and then carefully lower it into the steamer or on to the rack. Turn the heat to low and cover the wok or pan tightly. Steam gently for 1 hour or until the pork is done. Serve this dish on the plate on which it is steamed.

braised pork belly

Pork belly is an inexpensive cut of pork which is very popular in Chinese cuisine and it has always been a favourite of mine. At first glance it might look rather fatty and unappetizing, but its gelatinous texture is highly prized by the Chinese and, when it is properly cooked, the taste is unbeatable. In this recipe the long simmering process renders down most of the fat, leaving a juicy, delicious dish which goes very well with plain steamed rice.

Region: Shanghai
Method: Braising

Serves 6

1.5 kg (3 lb) belly pork, including the bones

1 tablespoon salt

3 tablespoons groundnut (peanut) oil

FOR THE BRAISING LIQUID

6 slices fresh ginger

1.2 litres (2 pints) Chicken Stock (page 59)

600 ml (1 pint) Shaoxing rice wine or dry sherry

150 ml (5 fl oz) light soy sauce

150 ml (5 fl oz) dark soy sauce

150 g (5 oz) Chinese rock sugar or ordinary sugar

2 teaspoons five-spice powder

2 teaspoons freshly ground white pepper

3 tablespoons whole yellow bean sauce

3 tablespoons hoisin sauce

6 spring onions

This joint can be cooked with its bones left in. If you ask your butcher to remove the bones, be sure to add them to the pot with the braising liquid for greater flavour. Rub the fresh pork belly with the salt and let it stand for 1 hour. Then carefully rinse off the salt. (This helps to clean the pork and to firm it up by drawing out some of the meat's moisture.) Pat the meat dry with kitchen paper.

Heat a wok or large frying pan until it is very hot. Add the oil and when it is very hot and slightly smoking, brown the pork, rind side only, until it is crisp and brown (cover the wok to prevent splattering). Add more oil if necessary. Cut the fresh ginger into slices 7.5 cm x 5 mm (3 x ¼ inch). Put the ginger together with the rest of the braising liquid ingredients into a large pan or casserole. Bring the liquid to a simmer and then add the pork. Cover the pan and simmer it slowly for 2 to 2½ hours or until the pork is very tender.

When the pork is cooked, remove it from the pot and let it cool slightly. (The braising sauce liquid can now be cooled and frozen for re-use. Remove any surface fat before transferring it to the freezer.) Then slice the meat thinly. The Chinese would serve the pork rind and fat as well as the meat, but do remove it if you prefer. If you like, some of the braising liquid may be thickened with a little cornflour and served as a sauce over the sliced pork. If you do this be sure to remove all traces of fat from the sauce before thickening it.

rainbow beef in lettuce leaves

Some have speculated that this dish is not traditionally Chinese but rather an invention of some Hong Kong restaurant. Whatever the truth may be, it doesn't alter the fact that it is a truly delicious and popular dish. Various colourful vegetables constitute the 'rainbow' and they are stir-fried with beef and garnished with crispy bean thread (transparent) noodles and hoisin sauce to create an unusual combination of tastes and textures.

This dish makes a good starter for a dinner party or festive occasion. The rainbow beef mixture, crispy noodles and lettuce leaves are served on individual platters and the hoisin sauce in a small bowl. Each guest puts a helping of each ingredient into a hollow lettuce leaf (rather like stuffing a pancake) and eats it with his or her fingers.

Region: Hong Kong
Method: Stir-frying

Serves 4 to 6

450 g (1 lb) minced beef

1 tablespoon Shaoxing rice wine or dry sherry

1 tablespoon light soy sauce

2 teaspoons sesame oil

2 teaspoons cornflour

100 g (4 oz) carrots

100 g (4 oz) canned bamboo shoots

100 g (4 oz) courgettes

100 g (4 oz) red or green pepper (about 1)

15 g (½ oz) Chinese dried mushrooms

225 g (8 oz) iceberg lettuce

25 g (1 oz) bean thread (transparent) noodles

300 ml (10 fl oz) groundnut (peanut) oil (see Deep-Fat Fryers, page 42)

1 tablespoon groundnut (peanut) oil

1 tablespoon finely chopped garlic

1 tablespoon finely chopped shallot

3 tablespoons finely chopped spring onions

2 teaspoons dark soy sauce

2 teaspoons Shaoxing rice wine or dry sherry

2–3 tablespoons hoisin sauce

2 tablespoons oyster sauce

½ teaspoon salt

¼ teaspoon freshly ground black pepper

FOR THE ACCOMPANIMENT

4 tablespoons hoisin sauce

Put the minced beef into a bowl together with the Shaoxing rice wine or dry sherry, light soy sauce, sesame oil and cornflour and mix well. Leave the beef to marinate for about 20 minutes.

Meanwhile peel and cut the carrots into 5 cm (2 inch) long, fine shreds. Cut the bamboo shoots, courgettes and pepper into 5 cm (2 inch) fine shreds. Soak the dried mushrooms in warm water for 20 minutes, drain them and squeeze out any excess liquid. Trim off the stems and shred the caps into 5 cm (2 inch) long strips. Separate and wash the lettuce leaves, wiping off any excess water and set them aside.

In a large wok or deep-fat fryer, heat 300 ml (10 fl oz) of oil until it is slightly smoking. Deep-fry the noodles until they are crisp and puffed up. Drain them on kitchen paper. (Leave the oil to cool; it can be saved for future use.)

Put 1 tablespoon of the oil in which you have fried the noodles into a very hot wok or frying pan and when the oil begins to smoke, stir-fry the beef for about 1 minute. Remove the beef and put it into a bowl. Wipe the wok or pan clean. Re-heat the wok or pan over high heat and when it is hot, add 1 tablespoon of fresh oil. When it is slightly smoking, add the garlic, shallots and spring onions and stir-fry for 10 seconds. Then add the carrots and stir-fry for another minute. Now add the bamboo shoots, courgettes, peppers, mushrooms, the soy sauce, Shaoxing rice wine or dry sherry, hoisin sauce, oyster sauce, salt and pepper. Stir-fry the mixture for 3 minutes and then return the beef to the pan and stir so that the beef is just coated. Turn on to a warm serving platter. Arrange the lettuce and noodles on separate platters, put the hoisin sauce into a small bowl, and serve at once.

stewed beef northern-style

Region: Beijing
Method: Braising

Beef in China is often tough and braising is therefore the preferred method of cooking it. Chinese cooks long ago learned to make a virtue of this necessity by using spices and seasonings during the long braising process to imbue the meat with subtle and complex flavours. This recipe is really a Chinese version of beef stew and uses many of the favourite seasonings of northern China. Be sure to use an inexpensive cut of beef such as brisket or shin. One of the ingredients is Chinese white radish, sometimes called mooli. It can be bought in many greengrocers and in Chinese and Asian grocers. But you could use turnips or carrots instead. This is a perfect dish for a cold winter's night. Plain steamed rice makes a delicious accompaniment.

Serves 4 to 6

1.5 kg (3 lb) stewing beef such as brisket or shin

4 spring onions

2 tablespoons groundnut (peanut) oil

6 slices fresh ginger

4 cloves garlic, peeled and lightly crushed

4 dried red chillies

450 g (1 lb) Chinese white radish (mooli)

FOR THE BRAISING SAUCE

900 ml (1½ pints) Chicken Stock (page 59)

50 g (2 oz) Chinese rock sugar or ordinary sugar

1½ tablespoons light soy sauce

2 tablespoons dark soy sauce

3 tablespoons Shaoxing rice wine or dry sherry

4 whole star anise

2 teaspoons five-spice powder

5 tablespoons hoisin sauce

1 tablespoon whole yellow bean sauce

2 tablespoons fermented beancurd (optional)

Cut the beef into 5 cm (2 inch) cubes. Slice the spring onions at a slight diagonal into 5 cm (2 inch) segments. Heat a wok or large frying pan until it is hot. Add the oil and when it is very hot and slightly smoking, add the beef. Pan-fry until it is brown. (This should take about 10 minutes.) Then pour off any excess fat, leaving 1 tablespoon of oil in the pan. Add the spring onions, ginger, garlic and chillies and stir-fry with the beef for about 5 minutes.

Transfer this mixture to a large flameproof casserole or pan. Add the braising sauce ingredients. Bring the liquid to the boil, skim off any fat from the surface and turn the heat as low as possible. Cover and braise for 1½ hours.

Meanwhile, peel the Chinese white radish and cut it at a slight diagonal into 5 cm (2 inch) chunks. Add these to the meat and continue to cook the mixture for another 30 minutes or until the beef is quite tender. Then turn the heat up to high and rapidly reduce the liquid for about 15 minutes. The sauce should thicken slightly. It can be served immediately or cooled and re-heated later.

beef in oyster sauce

This was one of the most popular dishes in our family's restaurant. A good brand of oyster sauce does not taste at all fishy. Rather, it has a meaty flavour and goes very well with beef or pork. This simple dish is easy to make and is delicious served with plain steamed rice and Chinese Leaves in Soy Sauce (page 206).

Region: Canton
Method: Stir-frying

Serves 4

450 g (1 lb) lean beef steak

1 tablespoon light soy sauce

2 teaspoons sesame oil

1 tablespoon Shaoxing rice wine or dry sherry

2 teaspoons cornflour

3 tablespoons groundnut (peanut) oil

3 tablespoons oyster sauce

FOR THE GARNISH

1½ tablespoons finely chopped spring onions

Cut the beef into thin slices 5 cm (2 inches) long and put them in a bowl. Add the soy sauce, sesame oil, Shaoxing rice wine or dry sherry and cornflour. Leave the beef to marinate for 20 minutes.

Heat a wok or large frying pan until it is very hot. Add the oil and when it is very hot and slightly smoking, add the beef slices and stir-fry for 5 minutes or until they are lightly browned. Remove them and drain them well in a colander set inside a bowl. Discard the drained oil.

Wipe the wok or pan clean and re-heat it over a high heat until it is hot. Add the oyster sauce and bring it to a simmer. Return the drained beef slices to the pan and toss them thoroughly with the sauce. Turn the mixture on to a warm serving platter, garnish with the spring onions and serve at once.

stir-fried beef with orange

This is a dish from northern and western China. The Chinese always use dried peel — the older the skin, the more prized the flavour. It's easy to make your own dried peel (see page 25), but I have often made this dish with fresh orange peel and find that the tartness works just as well with the robust flavour of the beef. This is an easy dish to make and is a pleasant change of flavour from the usual stir-fried beef recipes. Serve it with rice and Sweetcorn Soup with Crabmeat (page 75).

Serves 4

450 g (1 lb) lean beef steak

1 tablespoon dark soy sauce

1 tablespoon Shaoxing rice wine or dry sherry

1½ teaspoons finely chopped fresh ginger

2 teaspoons cornflour

2 teaspoons sesame oil

65 ml (2½ fl oz) groundnut (peanut) oil

2 dried red chillies, cut in half lengthways

1 tablespoon dried citrus peel, soaked and coarsely chopped (page 25)

2 teaspoons whole Sichuan peppercorns, roasted and finely ground (page 35), optional

1 tablespoon dark soy sauce

½ teaspoon salt

½ teaspoon freshly ground black pepper

1½ teaspoons sugar

2 teaspoons sesame oil

Cut the beef into thin slices 5 cm (2 inches) long, cutting against the grain. Put the beef into a bowl and add the soy sauce, Shaoxing rice wine or dry sherry, fresh ginger, cornflour and sesame oil. Mix well and then leave the beef to marinate for about 20 minutes.

Heat a wok or large frying pan until it is very hot. Add the oil and when it is very hot and slightly smoking, remove the beef from the marinade with a slotted spoon. Add it to the pan and stir-fry it for 2 minutes until it browns. Remove it and leave to drain in a colander or sieve. Pour off most of the oil, leaving about 2 teaspoons. Re-heat the wok or pan over a high heat, add the dried chillies and stir-fry them for 10 seconds. Then return the beef to the pan, add the rest of the ingredients and stir-fry for 4 minutes, mixing well. Serve the dish at once.

stir-fried beef with ginger

This typical Cantonese dish is one of the quickest and tastiest ways to cook beef. The ginger adds a subtle and fragrant spiciness. Serve it with Ham and Bean Sprout Soup (page 68) and Lettuce with Oyster Sauce (page 210).

Region: Canton
Method: Stir-frying

Serves 4

450 g (1 lb) lean beef steak

½ teaspoon salt

2 teaspoons light soy sauce

2 teaspoons Shaoxing rice wine or dry sherry

1 teaspoon sesame oil

1 teaspoon cornflour

3 tablespoons finely shredded fresh ginger

1½ tablespoons groundnut (peanut) oil

2 teaspoons groundnut (peanut) oil

2 tablespoons Chicken Stock (page 59) or water

1½ teaspoons salt

1 teaspoon freshly ground white pepper

1 teaspoon sugar

Put the beef in the freezing compartment of the refrigerator for 20 minutes. This will allow the meat to stiffen slightly and make it easier to cut. Then cut it into thin slices 4 cm (1½ inches) long. Put the beef slices into a bowl and add the salt, soy sauce, Shaoxing rice wine or dry sherry, sesame oil and cornflour. Mix well and leave the beef to marinate for about 20 minutes. Finely shred the ginger and set it aside.

Heat a wok or large frying pan until it is very hot. Add the oil and when it is very hot and slightly smoking, remove the beef from the marinade with a slotted spoon and stir-fry it for about 2 minutes. Remove the beef slices. Wipe the wok or pan clean and re-heat it. Add 2 teaspoons of oil and when it is very hot and slightly smoking, stir-fry the ginger for a few seconds. Then add the stock or water, salt, white pepper and sugar. Bring the mixture to the boil. Return the beef to the pan and stir well until hot through. Serve at once.

stir-fried pepper beef with mangetout

This is my adaptation of a stir-fried beef dish which is popular in Chinese restaurants in the West. What makes this recipe so adaptable is that any fresh vegetable can be substituted for the mangetout, which are known as snow peas in America and Australia. The dish is extremely simple to make. Try it with plain steamed rice and Steamed Fish with Garlic, Spring Onions and Ginger (page 160) for a delicious and typical Chinese family meal.

Region: Canton
Method: Stir-frying

Serves 4

450 g (1 lb) lean beef steak
2 teaspoons light soy sauce
2 teaspoons Shaoxing rice wine or dry sherry
2 teaspoons sesame oil
½ teaspoon salt
¼ teaspoon freshly ground black pepper
2 teaspoons cornflour
100 g (4 oz) red or green pepper (about 1)
3 tablespoons groundnut (peanut) oil
225 g (8 oz) mangetout, trimmed
150 ml (5 fl oz) Chicken Stock (page 59) or water
2 tablespoons oyster sauce

Cut the beef into thin slices 5 cm (2 inches) long. Put the beef into a bowl and add the light soy sauce, Shaoxing rice wine or dry sherry, sesame oil, salt, pepper and cornflour. Mix well and then leave the beef to marinate for 20 minutes. Cut the pepper into 5 cm (2 inch) strips.

Heat a wok or large frying pan until it is very hot. Add the oil and when it is very hot and slightly smoking, remove the beef from the marinade with a slotted spoon, add the beef and stir-fry for 3 minutes. Remove the beef slices; drain and reserve the oil. Wipe the wok or pan clean, then re-heat it. Return 1 tablespoon of drained oil to the pan and when it is very hot, add the pepper and mangetout and stir-fly for 2 minutes. Then add the stock and oyster sauce. Bring the mixture to the boil. Return the beef to the pan and stir well. Turn on to a warm serving platter and serve at once.

steamed beef meatballs

Since my days as an apprentice in our family restaurant, I have always enjoyed these steamed meatballs. The secret of making them light and fluffy lies in the egg white and cornflour. We used to mince the beef by hand with two cleavers, one in each hand, adding egg white and cornflour as we chopped until it was all fully incorporated into the meat. Then we added the seasonings and continued to chop until the meat was almost a light paste. Such chopping requires concentration! But when we finished, we all sat about chatting as we rolled the meat into balls. Today with a blender or food processor, this long process takes only a few minutes. The texture will be smoother, of course, but it does mean a lot less work. The meatballs re-heat well by steaming and are perfect for dinners, for parties or with drinks.

Region: Canton
Method: Steaming

Serves 4

350 g (12 oz) minced beef
2 egg whites
5 tablespoons very cold water
1 teaspoon salt
1½ tablespoons light soy sauce
2 teaspoons freshly ground black pepper
1 tablespoon sesame oil
3 tablespoons finely chopped fresh coriander
3 tablespoons finely chopped spring onions
1 teaspoon cornflour
2 teaspoons sugar

Mix the beef in a food processor for a few seconds. Slowly add the egg whites and cold water and mix them for a few more seconds until they are fully incorporated. Add the rest of the ingredients and mix for about a minute until the meat mixture has become a light paste. Using your hands, form the mixture into 4 cm (1½ inch) balls – about the size of a golf ball. (This recipe makes about 12 balls.)

Next set up a steamer or put a rack into a wok or deep pan and fill it with 5 cm (2 inches) of water. Bring the water to the boil over a high heat. Put the meatballs on to a heatproof plate and then carefully lower it into the steamer or on to the rack. Turn the heat to low and cover the wok or pan tightly. Steam the meatballs gently for about 15 minutes. Pour off any liquid which has accumulated on the plate. Put the steamed meatballs on a warm serving platter and serve at once.

minced beef with scrambled eggs

Regions: Canton and Fujian
Method: Stir-frying

Eggs are commonly found in many home-cooked dishes in China. They are an inexpensive and easy-to-prepare food. Although they are rather bland alone, they combine well with many ingredients to make hearty dishes. Here minced beef is marinated, stir-fried and then mixed with the stir-fried eggs. It is akin to a Western-style omelette and, like that dish, it makes for a quick and delicious meal. Serve with plain rice and stir-fried vegetables.

Serves 4

225 g (8 oz) minced beef

FOR THE MARINADE

2 teaspoons light soy sauce

2 teaspoons Shaoxing rice wine or dry sherry

2 teaspoons sesame oil

1 teaspoon sugar

½ teaspoon salt

¼ teaspoon freshly ground black pepper

1 tablespoon groundnut (peanut) oil

6 eggs, beaten

2 teaspoons sesame oil

¼ teaspoon salt

¼ teaspoon freshly ground black pepper

1 teaspoon light soy sauce

4 tablespoons finely chopped spring onions

1½ tablespoons groundnut (peanut) oil

FOR THE GARNISH

2 tablespoons finely chopped spring onions

Put the beef in a bowl with the soy sauce, rice wine or dry sherry, sesame oil, sugar, salt and pepper and mix well. Leave the beef to marinate for 20 minutes. **Heat a wok** until it is very hot. Add 1 tablespoon of oil and when it is very hot and slightly smoking, add the beef. Stir-fry the mixture for 2 minutes. Remove the beef and drain well in a colander or sieve.

Combine the eggs with the sesame oil, salt, pepper, soy sauce and spring onions. Wipe the wok or pan clean and re-heat it over high heat until it is hot. Add 1½ tablespoons of oil and when the oil begins to slightly smoke, swirl the oil around all sides of the wok. Add the egg mixture and stir-fry over high heat, folding and lifting the egg mixture, until the egg begins to set slightly. Return the beef to the mixture and continue to stir-fry for another minute to finish cooking the eggs and to re-heat the beef.

Turn the mixture on to a warm serving platter, garnish with the spring onions and serve at once.

stir-fried lamb with garlic

Lamb is especially delicious when it is stir-fried. This way of preparing it with a lot of garlic and spring onions to balance its strong taste is a popular one. The tenderest parts of the lamb, such as steaks or chops, are best for this dish. Serve it with rice and Braised Spicy Aubergines (page 191).

Region: Beijing
Method: Stir-frying

Serves 4

450 g (1 lb) lean lamb steaks or fillet, or boned, loin chops

1 tablespoon Shaoxing rice wine or dry sherry

2 teaspoons dark soy sauce

1 tablespoon light soy sauce

2 teaspoons sesame oil

1½ teaspoons cornflour

1 tablespoon groundnut (peanut) oil

2 spring onions, white part only, finely chopped

6 cloves garlic, peeled and thinly sliced

2 teaspoons finely chopped fresh ginger

1 teaspoon Sichuan peppercorns, roasted and freshly ground (page 35)

Cut the lamb into thin slices and put it into a bowl. Mix in the Shaoxing rice wine or dry sherry, soy sauces, sesame oil and cornflour and leave the lamb to marinate for 20 minutes. Then drain off the marinade, and set the lamb aside.

Heat a wok or large frying pan until it is very hot. Add the oil and when it is very hot and slightly smoking, add the marinated lamb pieces with just a little of the marinade. Stir-fry for 2 minutes. Now add the spring onions, garlic and ginger and continue to stir fry for another 4 minutes. Turn on to a warm serving platter, sprinkle with the peppercorns and serve at once.

mongolian hot pot

This Northern dish is similar in style to a European fondue. It was introduced into China after the Mongolian conquest in the thirteenth century and could soon be found throughout China with regional touches added. Beef was sometimes substituted for the traditional lamb and the Cantonese developed their 'Chrysanthemum Fire Pot' which includes edible flower petals. In this recipe, which follows the traditional method, thin slices of lamb and vegetables are simmered in a broth. Each diner cooks his or her own food at the table in the pot of stock. The cooked food is then dipped into various sauces before being eaten. Towards the end of the meal, bean thread (transparent) noodles are cooked in the remaining broth which is then drunk as a soup. The Chinese use a special charcoal-burning 'fire pot' for this dish, but you could use either a large fondue pot or a small portable electric element and heatproof pot instead. (If you have an authentic Chinese fire pot, only use it in a well ventilated room with the windows open, or use it out of doors. Otherwise the carbon monoxide fumes arising from the charcoal can be dangerous.)

Region: Beijing
Method: Simmering

Serves 4 to 6

1–1.5 kg (2–3 lb) lean lamb

175 g (6 oz) bean thread (transparent) noodles

225 g (8 oz) spinach

225 g (8 oz) Chinese leaves

1.2 litres (2 pints) Chicken Stock (page 59)

2 tablespoons light soy sauce

2 teaspoons dark soy sauce

1½ tablespoons Shaoxing rice wine or dry sherry

1 tablespoon sesame oil

1 teaspoon salt

½ teaspoon freshly ground black pepper

1 teaspoon sugar

2 teaspoons finely chopped fresh ginger

3 tablespoons finely chopped spring onions

1 tablespoon chopped garlic

3 tablespoons finely chopped fresh coriander

FOR THE DIPPING SAUCE

3 tablespoons sesame paste or smooth peanut butter

1½ tablespoons light soy sauce

1 tablespoon dark soy sauce

2 tablespoons Shaoxing rice wine or dry sherry

2 teaspoons chilli bean sauce

1 tablespoon sugar

1 tablespoon hot water

Using a cleaver or sharp knife, slice the lamb into very thin slices. Soak the bean thread (transparent) noodles in warm water for 5 minutes, then drain them and cut them into 12.5 cm (5 inch) lengths. Separate the spinach leaves from the stalks and wash them well. Discard the stalks. Cut the Chinese leaves into 7.5 cm (3 inch) pieces. Combine all the ingredients for the dipping sauce in a small bowl and mix them well.

Everyone should have their own small portion of dipping sauce. Serve each guest a plate containing their share of lamb, spinach and Chinese leaves. When you are ready to begin, bring the stock to the boil and light the fondue. Ladle the stock into the fondue and put the soy sauces, Shaoxing rice wine or dry sherry, sesame oil, salt and pepper, sugar, ginger, spring onions, garlic and coriander into the stock.

Each person selects a piece of food and cooks it quickly in the pot. When all the meat and vegetables have been eaten, add the noodles to the pot, let them heat through, then ladle the soup into soup bowls.

This dish also works successfully with other foods such as steak, fish balls, oysters, prawns, squid, mushrooms and lettuce, although it would be more like the Cantonese Chrysanthemum Pot than a Mongolian Hot Pot.

peking braised lamb

The Chinese usually cook mutton and goat rather than lamb, which is scarce, and have many exciting ways of braising both these meats with spices which help to mask their strong taste. This tasty and filling family dish is perfect for the winter. It goes well with plain steamed rice and Chinese Leaves in Soy Sauce (page 206).

Region: Beijing
Method: Braising

Serves 4

450 g (1 lb) boned shoulder of lamb
2 spring onions
2 slices fresh ginger
1 tablespoon groundnut (peanut) oil
1/2 small onion, finely chopped

FOR THE BRAISING SAUCE
900 ml (11/2 pint) Chicken Stock (page 59)
2 whole star anise
50 g (2 oz) Chinese rock sugar or ordinary sugar
2 tablespoons dark soy sauce
3 tablespoons Shaoxing rice wine or dry sherry
1 Chinese cinnamon bark or cinnamon stick
11/2 tablespoons sesame paste or smooth peanut butter
2 tablespoons hoisin sauce

Cut the lamb into 5 cm (2 inch) cubes. Blanch it by plunging it into boiling water for 5 minutes. Then remove the lamb and discard the water. Slice the spring onions diagonally into 7.5 cm (3 inch) pieces. Slice the ginger diagonally into pieces 7.5 cm x 5 mm (3 x 1/4 inch).

Heat a wok or large frying pan until it is very hot. Add the oil and when it is very hot and slightly smoking, add the pieces of lamb. Stir-fry them until they are brown. Now add the spring onions, ginger and onion to the pan and continue to stir-fry for 5 minutes. Transfer this mixture to a large casserole or pot and add the braising sauce ingredients. Bring the liquid to the boil, skim off any fat from the surface, then turn the heat down as low as possible. Cover and braise for 11/2 hours or until the lamb is quite tender. (The remaining liquid can be frozen and re-used another time to braise lamb.) Arrange the cooked meat on a warm serving platter and serve.

stir-fried lambs' kidneys

Lambs' kidneys are delicious when they are stir-fried. As a young cook, I was taught a wonderful technique for cleaning kidneys which I use to this day. First the kidneys should be scored and tossed in bicarbonate of soda; this helps to tenderize them and to neutralize their acidity. Then the bicarbonate of soda should be rinsed off the kidneys before they are tossed in a mixture of vinegar and salt to remove any remaining bitterness. The result is a clean and fresh-tasting kidney. Serve this dish with Sweetcorn Soup with Crabmeat (page 75) and plain steamed rice.

Region: Sichuan
Method: Stir-frying

Serves 4

450 g (1 lb) lambs' or pigs' kidneys
1½ teaspoons bicarbonate of soda
2 teaspoons Chinese white rice vinegar or cider vinegar
1 teaspoon salt
1 tablespoon groundnut (peanut) oil
3 dried red chillies, 1 split in half lengthways
1 tablespoon finely chopped garlic
1 tablespoon dark soy sauce
2 teaspoons Shaoxing rice wine or dry sherry
½ teaspoon whole Sichuan peppercorns, roasted and finely ground (page 35), optional
1 teaspoon sugar
½ teaspoon salt
1 teaspoon sesame oil

FOR THE GARNISH
2 teaspoons finely chopped spring onions

Using a sharp knife, remove the thin outer kidney membrane. Then, with a sharp cleaver or knife, split the kidneys in half by cutting them horizontally. Now cut away the small knobs of fat and any tough membrane surrounding them. Next, score the kidneys in a criss-cross pattern (see diagram below) and cut them into thin slices. Toss the kidney slices with the bicarbonate of soda and let them sit for about 20 minutes. Then rinse them thoroughly with cold water and toss them with the vinegar and salt. Put them in a colander and let them drain for at least 30 minutes, preferably longer.

Blot the kidney slices dry with kitchen paper. Heat a wok or large frying pan until it is very hot. Add the oil and when it is very hot and slightly smoking, add the dried chillies. Stir-fry for about 20 seconds to flavour the oil. Then add the kidney slices and stir-fry for about 1 minute, coating the kidneys with the oil. Now add the rest of the ingredients and toss them together well with the kidneys. Continue to stir-fry the mixture for about 2 minutes or until the kidney edges begin to curl. Turn the mixture on to a warm serving platter, garnish with the spring onions and serve at once.

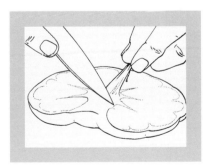 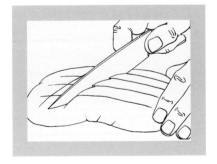

hot and sour kidneys

Region: Sichuan
Method: Stir-frying

Pigs' kidneys are tender and tasty when stir-fried in this hot and sour sauce. The contrasting flavours of the sauce perfectly complement the strong taste of the kidneys. As with the Stir-Fried Lambs' Kidneys recipe (page 113), I suggest you marinate the kidneys in bicarbonate of soda and then toss them in vinegar and salt. This dish is inexpensive to make and goes well with plain steamed rice and any stir-fried vegetable to make a nutritious family meal.

Serves 4

450 g (1 lb) pigs' kidneys

1 teaspoon bicarbonate of soda

2 teaspoons Chinese white rice vinegar or cider vinegar

1 teaspoon salt

1 tablespoon groundnut (peanut) oil

1 tablespoon finely chopped fresh ginger

FOR THE SAUCE

2 teaspoons finely chopped garlic

2 teaspoons finely chopped fresh ginger

1 tablespoon chilli bean sauce

1 tablespoon Chinese white rice vinegar or cider vinegar

2 teaspoons sugar

1 tablespoon dark soy sauce

1 teaspoon whole Sichuan peppercorns, roasted and freshly ground (page 35), optional

1½ tablespoons Chicken Stock (page 59) or water

FOR THE GARNISH

2 tablespoons chopped spring onions

Using a sharp knife, remove the thin outer kidney membrane. Then, with a sharp cleaver or knife, split the kidneys in half horizontally (see opposite). Now cut away the small knobs of fat and any tough membrane surrounding them. Score the kidneys in a criss-cross pattern and cut into 2.5 cm (1 inch) slices. Toss the kidney slices with the bicarbonate of soda and let them sit for about 20 minutes. Then rinse them thoroughly with cold water and toss them with the vinegar and salt. Put them in a colander and drain for at least 30 minutes, preferably longer.

Blot the kidney slices dry with kitchen paper. Heat a wok or large frying pan until it is very hot. Add the oil, and when it is very hot and slightly smoking add the ginger. Stir-fry for about 20 seconds to flavour the oil. Then add the kidney slices and stir-fry them for about 1 minute. Now add the sauce ingredients and toss them together well with the kidneys. Continue to stir-fry the mixture for about 2 minutes or until the kidney edges begin to curl. Turn the mixture on to a warm serving platter, garnish with the spring onions and serve at once.

stir-fried liver in spicy sauce

Pigs' liver is another Chinese speciality which is delicious when it is properly prepared. My uncle used to make a delectable pigs' liver dish with vegetables. His secret was to cut the liver into thin slices, to stir-fry them quickly and then to drain them to get rid of any bitter juices. Growing up in America, however, my personal preference is calves' liver. This dish is an adaptation of the traditional pigs' liver recipe. Here it is paired with a robust and tasty sauce containing spices which help to balance the rich flavour of the liver. Cooked this way, the liver tastes a little like beef. I like to serve this dish with plain steamed rice and some green vegetables.

Region: Canton
Method: Stir-frying

Serves 4

225 g (8 oz) fresh liver, such as calves' or pigs'
3 spring onions
150 ml (5 fl oz) groundnut (peanut) oil

FOR THE MARINADE
1 egg white
1 tablespoon Shaoxing rice wine or dry sherry
2 teaspoons sesame oil
2 teaspoons salt
1/2 teaspoon freshly ground white pepper
2 teaspoons finely chopped fresh ginger
2 teaspoons cornflour

FOR THE SAUCE
2 teaspoons light soy sauce
2 teaspoons Shaoxing rice wine or dry sherry
2 teaspoons sugar
1 1/2 tablespoons whole yellow bean sauce
2 teaspoons chilli bean sauce

Cut the liver into thin slices 7.5 cm (3 inches) long and place in a bowl. Add the egg white, rice wine or sherry, sesame oil, salt, pepper, ginger and cornflour and mix well. Leave the liver to marinate in the refrigerator for at least 20 minutes. Cut the spring onions into 5 cm (2 inch) diagonal pieces. In a separate bowl mix together the sauce ingredients.

Heat a wok or large frying pan until it is very hot. Add the oil and when it is very hot and slightly smoking, remove the liver with a slotted spoon and stir-fry for 2 minutes. Drain the liver, leaving about 2 teaspoons of the oil in the wok or pan.

Re-heat the wok or pan and add the spring onions. Stir-fry them for 1 minute and then add the sauce ingredients. When the sauce comes to the boil, return the liver to the wok or pan and toss it well, coating it with the sauce. Stir-fry for 30 seconds and serve at once.

Chicken is the most highly regarded of all poultry in China. To impress a guest a Chinese hostess might announce that she has killed a chicken in his or her honour. It is frequently served on special occasions, on birthdays and at festivals and banquets. At our family gatherings, chicken was always the centrepiece. Early every Sunday morning my mother would bring home a live chicken from the market in Chinatown in Chicago where we lived. Its noisy clucking would usually wake me up. The chicken would be quickly dispatched and then prepared in one of many ways. One of my favourites was when it had been slowly poached, then steeped and finally served with a soy sauce and spring onion dipping sauce.

In China most homes do not have ovens and poultry is usually roasted by professional cooks and sold in speciality food shops. Home-cooked chicken is braised, stir-fried, deep-fried, steamed or simmered. One of the virtues of chicken is that its mild but distinctive flavour blends very well with other seasonings, spices and sauces. It is a very versatile bird and is as popular in China as pork.

The Chinese prefer to buy their chickens live to ensure that they are at their freshest when cooked. Obviously this is not practical in the West. In Europe and North America there are plentiful supplies of relatively inexpensive chicken but because of modern farming methods, commercially-produced chickens tend to lack taste. Frozen chicken is especially bland and should be avoided whenever possible. Try to buy a fresh chicken for Chinese cooking. It should have a healthy pinkish colour, a fresh smell, and be firm in texture. If possible buy free-range or corn-fed chickens. Not only have they been raised by more humane methods but their taste is far superior. In China, whole cooked chickens are never carried to the table to be carved, but are always chopped into bite-sized pieces before being arranged on a platter. However, a number of the recipes in this chapter can be made with chicken pieces rather than with a whole chicken. All parts of the chicken are used in China. The dark meat from the thighs and drumsticks is especially prized for its sturdier flavour. Roasting chickens are the most suitable for frying, steaming and braising. If possible use boiling fowl for stock to give you a rich liquid with a good flavour. Poussins are also suitable for stir-fried dishes.

Fresh chicken should be cooked as soon as possible after buying. Keep it cold until you are ready to use it. If you wish to store the chicken, first remove any wrapping and the giblets. Rinse it carefully in cold water and blot it completely dry with kitchen paper. Wrap it loosely in cling film and put it in the refrigerator where it will keep for up to two days.

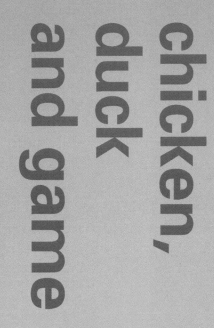

chicken, duck and game

Duck is also popular in Chinese cookery with Peking Duck being one of the most famous of all Chinese dishes. Like chicken, it is never roasted at home. In domestic kitchens duck is cut up and then braised or stir-fried. It is also steamed and then deep-fried, a process which results in a very tender fat-free duck. Fresh duck is always preferable to frozen and should be stored in the same way as chicken. Use Cherry Valley ducks and not English ducks for Chinese recipes. They are less fat and more appropriate for Chinese cooking. If you use frozen duck, be sure to defrost it thoroughly before cooking.

Game birds are widely used in Chinese cookery, but because their flavour tends to be strong they are frequently stewed or put into soups together with medicinal herbs and seasonings. Pigeon and quail are two birds which are readily available in the West and which are ideal for Chinese cooking.

Left:
Stir-fried quails
(*page 151*)

chicken pieces in black bean sauce

This recipe is a favourite one for me, mainly because it evokes childhood memories of the fragrance of black bean sauce mixed with garlic which often greeted me at the door when I came home from school. My mother used to make this dish with chicken wings, one of the tastiest parts of the chicken. Wings are ideal for stir-frying because they cook quickly, but other parts of the chicken work just as well. Here I use another favourite; boneless chicken thigh. The tender, juicy flesh makes this ideal for the recipe. Serve this dish with plain rice and Stir-Fried Spinach with Garlic (page 216). It can be cooked ahead of time and re-heated and it is also delicious served cold.

Region: Canton
Methods: Stir-frying and braising

Serves 4

450 g (1 lb) boneless chicken thighs
1 tablespoon light soy sauce
1½ tablespoons Shaoxing rice wine or dry sherry
½ teaspoon salt
1 teaspoon sugar
1 teaspoon sesame oil
2 teaspoons cornflour
1 tablespoon groundnut (peanut) oil
1 tablespoon finely chopped fresh ginger
1½ tablespoons finely chopped garlic
1 tablespoon finely chopped shallots
1½ tablespoons finely chopped spring onions
2½ tablespoons black beans, rinsed and coarsely chopped
150 ml (5 fl oz) Chicken Stock (page 59) or water

FOR THE GARNISH
2 tablespoons finely chopped spring onions

If you are using chicken pieces, cut them into 5 cm (2 inch) chunks. Mix the soy sauce, Shaoxing rice wine or dry sherry, salt, sugar, sesame oil and cornflour together and pour it over the chicken pieces. Leave the chicken to marinate for about 1 hour, then drain the chicken and discard the marinade.

Heat a wok or large frying pan until it is very hot. Add the oil and when it is very hot and slightly smoking, add the chicken. Stir-fry it for 5 minutes or until the chicken begins to brown. Add the ginger, garlic, shallots, spring onions and black beans and stir-fry for 2 minutes then add the stock. Bring the mixture to the boil and then reduce the heat. Cover the wok or pan and simmer for 15 minutes or until the chicken is cooked. Garnish with spring onions and serve.

garlic chicken with cucumber

Cucumbers are rarely served raw in China; they are delicious cooked. In this recipe they are stir-fried with delicate chicken breasts and flavoured with garlic and chilli. This is an uncomplicated dish which goes well with Honey Glazed Pork (page 93) or Tomato Eggflower Soup (page 62).

Regions: Sichuan and Beijing
Method: Stir-frying

Serves 4

450 g (1 lb) boneless chicken breasts, skinned

450 g (1 lb) cucumber

2 teaspoons salt

1 tablespoon groundnut (peanut) oil

1½ tablespoons finely chopped garlic

1 tablespoon finely chopped spring onions

1 tablespoon light soy sauce

1 tablespoon Shaoxing rice wine or dry sherry

2 teaspoons chilli bean sauce or chilli powder

2 teaspoons sesame oil

Cut the chicken into 2.5 cm (1 inch) cubes and set aside. Peel the cucumber, halve it and remove the seeds with a teaspoon. Then cut it into 2.5 cm (1 inch) cubes, sprinkle with the salt and put the cucumber into a colander to drain for 20 minutes. (This removes the excess moisture from the cucumber.) Next rinse the cucumber cubes in cold running water and blot them dry with kitchen paper.

Heat a wok or large frying pan until it is very hot. Add the oil and when it is very hot and slightly smoking, add the chicken cubes and stir-fry them for a few seconds. Add all the other ingredients except the cucumber and continue to stir-fry for another 2 minutes. Now add the cucumber cubes and keep stir-frying the entire mixture for another 3 minutes. Serve at once.

curried chicken with peppers

Curry blends well with chicken especially when used in the style of southern Chinese cuisine, namely as a light and subtle sauce which does not overpower the delicate chicken flavour. The chicken is velveted to preserve its juiciness and taste. You can use the traditional oil method or, for a less fattening alternative, substitute water instead. The peppers provide the dish with a crunchy texture that makes a wonderful complement to the soft tender chicken. Serve this with Tomato Eggflower Soup (page 62) and plain steamed rice.

Region: Canton
Methods: Velveting and stir-frying

Serves 4

450 g (1 lb) boneless chicken breasts, skinned

1 egg white

1 teaspoon salt

2 teaspoons cornflour

225 g (8 oz) red or green peppers

300 ml (10 fl oz) groundnut (peanut) oil or water

1 tablespoon groundnut (peanut) oil

1 tablespoon finely chopped garlic

150 ml (5 fl oz) Chicken Stock (page 59)

1½ tablespoons Madras curry paste

2 teaspoons sugar

1½ tablespoons Shaoxing rice wine or dry sherry

1½ tablespoons light soy sauce

1 teaspoon cornflour, blended with 1 tablespoon water

Cut the chicken breasts into 2.5 cm (1 inch) cubes. Combine them with the egg white, salt and 2 teaspoons of corn-flour in a small bowl and put the mixture into the refrigerator for about 20 minutes. Wash and de-seed the peppers and cut them into 2.5 cm (1 inch) cubes.

Heat a wok or frying pan until it is very hot. Add the oil and when it is very hot and slightly smoking, remove the wok from the heat. Immediately add the chicken pieces, stirring vigorously to prevent them from sticking. After about 2 minutes when the chicken pieces turn white, quickly drain the chicken and all the oil in a stainless steel colander set in a bowl. Discard the oil.

(If you use water instead of oil, bring it to a boil in a saucepan. Remove the pan from the heat and immediately add the chicken pieces, stirring vigorously to prevent them from sticking. After about 2 minutes when the chicken pieces turn white, drain the chicken and the water in a stainless steel colander set in a bowl. Discard the water.)

Wipe the wok or pan clean and re-heat until it is very hot. Add 1 tablespoon of oil and when it is very hot and slightly smoking, add the peppers and garlic and stir-fry for 2 minutes. Add the rest of the ingredients and cook for 2 minutes. Add the chicken and stir-fry for another 2 minutes to coat with the sauce.

spicy chicken with peanuts

This is a classic western Chinese dish which is better known in China as Gongbao Chicken. According to one legend, the dish was named after a Chinese official, Ding Baozhen, who was Governor of Sichuan province in the nineteenth century. There are many versions of this recipe; this one is close to the original and is also quick and easy to make. Rice and Stir-Fried Chinese Greens (page 206) would go well with it.

Region: Sichuan
Method: Stir-frying

Serves 4

225 g (8 oz) boneless chicken breasts

1½ tablespoons groundnut (peanut) oil

1 dried red chilli, split lengthways

75 g (3 oz) raw peanuts, shelled (page 31)

FOR THE SAUCE

1 tablespoon Chicken Stock (page 59) or water

1 tablespoon Shaoxing rice wine or dry sherry

2 teaspoons dark soy sauce

1 teaspoon sugar

1 teaspoon finely chopped garlic

2 teaspoons finely chopped spring onions

½ teaspoon finely chopped fresh ginger

1 teaspoon Chinese white rice vinegar or cider vinegar

½ teaspoon salt

1 teaspoon sesame oil

Cut the chicken into 2.5 cm (1 inch) cubes. Heat a wok or large frying pan until it is very hot. Add the oil and when it is very hot and slightly smoking, add the chilli and stir-fry for a few seconds. (You may remove it when it turns black or leave it in.) Add the chicken cubes and peanuts and stir-fry them for 1 minute. Remove the chicken, peanuts and chilli – if not removed earlier – from the pan.

Put all the sauce ingredients except the sesame oil into the pan. Bring the sauce to the boil, and then turn the heat down. Return the chicken, peanuts and chilli to the pan and cook for about 2 minutes in the sauce, mixing well all the time. Finally, add the sesame oil and give the mixture a good stir. Remove the chilli and turn the mixture onto a warm serving platter. Serve at once.

stir-fried chicken shreds

This is a simple recipe which is quick and easy to make and is very suitable for family meals. The secret of cooking the chicken shreds without drying them out is to velvet them quickly in oil or water until they turn opaque and then remove them at once. You can substitute other vegetables such as asparagus, carrots or green peas for the ones I have used, if you prefer. This dish goes nicely with rice and Ham and Marrow Soup (page 72).

Region: Fujian
Methods: Velveting and stir-frying

Serves 4

450 g (1 lb) boneless chicken
breasts, skinned

1 egg white

1 teaspoon salt

2 teaspoons cornflour

175 g (6 oz) fresh bean sprouts

100 g (4 oz) mangetout, trimmed

175 g (6 oz) water chestnuts, peeled if
fresh, rinsed if canned (page 37)

4 whole spring onions

300 ml (10 fl oz) groundnut (peanut) oil
or water

1 tablespoon groundnut (peanut) oil

1 tablespoon light soy sauce

2 teaspoons Shaoxing rice wine or
dry sherry

1½ teaspoons salt

1 teaspoon sugar

2 teaspoons sesame oil

Cut the chicken into very thin shreds and mix with the egg white, salt and cornflour in a bowl. Stir well and place in the refrigerator for about 20 minutes.

Meanwhile, trim the bean sprouts, finely shred the mangetout lengthways, shred or slice the water chestnuts and finely shred the spring onions.

Heat a wok or large frying pan until it is very hot. Add the oil and when it is very hot and slightly smoking, remove the wok from the heat. Immediately add the chicken, stirring vigorously to prevent it from sticking. When the chicken turns white, about 2 minutes, drain the chicken and all the oil in a stainless steel colander set in a bowl. Discard the oil.

(If you use water instead of oil, bring it to a boil in a saucepan. Remove the saucepan from the heat and immediately add the chicken pieces, stirring vigorously to prevent them from sticking. When the chicken turns white, about 2 minutes, drain the chicken and all the water in a stainless steel colander set in a bowl. Discard the water.)

Heat the wok or pan until it is hot. Add 1 tablespoon of oil and the vegetables and stir-fry for 1 minute. Add the soy sauce, rice wine, salt and sugar and stir-fry for 2 minutes. Return the chicken to the wok with the sesame oil and heat through.

chicken with garlic vinegar sauce

The secret here is to steam the chicken to keep it moist and then deep-fry it without batter. The result is a juicy chicken with a crispy skin. Served with a piquant garlic sauce, it goes well with steamed rice and Stir-Fried Ginger Broccoli (page 199).

Region: Beijing
Methods: Steaming and deep-frying

Serves 4 to 6

4 slices fresh ginger
4 spring onions
1 x kg (2½ lb) chicken
2 teaspoons salt
900 ml (1½ pints) groundnut (peanut) oil (see Deep-Fat Fryers, page 42)

FOR THE SAUCE

1 tablespoon finely chopped garlic
2 tablespoons Chinese white rice vinegar or cider vinegar
2 tablespoons light soy sauce
2½ tablespoons finely chopped spring onions, white part only

Cut the ginger into slices 7.5 cm x 5 mm (3 x ¼ inch). Cut the spring onions into 7.5 cm (3 inch) pieces. Rub the chicken with salt and stuff the cavity with the ginger and spring onions. Let it sit at room temperature for 30 minutes.

Next set up a steamer or put a rack into a wok or deep pan and fill it with 5 cm (2 inches) of water. Bring the water to the boil over a high heat. Put the chicken on to a heatproof plate and then carefully lower it into the steamer or on to the rack. Turn the heat to low and cover the wok or pan tightly. Steam gently for 1 hour or until the chicken is cooked through to the bone. Top up with boiling water from time to time.

Place the chicken on a rack over a tray or roasting pan and leave in a cool, well-ventilated place to dry for about 3 hours. (To speed up the process, place it in front of a fan for 2 hours.) When the chicken has dried, the skin should feel like parchment paper. Cut it in half lengthways, then wipe the cavity dry with kitchen paper.

Mix together the sauce ingredients and set aside. Heat a wok or deep frying pan until it is very hot. Add the oil and when it is hot and slightly smoking, deep-fry one half until it is golden and crisp. Remove and then do the other half. Drain on kitchen paper. When it is cool enough, cut into bite-sized pieces. Place on a warm platter and pour the sauce over. Serve at once.

walnut chicken

This recipe pairs the crunchy texture of walnuts with the softness of chicken in a classic stir-fry dish. For a variation, try this recipe with other nuts such as pine nuts or almonds but be sure the nuts you use are very fresh. Stale nuts tend to go soft and will ruin both the texture and the flavour of the combination. I like to serve this dish with Fried Stuffed Cucumbers (page 209) and Sweetcorn Soup with Crabmeat (page 75).

Regions: Fujian, Beijing and Canton
Methods: Velveting and stir-frying

Serves 4

450 g (1 lb) boneless chicken breasts, skinned

1 egg white

1 teaspoon salt

2 teaspoons cornflour

75 g (3 oz) walnuts, shelled halves or pieces

300 ml (10 fl oz) groundnut (peanut) oil or water

1 tablespoon groundnut (peanut) oil

2 teaspoons finely chopped garlic

1 teaspoon finely chopped fresh ginger

2 tablespoons finely chopped spring onions

2 tablespoons Shaoxing rice wine or dry sherry

1½ tablespoons light soy sauce

Cut the chicken breasts into 2.5 cm (1 inch) cubes. Combine the chicken with the egg white, salt and cornflour in a small bowl and put it in the refrigerator for about 20 minutes. Blanch the walnuts in a small pan of boiling water for 5 minutes; then drain them.

Heat a wok or large frying pan until it is very hot. Add the oil and when it is very hot and slightly smoking, remove the wok from the heat. Immediately add the chicken pieces, stirring vigorously to prevent them from sticking. After about 2 minutes when the chicken pieces turn white, quickly drain the chicken and all the oil in a stainless steel colander set in a bowl. Discard the oil.

(If you use water instead of oil, bring it to a boil in a saucepan. Remove the saucepan from the heat and immediately add the chicken pieces, stirring vigorously to prevent them from sticking. After about 2 minutes when the chicken pieces turn white, quickly drain the chicken and all the water in a stainless steel colander set in a bowl. Discard the water.)

If you have used the wok or pan, wipe it clean. Heat it until it is very hot and add 1 tablespoon of oil. Add the walnuts and stir-fry them for 1 minute. Remove and set aside. Add the garlic, ginger and spring onions to the pan and stir-fry for a few seconds. Return the walnuts to the pan and then add the rest of the ingredients. Return the chicken to the wok and stir-fry the mixture for another 2 minutes. Serve at once.

lemon chicken

The southern Chinese have made a speciality of chicken cooked with lemon. Unlike many versions which employ a cloyingly sweet sauce, this recipe balances tartness with sweetness. Sometimes the lemon chicken is steamed, but I think it is equally good stir-fried, especially if the chicken is velveted beforehand. Serve it with plain steamed rice and Cold Sesame Broccoli (page 200).

Region: Canton
Methods: Velveting and stir-frying

Serves 4

450 g (1 lb) boneless chicken breasts, skinned
1 egg white
1 teaspoon salt
1 teaspoon sesame oil
2 teaspoons cornflour
280 ml (10 fl oz) groundnut (peanut) oil or water

FOR THE SAUCE
65 ml (2½ fl oz) Chicken Stock (page 59) or water
3 tablespoons fresh lemon juice
1 tablespoon sugar
1 tablespoon light soy sauce
1½ tablespoons Shaoxing rice wine or dry sherry
1 tablespoon finely chopped garlic
2 dried red chillies, halved
1 teaspoon cornflour, blended with 1 teaspoon water
2 teaspoons sesame oil

FOR THE GARNISH
2 tablespoons finely chopped spring onions

Cut the chicken into thin strips about 7.5 cm (3 inches) long. Combine them with the egg white, salt, sesame oil and corn-flour in a bowl and put it into the refrigerator for about 20 minutes.

Heat a wok or frying pan until it is very hot. Add the oil and when it is very hot and slightly smoking, remove the wok from the heat. Immediately add the chicken, stirring vigorously to keep it from sticking. After about 2 minutes when the chicken pieces turn white, quickly drain the chicken and all the oil in a stainless steel colander set in a bowl. Discard the oil.

(If you use water instead of oil, bring it to a boil in a saucepan. Remove the saucepan from the heat and immediately add the chicken pieces, stirring vigorously to prevent them from sticking. After about 2 minutes when the chicken pieces turn white, quickly drain the chicken and all the water in a stainless steel colander set in a bowl. Discard the water.)

Wipe the wok or pan clean and re-heat it. Add the stock, lemon juice, sugar, soy sauce, Shaoxing rice wine or dry sherry, garlic and chillies and bring the mixture to the boil over a high heat. Add the cornflour mixture and simmer for 1 minute. Return the chicken strips to the sauce and stir-fry them long enough to coat them all with the sauce. Stir in the sesame oil and mix once again. Then turn on to a warm serving platter, garnish with the spring onions and serve at once.

shredded chicken with sesame seeds

This is my version of a fragrant Sichuan dish popularly known as 'Strange Taste Chicken' because it incorporates so many flavours, being hot, spicy, sour, sweet and salty all at the same time. It is delicious as a hot dish but I find it an excellent cold dish as well. I simply let it cool and serve it at room temperature. The sesame seeds add a crunchy texture which contrasts nicely with the tender chicken. Serve with Ham and Marrow Soup (page 72) and Stir-Fried Broccoli with Hoisin Sauce (page 200).

Region: Sichuan
Method: Stir-frying

Serves 3 to 4

450 g (1 lb) boneless chicken breasts, skinned

1 egg white

½ teaspoon salt

2 teaspoons cornflour

300 ml (10 fl oz) groundnut (peanut) oil or water

1 tablespoon groundnut (peanut) oil

1 tablespoon white sesame seeds

FOR THE SAUCE

2 teaspoons dark soy sauce

2 teaspoons Chinese black rice vinegar or cider vinegar

2 teaspoons chilli bean sauce

2 teaspoons sesame oil

2 teaspoons sugar

1 tablespoon Shaoxing rice wine or dry sherry

1 teaspoon whole Sichuan peppercorns, roasted (page 35)

1½ tablespoons finely chopped spring onions

Cut the chicken breasts into strips about 7.5 cm (3 inches) long. Combine them with the egg white, salt and cornflour in a small bowl and place in the refrigerator for about 20 minutes.

Heat a wok or large frying pan until it is very hot. Add the oil and when it is very hot and slightly smoking, remove the wok from the heat. Immediately add the chicken pieces, stirring vigorously to prevent them from sticking. After about 2 minutes when the chicken pieces turn white, quickly drain the chicken and all the oil in a stainless steel colander set in a bowl. Discard the oil.

(If you use water instead of oil, bring it to a boil in a saucepan. Remove the saucepan from the heat and immediately add the chicken pieces, stirring vigorously to prevent them from sticking. After about 2 minutes when the chicken pieces turn white, quickly drain the chicken and all the water in a stainless steel colander set in a bowl. Discard the water.)

If you are using the wok or pan, wipe it clean. Heat it until it is hot, then add 1 tablespoon of oil. Immediately add the sesame seeds and stir-fry them for 30 seconds or until they are slightly brown. Then add the sauce ingredients and bring to the boil. Return the cooked chicken to the pan and stir-fry the mixture for another 2 minutes, coating the pieces thoroughly with the sauce and sesame seeds. Serve at once or let it cool and serve at room temperature.

drunken chicken

This dish is called Drunken Chicken with good reason! You do need quite a lot of rice wine to cover the fowl during the steeping process, but it can be re-used. I think this traditional dish tastes best when it is made with Chinese Shaoxing rice wine rather than sherry. Because it can be prepared at least two days ahead, it makes an ideal dish for a party or a large gathering or special occasion.

Region: Shanghai
Methods: Simmering and steeping

Serves 4

3 slices fresh ginger
1.2 litres (2 pints) Chicken Stock (page 59)
3 tablespoons light soy sauce
1 tablespoon salt
1 spring onion
1 x 1.5–1.75 kg (3–3½ lb) chicken
1.2 litres (2 pints) Shaoxing rice wine or dry sherry

Cut the ginger into slices 5 cm x 5 mm (2 x ¼ inch). Fill a large casserole or saucepan with the stock, bring it to the boil, then add the ginger, soy sauce, salt, whole spring onion and the chicken. (If they are not covered by the liquid, add a little more stock or water.) Bring the liquid back to the boil and turn the heat down. Simmer for 30 minutes, skimming any fat or scum off the surface all the time. Turn off the heat, cover the casserole or pan tightly and let the chicken sit in the liquid for 30 minutes.

Transfer the cooked chicken to a large plate and let it cool. (The cooking liquid can now be skimmed of all fat, saved and used as a base for stock or to cook rice.) Cut the chicken in half lengthways and place it in a bowl. Cover the chicken halves with the Shaoxing rice wine and leave it for 2 days in the refrigerator, turning it over from time to time.

After 2 days remove the chicken and arrange it on a serving platter. Pour some of the wine over the chicken to moisten it. The remaining wine can be kept in the refrigerator and used for cooking other dishes which call for Shaoxing rice wine.

Left:
Fresh ginger
(*page 27*)

cashew chicken

This dish exemplifies the Chinese penchant for contrasting textures. Here, tender succulent pieces of chicken are used with sweet, crunchy cashew nuts. The original Chinese version would have been made with peanuts. Nevertheless this dish uses the best Chinese cooking principles: velveting to seal in the juices of the chicken, and then stir-frying with spices to flavour it.

Region: Canton
Methods: Velveting and stir-frying

Serves 4

450 g (1 lb) boneless chicken breasts, skinned

1 egg white

1 teaspoon salt

2 teaspoons cornflour

300 ml (10 fl oz) groundnut (peanut) oil or water

2 teaspoons groundnut (peanut) oil

50 g (2 oz) cashew nuts

1 tablespoon Shaoxing rice wine or dry sherry

1 tablespoon light soy sauce

FOR THE GARNISH

1 tablespoon finely chopped spring onions

Cut the chicken into 1 cm (½ inch) cubes. Mix with the egg white, salt and cornflour in a small bowl and put it in the refrigerator for 20 minutes.

Heat a wok or large frying pan until it is very hot. Add the oil and when it is very hot and slightly smoking, remove the wok from the heat. Immediately add the chicken, stirring vigorously to prevent it from sticking. After about 2 minutes when the chicken turns white, drain the chicken and all the oil in a stainless steel colander set in a bowl. Discard the oil.

(If you use water instead of oil, bring it to a boil in a saucepan. Remove from the heat and immediately add the chicken, stirring vigorously to prevent it from sticking. After about 2 minutes when the chicken turns white, drain into a stainless steel colander set in a bowl. Discard the water.)

If you have used the wok or pan, wipe it clean. Heat it until it is very hot, add the 2 teaspoons of oil and the cashew nuts and stir-fry them for 1 minute. Add the rest of the ingredients. Return the chicken to the wok and stir-fry the mixture for another 2 minutes. Garnish the dish with the spring onions and serve at once.

hot spiced chicken

This hot and spicy chicken dish can easily be made in advance and re-heated. It is a good example of the combination of contrasting flavours which characterize the spicy cuisine of western China. The finished dish has a wonderful fragrance and an equally delightful taste.

Serves 4

450 g (1 lb) boneless chicken thighs, skin removed, cut into 2.5 cm (1 inch) cubes

1 teaspoon salt

4 spring onions

150 ml (5 fl oz) groundnut (peanut) oil

3 dried red chillies, halved lengthways

1 teaspoon groundnut (peanut) oil

2 teaspoons finely chopped fresh ginger

1 tablespoon chilli bean sauce

300 ml (10 fl oz) Chicken Stock (page 59)

2 teaspoons whole Sichuan peppercorns, roasted and freshly ground (page 35)

2 teaspoons sugar

2 tablespoons dark soy sauce

Rub the chicken thighs with the salt and let them sit for about 30 minutes. Cut the spring onions into 5 cm (2 inch) pieces. Heat a wok or large frying pan until it is very hot. Add the oil and when it is very hot and slightly smoking, add the dried chillies and stir-fry for a few seconds. (You may remove them when they turn black or leave them in.) Turn the heat down. Add the chicken pieces to the pan and slowly brown them. Drain the cooked pieces in a colander set over a stainless bowl. Wipe the pan clean.

Heat the wok or pan until it is very hot and add 1 teaspoon oil. Fry the spring onions, ginger and chilli bean sauce, taking care not to have the heat too high or the sauce will burn. A few seconds later add the chicken stock, Sichuan peppercorns, sugar and soy sauce. Then turn the heat down low and add the chicken pieces to the pan. Cover, and cook the chicken in this sauce for 20 to 30 minutes, turning the pieces from time to time. Remove any surface fat then serve the chicken with the sauce.

paper-wrapped chicken

This unusual method of cooking chicken is ingenious: a thin slice of chicken is sandwiched between flavourful ingredients and wrapped in greaseproof paper then deep-fried. As the package cooks, the mixture steams and the flavours meld, the result being a most delicious and unique starter. The package must be wrapped carefully so the oil does not seep in. Some Chinese restaurants cheat by using a quick marinade of hoisin and soy sauce, then wrapping the chicken in aluminium foil. Although this method takes a little more work, the outcome is worth the effort. It is one of those special dishes that is also a dinner-time conversation piece.

Region: Canton
Method: Deep-frying

Serves 8 as a starter

250 g (9 oz) boneless chicken breasts, skinned

FOR THE MARINADE

2 tablespoons oyster sauce

1 tablespoon light soy sauce

1 tablespoon dark soy sauce

1 tablespoon Shaoxing rice wine or dry sherry

2 teaspoons sugar

1 teaspoon sesame oil

Salt and freshly ground black pepper

30 shreds red chilli peppers, 4 cm (1½ inches) long

60 shreds spring onions, 4 cm (1½ inches) cut diagonally

30 shreds fresh ginger, peeled, 4 cm x 5 mm (1½ x ¼ inch)

30 pieces thinly sliced water chestnuts, peeled if fresh, rinsed if canned (page 37)

60 pieces fresh coriander leaves

30 pieces Parma ham, cut into 8 cm (3 inch) squares

FOR THE WRAPPING

30 pieces greaseproof paper, cut into 15 cm (6 inch) squares

1.2 litres (2 pints) groundnut (peanut) oil

Cut the chicken into 30 4 cm x 5 mm (1½ x ¼ inch) pieces and combine it with the marinade in a glass bowl. Let it marinate in the refrigerator at least 1 hour.

Place a piece of greaseproof square with a corner towards you and fold the tip in slightly. Put in the centre of the square the following: a shred of chilli, fresh coriander leaf, chicken, ham, two shreds of spring onion, a shred of ginger, a slice of water chestnut and finally another fresh coriander leaf. Fold the first corner over the ingredients, then fold in the sides. Then fold the entire package in half, leaving a flap at the corner away from you. Finally tuck the flap in to secure the package. Repeat until all the packages are filled.

Heat a wok until it is very hot. Add the oil and when it is very hot and slightly smoking, add about 10 packages and deep-fry for about 3 minutes. Remove them with a slotted spoon and drain well. Deep-fry the rest of the packages in two batches in the same way.

When they are completely finished, arrange them on a warm serving platter and let each of your guests unwrap his or her package.

braised chicken with leeks

Leeks are popular in northern and eastern Chinese cooking. They have a flavour which is less pronounced than that of garlic or onions and which blends well with the mild taste of chicken. Leeks need to be thoroughly washed and I find it easier to do this after they have been chopped. This warm rich dish is perfect for cold winter days. I like to cook it in a Chinese clay pot but any heavy casserole will do. Serve with plain steamed rice or plain boiled noodles and Ginger and Spring Onion Sauce (page 39).

Regions: Beijing and Shanghai
Methods: Stir-frying and braising

Serves 4

450 g (1 lb) boneless chicken thighs, skinned
2 teaspoons sesame oil
2 teaspoons Shaoxing rice wine or dry sherry
2 teaspoons light soy sauce
1½ teaspoons cornflour
225 g (8 oz) leeks
1 tablespoon groundnut (peanut) oil
2 spring onions, finely shredded
1 tablespoon finely shredded fresh ginger
½ teaspoon salt
½ teaspoon freshly ground black pepper
210 ml (7½ fl oz) Chicken Stock (page 59)
2 teaspoons Shaoxing rice wine or dry sherry
1 tablespoon dark soy sauce
2 teaspoons sesame oil
1 teaspoon sugar

Pat the chicken pieces dry with kitchen paper. Using a heavy cleaver or knife, cut them into smaller pieces about 5 x 2.5 cm (2 x 1 inch) and put them into a bowl. Add the sesame oil, Shaoxing rice wine or dry sherry, light soy sauce and cornflour and mix well. Leave the chicken to marinate for 20 minutes.

Trim the leeks and discard any yellow parts. Cut the leeks at the point where they begin to turn green and discard the green parts. Then split the white parts in half and cut them at a slight diagonal into 6 cm (2½ inch) segments. Now wash them well in cold water until there is no trace of dirt.

Heat a wok or large frying pan until it is very hot. Add the oil and when it is very hot and slightly smoking, add the spring onion and ginger. Quickly lift the chicken out of the marinade, using a slotted spoon, and add to the pan with the leeks, salt and pepper. Stir-fry for about 5 minutes until they are thoroughly browned and then remove them from the pan with a slotted spoon and discard any remaining oil or fat.

Bring the stock to the boil in a medium-sized pan and add the Shaoxing rice wine or dry sherry, dark soy sauce, sesame oil and sugar; then add the browned chicken and vegetables. Skim off any scum and reduce the heat to a simmer. Cover the pan tightly and braise for about 25 minutes. Before serving, skim off any fat. Serve at once or cool and refrigerate.

twice-cooked chicken

This eastern Chinese recipe involves a two-step cooking process. First the chicken is marinated and steamed. This cooks the flesh but retains the moisture and flavour of the bird. The chicken pieces are then dried and deep-fried to a golden, crispy brown.

Region: Fujian
Methods: Steaming and deep-frying

Serves 4 to 6

750 g (1½ lb) chicken thighs, boned, skinned and cut into 5 cm (2 inch) cubes
600 ml (1 pint) groundnut (peanut) oil (see Deep-Fat Fryers, page 42)

FOR THE MARINADE

1 tablespoon Shaoxing rice wine or dry sherry
1½ tablespoons light soy sauce
1 tablespoon dark soy sauce
1 tablespoon shrimp paste
1 tablespoon finely chopped spring onions
2 teaspoons finely chopped fresh ginger
1 teaspoon whole Sichuan peppercorns, roasted and freshly ground (page 35), or 1 teaspoon freshly ground black peppercorns
2 teaspoons sugar
2 teaspoons salt
Cornflour for dusting

FOR DIPPING
Roasted Salt and Pepper (page 39)

Combine all the marinade ingredients, except the cornflour, together in a bowl. Rub the marinade mixture all over the chicken pieces and let them sit in a cool place for 1 hour.

Set up a steamer or put a rack into a wok or deep pan and fill it with 5 cm (2 inches) of water. Bring the water to the boil over a high heat. Put the chicken on to a heatproof plate and then carefully lower it into the steamer or on to the rack. Turn the heat to low and cover the wok or pan tightly. Steam gently for 30 minutes.

Remove the cooked chicken and let it cool and dry completely.

This may take an hour or more. (The dish can be made a day ahead up to this point.)

Heat the oil in a deep-fat fryer or large wok until it is hot. Dust the pieces of dried, steamed chicken with cornflour, shaking off any excess. Deep-fry the chicken, a few pieces at a time, until the pieces are golden brown and heated right through. Drain the pieces on kitchen paper. Serve the chicken hot with the Roasted Salt and Pepper on the side.

soy sauce chicken

My friends are often surprised at their first taste of Soy Sauce Chicken. Instead of the saltiness they expect, given the name of the dish, they taste tender, succulent chicken bathed in a rich and subtle sauce. The technique of steeping used here ensures that the chicken is moist and tender, and allows the rich flavours of the sauce to permeate the meat gently. The chicken may be served hot but I think it is best cooled and served at room temperature, or refrigerated and served cold. It also makes a delicious picnic dish or a wonderful cold starter. The steeping liquid may be used as a sauce, and the rest may be frozen and re-used for making more Soy Sauce Chicken.

Regions: Canton and Fujian
Methods: Simmering and steeping

Serves 4 to 6

6 slices fresh ginger

1 x 1.5–1.75 kg (3–3½ lb) free-range or corn fed chicken

6 spring onions

2 tablespoons salt

1 teaspoon freshly ground black pepper

FOR THE SAUCE

1.75 litres (3 pints) Chicken Stock (page 59) or water

600 ml (1 pint) dark soy sauce

150 ml (5 fl oz) light soy sauce

300 ml (10 fl oz) Shaoxing rice wine or dry sherry, or 150 ml (5 fl oz) dry sherry mixed with 150 ml (5 fl oz) Chicken Stock (page 59)

175 g (6 oz) Chinese rock sugar or ordinary sugar

5 whole star anise

5 Chinese cinnamon bark or cinnamon sticks

3 tablespoons cumin seeds

FOR THE GARNISH

Fresh coriander sprigs

First make the sauce by combining all the sauce ingredients in a very large pan and bringing the liquid to a simmer. Meanwhile, cut the ginger into 5 cm x 5 mm (2 x ¼ inch) slices. Stuff the cavity of the chicken with the whole spring onions, ginger slices, salt and pepper. Put the chicken into the pan breast-side down with the sauce mixture. If the liquid does not cover the chicken, add a little more stock. Bring it back to a simmer and simmer for about 30 minutes, skimming all the while. Turn the chicken over so the breast is touching the bottom of the pan. Turn off the heat, cover the pan tightly and leave for 1 hour.

After this time, remove the chicken from the liquid with a slotted spoon and put it on a plate to cool. It can now be put into the refrigerator or cut up into pieces and served. Remove any surface fat from the sauce then spoon it over the chicken pieces. Garnish with fresh coriander sprigs before serving.

steeped chicken

This is a classic Cantonese dish, sometimes called White-Cut Chicken, which my mother often made. The technique used is called steeping, which applies to delicate foods, such as chicken. Here the gentlest possible heat is used so that the flesh of the chicken remains extremely moist and flavourful with a satiny, almost velvet-like texture. It is not a difficult dish to make. The chicken simmers in liquid for a few minutes, then the heat is turned off, the pan tightly covered and the chicken left to steep to finish cooking. Save the water the chicken is steeped in for cooking rice or for chicken stock.

The pure, simple flavours call for a suitably pungent dipping sauce. Scallions and ginger root, jolted to the full fragrance by a quick dousing of hot groundnut (peanut) oil, offer the perfect flavour combination.

Serves 4

1 x 1.5–1.75 kg (3½–4 lb) free-range or corn fed chicken

1 tablespoon salt

6 slices fresh ginger

6 spring onions

Freshly ground black pepper

FOR THE CANTONESE-STYLE DIPPING SAUCE

4 tablespoons finely chopped spring onions, white part only

2 teaspoons finely chopped fresh ginger

2 teaspoons salt

2 tablespoons groundnut (peanut) oil

Rub the chicken evenly with the salt. Place the chicken in a large saucepan, cover with water and bring to a boil. Add the ginger, spring onions and pepper. Cover tightly, reduce the heat and simmer for 20 minutes. Turn off the heat and leave covered tightly for 1 hour.

To make the sauce: mix all the ingredients except the oil in a heatproof bowl. Heat a wok or small pan until it is very hot. Add the oil and when it is very hot and slightly smoking, pour it on the sauce ingredients and mix well.

Transfer the chicken to a chopping board. Strain and save the liquid which can be used as a base for making stock or to cook rice. Cut the chicken into bite-sized pieces and arrange it on a warm serving platter. Serve the sauce on the side.

mango chicken

This might be called 'Nouvelle Hong Kong' or Southeast Asia meets Hong Kong. It is an exotic and unlikely combination. I have eaten this dish several times in Hong Kong and found it delicious every time. The rich sweetness and soft texture of the mango works extremely well with the delicate taste of the chicken. The mango is cooked for a short time, just enough to warm it through. Mangoes are very popular in Hong Kong. They are imported from Thailand and the Philippines and are one of the best liked of all tropical fruits and, as this recipe indicates, mix well with other distinctively-flavoured foods.

Region: Hong Kong
Methods: Velveting and stir-frying

Serves 4

450 g (1 lb) boneless chicken breasts, skinned and cut into 2.5 cm (1 inch) pieces
1 egg white
1 teaspoon sesame oil
1 teaspoon salt
2 teaspoons cornflour
Freshly ground black pepper to taste
600 ml (1 pint) groundnut (peanut) oil or water
1½ tablespoons groundnut (peanut) oil
1 tablespoon finely chopped fresh ginger
1 tablespoon finely chopped garlic
1½ tablespoons Shaoxing rice wine or dry sherry
1 teaspoon salt
1 teaspoon sesame oil
2 mangoes, peeled and cut into 2.5 cm (1 inch) pieces

FOR THE GARNISH
1 tablespoon finely chopped fresh coriander

Mix the chicken with the egg white, sesame oil, salt, cornflour and pepper in a bowl. Refrigerate for about 20 minutes.

Heat a wok or large frying pan until it is very hot. Add the oil and when it is very hot and slightly smoking, remove the wok from the heat. Immediately add the chicken pieces, stirring vigorously to prevent them from sticking. After about 2 minutes when the chicken pieces turn white, quickly drain the chicken and all the oil in a stainless steel colander set in a bowl. Discard the oil.

(If you use water instead of oil, bring it to a boil in a saucepan. Remove the saucepan from the heat and immediately add the chicken pieces, stirring vigorously to prevent them from sticking. After about 2 minutes when the chicken pieces turn white, quickly drain the chicken and all the water in a stainless steel colander set in a bowl. Discard the water.)

Heat 1½ tablespoons of oil in the wok or pan. Add the ginger and garlic and stir-fry for 30 seconds. Add the Shaoxing rice wine or dry sherry, salt, sesame oil and mangoes. Stir-fry gently for 2 minutes or until the mangoes are heated through. Add the drained chicken and stir gently to mix well. Garnish with the coriander, turn on to a warm serving platter and serve at once.

crispy chicken

This is one of my favourite chicken dishes. It was a standard at all family gatherings on special occasions. Although it is usually served in restaurants, it can easily be made at home. The many exotic ingredients gives this chicken dish a special taste experience. Although it requires a bit of patience to make, much of the work can be done the day before. You can serve this as a centrepiece for a special dinner party.

Region: Canton
Methods: Simmering and
deep-frying

Serves 4 to 6

1 x 1.5 kg (3–3½ lb) free-range or corn fed chicken
1.2 litres (2 pints) groundnut (peanut) oil

FOR THE SIMMERING SAUCE
3.4 litres (6 pints) water
2 Chinese cinnamon bark or cinnamon sticks
250 ml (8 fl oz) dark soy sauce
3 tablespoons light soy sauce
120 ml (4 fl oz) Shaoxing rice wine or dry sherry
3 whole star anise
1 tablespoon fresh orange peel or dried citrus peel, soaked and finely chopped (page 25)
3 slices fresh ginger
2 spring onions
50 g (2 oz) Chinese rock sugar or ordinary sugar

FOR THE GLAZE
3 tablespoons honey
300 ml (10 fl oz) water
2 tablespoons dark soy sauce
2 tablespoons Chinese black rice vinegar or cider vinegar

FOR THE GARNISH
1 whole lemon, cut into wedges
Roasted Salt and Pepper (page 39)

Combine all the ingredients for the simmering sauce in a large casserole or pan and bring the mixture to the boil. Then turn the heat down to a simmer. Lower in the chicken, breast side down, and simmer it, uncovered, for 30 to 40 minutes or until the chicken is cooked through. Place the chicken on a rack over a tray or roasting pan and leave in a cool, well-ventilated place to dry for about 3 hours. When the chicken has dried the skin should feel like parchment paper. Cut it in half lengthways, then wipe the cavity dry with kitchen paper.

!n a wok or pan, bring the glaze ingredients to the boil and baste the skins of the chicken. Let the chicken dry again for another 2 hours, keeping it in a cool and airy place but not in the refrigerator.

Heat the oil in a deep-fat fryer or large wok and lower in one of the halves, skin-side down. Deep-fry until it is a rich, dark brown colour and very crisp. Remove from the pan and drain well on kitchen paper. Deep-fry the other half. Cut the chicken into bite-sized pieces, arrange on a platter and garnish with the lemon. Serve with Roasted Salt and Pepper.

chinese chicken salad

I have often enjoyed serving this salad either as a first course or as a main course for dinner on a warm summer night. It has been a success at picnics, too. It is easy to prepare and is served with a tasty dressing.

Regions: Beijing and Sichuan
Method: Steaming

Serves 4 to 6

1 x 1.25–1.5 kg (3–3½ lb) chicken, uncooked, or 1 plain roasted chicken
1 tablespoon salt
225 g (8 oz) fresh bean sprouts
275 g (10 oz) cucumber
100 g (4 oz,) carrots

FOR THE DRESSING

3 tablespoons sesame paste or smooth peanut butter
2 tablespoons chilli bean sauce
2 tablespoons finely chopped spring onions
1 tablespoon sesame oil
3 tablespoons Chinese white rice vinegar or cider vinegar
2 tablespoons light soy sauce
1½ tablespoons dark soy sauce
1½ tablespoons finely chopped garlic
1 teaspoon salt
½ teaspoon freshly ground white pepper
½ teaspoon ground Sichuan peppercorn
2 teaspoons sugar
150 ml (5 fl oz) Chicken Stock (page 59)

If you are using uncooked chicken, rub the chicken with 1 tablespoon of salt. Next set up a steamer or put a rack into a wok or deep pan and fill it with 5 cm (2 inches) of water. Bring the water to the boil over a high heat. Put the chicken on to a heatproof plate and then carefully lower it into the steamer or on to the rack. Turn the heat to low and cover the wok or pan tightly. Steam gently for 1 hour or until the chicken is cooked. Remove and allow the chicken to cool thoroughly.

Next prepare the vegetables. Trim the bean sprouts at both ends. Peel the cucumber, split it in half lengthways and remove the seeds with a teaspoon. Finely shred the cucumber into 7.5 cm (3 inch) lengths. Peel and finely shred the carrots into 7.5 cm (3 inch) lengths. Set the vegetables aside.

Take all the meat off the cooked chicken and shred it into fine strips using a sharp knife or cleaver. Arrange the chicken strips on a platter and surround them with the bean sprouts, cucumber and carrots. Combine all the ingredients for the dressing and mix them thoroughly. (I find an electric blender is quite useful for this but you could use a screw-top jar and shake everything in it well.) Pour the dressing all over the chicken and vegetables and mix well. Serve at once.

peking duck

The Chinese have a special reverence for duck, regarding it as a symbol of wholesomeness and fidelity. Of course its 'delectability' is its chief virtue. With Peking Duck, Chinese cooks mastered the art of making the most of the duck's rich, succulent flesh while minimizing its major flaw – its relatively large proportion of bone and fat. There is little doubt that this dish was first concocted in the Imperial kitchens. Its popularity spread as restaurants, staffed by former Imperial chefs, made it a speciality. The dish can now be found in all parts of China.

The preparation and cooking of Peking Duck in China is an art form. Specially raised ducklings are fed a rich diet of maize, sorghum, barley and soya beans for 1½ months before they are ready for the kitchen. After being killed and cleaned, air is pumped through the windpipe to separate the skin from the meat. (This allows the skin to roast separately and remain crisp while the fat melts, keeping the meat moist.) Hot water is then poured over the duck to close the skin pores and it is hung up to dry. During the drying process a solution of malt sugar is liberally brushed over the duck, which is then roasted in wood-burning ovens. The result is a shiny, crisp and aromatic duck with beautiful brown skin, moist flesh and no fat.

Preparing Peking Duck is a time-consuming task, but I have devised a simpler method which closely approximates the real thing. Just give yourself plenty of time and the results will be good enough for an emperor. Traditionally, Peking Duck is served with Chinese Pancakes, spring onions cut into brush shapes and sweet bean sauce. In Hong Kong and in the West, hoisin sauce is used instead. It is very similar to sweet bean sauce but contains vinegar. Each guest spoons some sauce on to a pancake. Then a helping of crisp skin and meat is placed on top with a spring onion brush and the entire mixture is rolled up like a stuffed pancake. It can be eaten using chopsticks or one's fingers. This makes an unforgettable dish for a very special dinner party.

Serves 4 to 6

1 x 1.6–1.8 kg (3½–4 lb) duck, fresh or
frozen, preferably Cherry Valley

FOR THE HONEY SYRUP MIXTURE

1 lemon

1.2 litres (2 pints) water

3 tablespoons honey

3 tablespoons dark soy sauce

150 ml (5 fl oz) Shaoxing rice wine or
dry sherry

TO SERVE

Chinese Pancakes (page 248)

6 tablespoons hoisin sauce or
sweet bean sauce

24 spring onion brushes (page 50)

If the duck is frozen, thaw it thoroughly. Rinse the duck well and blot it completely dry with kitchen paper. Insert a meat hook near the neck.

Using a sharp knife, cut the lemon into 5 mm (¼ inch) slices, leaving the rind on. Place them in a large pan with the rest of the honey syrup ingredients and bring the mixture to the boil. Turn the heat to low and simmer for about 20 minutes. Using a large ladle or spoon, pour this mixture over the duck several times, as if to bathe it, until the skin of the duck is completely coated. Hang the duck over a tray or roasting pan and leave in a cool, well ventilated place to dry, for about 4 to 5 hours, longer if possible. (To speed up the process place it in front of a fan for about 4 to 5 hours.) When the duck has dried, the skin should feel like parchment paper.

Pre-heat the oven to gas mark 9, 240°C (475°F). Meanwhile, place the duck on a roasting rack in a roasting pan, breast side up. Put 150 ml (5 fl oz) of water into the roasting pan. (This will prevent the fat from splattering.) Now put the duck into the oven and roast it for 15 minutes. Then turn the heat down to gas mark 4, 180°C (350°F) and continue to roast for 1 hour and 10 minutes.

Remove the duck from the oven and let it sit for at least 10 minutes before you carve it. Using a cleaver or a sharp knife, cut the skin and meat into pieces and arrange them on a warm serving platter. Serve at once with Chinese Pancakes, spring onion brushes and a bowl of hoisin sauce or sweet bean sauce.

crispy sichuan duck

Region: Sichuan
Methods: Steaming and deep-frying

In my family and in typical Chinese custom, duck was a treat reserved for special occasions and family banquets. I always remembered such feasts long afterwards. This duck recipe is one of my favourites, it is not surprising that it is so popular in Chinese restaurants in the West. Don't be intimidated by the long preparation process. Most of the steps are quite simple and can be done up to a day ahead – and the results are well worth the labour. The technique of steaming renders out most of the fat, leaving the duck meat moist and succulent. The final deep-frying gives the duck skin a crispy texture. This is a dish for a special dinner party and should be served with Steamed Buns (page 246) and Roasted Salt and Pepper (page 39).

Serves 4 to 6

1 x 1.6–1.8 kg (3½–4 lb) duck, fresh or frozen, preferably Cherry Valley

2 tablespoons five-spice powder

60 g (2½ oz) whole Sichuan peppercorns

25 g (1 oz) whole black peppercorns

3 tablespoons cumin seeds

200 g (7 oz) rock salt

4 slices fresh ginger

4 spring onions

Cornflour or taro flour for dusting

1.2 litres (2 pints) groundnut (peanut) oil

TO SERVE

Roasted Salt and Pepper (page 39)

Steamed Buns (page 246)

If the duck is frozen, thaw it thoroughly. Blot it with kitchen paper until it is thoroughly dry, then rub it inside and out with the five-spice powder, Sichuan peppercorns, black peppercorns and cumin seeds. Cover the outside of the duck on both sides with the rock salt. Make sure these are rubbed on evenly. Wrap well in cling film and place in the refrigerator for 24 hours.

After this time, brush the salt from the duck. Cut the ginger into slices 7.5 cm x 5 mm (3 x ¼ inch). Slice the spring onions into 7.5 cm (3 inch) lengths. Stuff the ginger and spring onions into the cavity of the duck, and place it on a heatproof china or glass plate.

Next set up a steamer or put a rack into a wok or deep pan and fill it with 5 cm (2 inches) of water. Bring the water to the boil over a high heat. Then carefully lower the duck into the steamer or on to the rack. Turn the heat to low and cover the wok or pan tightly. Steam gently for 2 hours, pouring off the excess fat from time to time. Top up with boiling water from time to time to keep the steam constant. Remove the duck and pour off all the fat and liquid which may have accumulated. Discard the ginger and spring onions. Keep the duck on a platter in a cool dry place for about 2 hours until it has thoroughly dried and cooled. At this point the duck can be refrigerated.

Just before you are ready to serve it, cut the duck into quarters. Dust the duck with either cornflour or taro flour, shaking off the excess. Heat the oil in a deep-fat fryer or wok. When the oil is slightly smoking, deep-fry the duck quarters in 2 batches until each is crisp and warmed right through. Drain the quarters on kitchen paper and then chop them into smaller serving pieces.

To eat Crispy Duck, dip a piece of duck meat in the Roasted Salt and Pepper mixture and then put the meat into a split, steamed bun and eat it rather like a sandwich.

braised duck

Region: Canton
Methods: Deep-frying and braising

The braising sauce used for this duck recipe is similar to the one used for Soy Sauce Chicken (page 136). The sauce can be frozen and re-used. Unlike chicken, duck needs long braising to cook it thoroughly and to render out the fat in the skin. You can see this braised duck in food shops in China, southeast Asia, Taiwan, Hong Kong and in Chinatowns in the USA and the UK, hanging picturesquely from hooks. It is easy to make at home and re-heats well, although I think it is best served at room temperature. It would go well with Hot Bean Thread Noodles (page 241) and Lettuce with Oyster Sauce (page 210).

Serves 4 to 6

1 x 1.6–1.8 kg (3¹/2–4 lb) duck, fresh or frozen, preferably Cherry Valley

1.2 litres (2 pints) groundnut (peanut) oil

FOR THE SAUCE

1.2 litres (2 pints) Chicken Stock (page 59) or water

1.2 litres (2 pints) dark soy sauce

300 ml (10 fl oz) light soy sauce

450 ml (15 fl oz) Shaoxing rice wine or dry sherry, or 210 ml (7¹/2 fl oz) dry sherry mixed with 210 ml (7¹/2 fl oz) Chicken Stock (page 59)

100 g (4 oz) Chinese rock sugar

5 whole star anise

3 Chinese cinnamon bark or cinnamon sticks

2 tablespoons fennel seeds

1 tablespoon cumin seeds

FOR THE GARNISH

Fresh coriander sprigs

Cut the duck in half lengthways. Dry the halves thoroughly with kitchen paper. Heat the oil in a wok or large frying pan until it is very hot and slightly smoking. Deep-fry the two halves of the duck, skin-side down. Turn the heat to medium and continue to fry slowly until the skin is browned. This should take about 15 to 20 minutes. Do not turn the pieces over but baste the duck as it fries. Drain the lightly browned duck on kitchen paper.

Combine all the sauce ingredients together in a large pan and bring the mixture to a boil. Add the duck halves and turn the heat down to a simmer. Cover the pan and slowly braise the duck for 1 hour or until it is tender.

Skim off the large amount of surface fat which will be left when the duck is cooked. (This procedure will prevent the duck from becoming greasy.) Remove the duck pieces with a slotted spoon, let them cool and then chop them into smaller pieces. Arrange on a warm serving platter, garnish with the fresh coriander and serve at once. Alternatively you can let the duck cool thoroughly and serve it at room temperature. Once the sauce has cooled, remove any lingering surface fat. The sauce can then be frozen and re-used to braise duck or chicken. This dish re-heats beautifully.

cantonese roast duck

One of the most delicious ways to cook duck is this Cantonese method of roasting it with a flavourful marinade inside the cavity. The method is ingenious, because not only does the marinade make a tasty duck, it also keeps the meat moist. The skin becomes very crispy and the duck juices combine with the marinade for a delicious duck sauce. This duck may be familiar to many who see it in the windows of Chinatowns throughout the world. It is easy to buy, but almost as easy to make at home. It makes a spectacular centrepiece for a dinner party.

Serves 4 to 6

1 x 1.6–1.8 kg (3½–4 lb) duck, fresh or frozen, preferably Cherry Valley

FOR THE MARINADE

1 tablespoon groundnut (peanut) oil

3 tablespoons finely chopped fresh ginger

5 cloves garlic, unpeeled and crushed

6 spring onions, cut into 7.5 cm (3 inch) segments

1 tablespoon whole yellow bean sauce

2 tablespoons light soy sauce

2 tablespoons Shaoxing rice wine or dry sherry

1½ tablespoons crushed Chinese rock sugar or ordinary sugar

3 whole star anise

1 tablespoon whole Sichuan peppercorns, roasted (page 35)

150 ml (5 fl oz) Chicken Stock (page 59)

10 whole sprigs fresh coriander

FOR THE BASTING MIXTURE

1.2 litres (2 pints) water

6 tablespoons honey

4 tablespoons dark soy sauce

3 tablespoons Shaoxing rice wine or dry sherry

2 tablespoons black rice vinegar or cider vinegar

If the duck is frozen, thaw it thoroughly. Rinse the duck well and blot it completely dry with kitchen paper. Insert a meat hook near the neck.

Heat a wok or large frying pan until it is very hot. Add the oil and when it is very hot and slightly smoking, add the ginger and garlic and stir-fry for 10 seconds. Then add the rest of the marinade ingredients. Bring the mixture to a simmer, remove from the heat and allow to cool thoroughly.

Pour the marinade into the duck cavity and skewer the tail opening with a steel or bamboo skewer. Tie this with strong string.

Combine the basting mixture in a medium-sized saucepan and bring the mixture to the boil. Using a large ladle or spoon, pour this mixture over the duck several times, as if to bathe it, until the skin of the duck is completely coated. Hang the duck over a tray or roasting pan and leave in a cool, well ventilated place to dry for about 8 hours, longer if possible. (To speed up the process, place it in front of a cold fan for about 4 to 5 hours.) When the duck has dried, the skin will feel like parchment paper.

Pre-heat the oven to gas mark 9, 240°C (475°F). Meanwhile, place the duck on a roasting rack in a roasting pan, breast side up. Put 150 ml (5 fl oz) of water into the roasting pan. (This will prevent the fat from splattering.) Now put the duck into the oven and roast it for 15 minutes. Then turn the heat down to gas mark 4, 180°C (350°F) and continue to roast for 1 hour and 10 minutes.

Remove the duck from the oven and let it sit for at least 10 minutes before you carve it. Carefully remove the skewer and drain the marinade. Using a cleaver or sharp knife, cut the duck into serving portions and arrange them on a warm serving platter. Skim the fat from the marinade and serve the marinade as a sauce with the duck.

deep-fried pigeons

Region: Canton
Methods: Braising and deep-frying

On Sundays in Hong Kong one of the most popular outings is to Shatin, a town in the New Territories, to play the famous Chinese game Mahjong and to eat pigeon. Pigeons have a rich, gamey taste. The southern Chinese like to braise them quickly, let them dry and then deep-fry them just before serving. The result is a moist, highly-flavoured pigeon with crisp skin. The secret to this dish lies in the braising liquid, which is used over and over again. In some restaurants it is used for years, like a vintage stock. This dish takes time and patience but it is not difficult to make and much of the work can be done several hours in advance. It is an impressive dish for any special dinner party. Serve it with rice, Braised Spicy Aubergines (page 191) and Roasted Salt and Pepper (page 39).

Serves 4 as a starter

2 x 225–350 g (8–12 oz) squab pigeons, cut in half lengthways

4 slices fresh ginger

900 ml (1½ pints) groundnut (peanut) oil (see Deep-Fat Fryers, page 42)

FOR THE BRAISING SAUCE

1.2 litres (2 pints) Chicken Stock (page 59)

5 tablespoons dark soy sauce

3 tablespoons light soy sauce

150 ml (5 fl oz) Shaoxing rice wine or dry sherry

3 tablespoons Chinese rock sugar

1 teaspoon salt

6 pieces fresh orange peel, or dried citrus peel, soaked and finely chopped (page 25)

3 Chinese cinnamon bark or cinnamon sticks

3 whole star anise (optional)

1 teaspoon freshly ground white pepper

2 teaspoons sesame oil

Bring a large pan of water to the boil. Blanch the pigeons in the boiling water for about 2 minutes. This helps to rid them of impurities and tightens the skin. Remove the pigeons from the pan and discard the water. Cut the ginger into 7.5 cm (3 inch) slices.

Combine all the braising sauce ingredients together in a large pan and bring it to the boil. Add the pigeons and the ginger. Lower the heat to a simmer and cover the pan tightly. Simmer for 30 minutes or until the pigeons are just tender. Remove them with a slotted spoon and place them on a rack over a tray or roasting pan and leave in a cool, well ventilated place to dry for about 2 hours. When the pigeons have dried the skin should feel like parchment paper. (The braising liquid, once cooled, can be stored and frozen for future use.)

Just before you are ready to serve them, heat the oil in a deep-fat fryer or large wok. When it is hot, lower in the pigeons and deep-fry them until they are crisp and deep brown in colour. Turn them over frequently with a slotted spoon so that all sides are thoroughly cooked and browned. This should take about 10 minutes. Drain the cooked pigeons on kitchen paper and let them cool for a few minutes. Using a heavy cleaver or knife, chop them into 4 to 6 pieces and arrange on a warm serving platter. Serve at once.

five-spice red-braised pigeons

In this recipe, the five-spice powder gives the pigeons a delicious flavour, while the soy braising sauce endows them with a rich brown colour. Chinese cooks often blanch pigeons before braising them to rid them of any impurities. Braising is a good technique to use as it keeps the pigeons moist. Squab pigeons are young, tender birds but if you prefer, you can substitute quails or other small game birds. This dish is excellent served cold and is perfect for an exotic picnic treat.

Regions: Fujian and Canton
Methods: Blanching and braising

Serves 4 as a starter

2 x 350 g–450 g (¾–1 lb) squab pigeons, cut in half lengthwise

FOR THE SAUCE

400 ml (14 fl oz) dark soy sauce

150 ml (5 fl oz) light soy sauce

3 tablespoons hoisin sauce

2 tablespoons five-spice powder

150 ml (5 fl oz) Shaoxing rice wine or dry sherry

50 g (2 oz) Chinese rock sugar or ordinary sugar

FOR THE GARNISH

2 tablespoons finely chopped spring onions

1 tablespoon finely chopped fresh ginger

Blanch the pigeons by immersing them in a large pan of boiling water for about 5 minutes. Remove them with a slotted spoon and discard the water.

Combine the sauce ingredients in a medium-sized pan and bring to the boil. Turn the heat down to a simmer and then add the pigeons. Cover the pan and braise the birds over a low heat for about 35 minutes or until they are tender. Then remove the pigeons with a slotted spoon and let them cool. (The braising sauce may be saved and frozen for the next time you cook this dish.) Chop the pigeons into bite-sized pieces and arrange them on a warm serving platter. Sprinkle the garnish ingredients on top and serve at once. If you want to serve the dish cold, let the pieces cool and then sprinkle them with the garnish ingredients. Refrigerate them, well-wrapped in cling film until you are ready to serve them.

stir-fried quails

Quails are popular in southeast as well as southern China because of their excellent flavour and their suitability for stir-frying. This technique seals in the taste and juices of the game birds and precludes overcooking. The bamboo shoots and water chestnuts provide a crunchy texture which complements the tenderness of the quail meat. This is an adaptation of a banquet dish from the Lee Gardens Rainbow Room Restaurant in Hong Kong. There, just the breasts of quails are served, an extravagance possible in a high-class restaurant staffed by expert chefs. I have found that this dish works equally well without the tedious job of boning these small birds. The robust flavours and rich colours of the dish make it a perfect starter or main course for a dinner party. Serve with Sweetcorn Soup with Crabmeat (page 75) and rice.

Regions: Fujian and Canton
Method: Stir-frying

Serves 4 as starter

4 x 100 g (4 oz) quails
225 g (8 oz) water chestnuts, peeled if fresh, rinsed if canned (page 37)
225 g (8 oz) canned bamboo shoots
6 spring onions
150 ml (5 fl oz) groundnut (peanut) oil
300 ml (10 fl oz) Chicken Stock (page 59)
2 tablespoons oyster sauce
2 teaspoons sugar
2 teaspoons cornflour mixed with 2 teaspoons water

FOR THE MARINADE

2 tablespoons Shaoxing rice wine or dry sherry
2 tablespoons light soy sauce
1 tablespoon cornflour
2 teaspoons sesame oil
1/2 teaspoon salt
1/2 teaspoon freshly ground white pepper

If the quails are frozen, thaw them thoroughly. Dry them inside and out with kitchen paper. Then, using a cleaver or heavy sharp knife, cut each quail into about 6 pieces. Put the pieces into a bowl with the marinade ingredients, mix them well and leave them to marinate for about 20 minutes.

Next prepare the vegetables. Slice the water chestnuts; rinse the bamboo shoots in cold water and slice these, too. Cut the spring onions at a slight diagonal into 7.5 cm (3 inch) pieces.

Heat a wok or large frying pan until it is very hot. Remove half the quail pieces from the marinade using a slotted spoon. Add half the groundnut (peanut) oil to the wok or pan and when it is slightly smoking, stir-fry the quail pieces for about 5 minutes or until they are brown. Transfer them to a colander or sieve to drain and discard the cooking oil. Re-heat the wok or pan and stir-fry the rest of the pieces in the same manner using the other half of the groundnut oil. Again, drain the quail in a colander or sieve, but leave about 1 tablespoon of oil in the wok or pan.

Re-heat the wok or pan over a high heat. Add the spring onions, fresh water chestnuts (if you are using them) and bamboo shoots and stir-fry them for about 2 minutes. Then add the rest of the ingredients, except canned water chestnuts (if you are using them) and bring the mixture to a boil. Return the quails to the wok or pan and cook for about 3 minutes. Make sure you coat all the quail pieces thoroughly with the sauce. If you are using canned water chestnuts add these now and cook for 2 more minutes. Serve at once.

Throughout the world, the consumption of all kinds of seafood has been rapidly growing over the past decade. Fish and shellfish are very nutritious and generally low in fat and cholesterol. In this preference for the 'harvest of the sea,' the world is catching up to the well-established Chinese custom.

Of the many remarkable and fortunate food experiences I had growing up as a young Chinese I count the extensive consumption of fresh fish and seafood as among the most pleasurable. In my family, fish and seafood were regarded with special affection whether as part of a simple family dinner or a large banquet. The first question always asked about fish, however, was: 'How fresh is it?'. From this early childhood experience I learned, as do all Chinese, to value good fresh fish and seafood.

Fish and seafood are understandably a major feature of Chinese cookery. China's long coastline gives it access to numerous saltwater varieties and its many rivers, lakes, streams and canals teem with freshwater fish and seafood all year round. It is estimated that there are several hundred species of fish and seafood which are used in Chinese cookery. Most are caught wild but a few species, such as carp, are raised on special fish farms and the practice of fish farming is growing exponentially. We Chinese prefer that no more than a few hours elapse between catching and cooking fish. Indeed, in many markets in southern China and Hong Kong, fish are sold live. You can select the fish of your choice while it swims around in special glass tanks and then take it straight home or to a restaurant to be cooked. The accent is always on freshness.

There are many cooking techniques which the Chinese use to ensure that the flesh of the fish or shellfish retains its natural juices and flavour. Steaming is a favourite method. Many Chinese chefs consider this to be the ideal way of cooking fish. It allows the fragrance and natural flavours of the fish to develop, while at the same time preserving the delicate texture, moistness and shape of the fish. Quick-braising is another popular method and deep-frying and shallow-frying are also often used.

The Chinese prefer to cook fish whole although fish fillets and steaks can be satisfactorily used instead. We believe that the flesh remains moist and the flavour is best when the whole fish is used, head and tail included. To serve a fish whole is also a symbol of prosperity. The head of the fish should always point in the direction of the guest of honour, a courtesy that assures him or her of good fortune.

Seafood is especially important in Chinese cuisine. Prawns, oysters, scallops, crab, lobster, squid and abalone are just some of the most popular varieties. Because seafood is so delicate it requires a minimum amount of handling and the simplest preparation. The most common techniques used are stir-frying, steaming, deep-frying and braising. Recipes for seafood are usually interchangeable; what works for prawns will work just as well for crab, lobster or scallops.

fish and shellfish

When fresh seafood is not available, Chinese cooks make imaginative use of dried seafood as the main ingredient or as a flavouring in soups, stir-fried dishes, braised dishes and stuffings. Drying concentrates the flavours of the seafood as well as preserving it.

The Chinese try to complement the delicate flavour, texture and colour of fish and seafood with contrasting flavourings and textures. For example, in the dish Sweet and Sour Prawns, the subtle taste and crisp texture of the prawns contrast nicely with the tasty spiciness of the sauce. Most Chinese recipes call for fresh, uncooked prawns. This is not as difficult for British cooks as in the past, when most prawns were sold cooked and were often frozen as well. If you must use cooked prawns, look for the best and largest variety you can find and just heat them through instead of cooking them for the full length of time called for in the recipe. Uncooked frozen prawns are a better substitute. Crabs can sometimes still be bought live, or at least freshly cooked. Instructions for dealing with live crab and crab cooked in the shell are given on page 183.

Fortunately the fish situation is much brighter. Cod and haddock are available everywhere, as well as many other varieties, such as sea bass and are perfect for deep-frying, stir-frying or braising. Plaice, Dover sole, lemon sole and flounder are perfect for steaming. Oily fish such as red mullet, carp and eel are best braised and trout should be shallow-fried. Get to know your fishmonger and be assertive in asking for the freshest fish and seafood. Fresh fish should be firm, have clear eyes, bright gills and a shiny sheen to the skin. Seafood should be firm and not smell fishy. Learn to be as finicky about selecting fish and seafood as the Chinese are. It will open up a whole new world of delicious healthy eating as well as of flavour for you.

fried fish with ginger

Ginger is the perfect complement to fish. The delicate but distinctive flavour of fish goes well with a little zest. Ginger is used rather as lemon is in European fish cookery. In this easy dish it imparts a subtle fragrance and light spicy counterpoint to the fish. Serve it with Braised Spicy Aubergines (page 191) and Garlic Chicken with Cucumber (page 120).

Region: Fujian
Method: Shallow-frying

Serves 4

450 g (1 lb) fresh, firm white fish fillets, such as cod, sea bass or halibut

1 teaspoon salt

Cornflour for dusting

150 ml (5 fl oz) groundnut (peanut) oil

3 tablespoons finely shredded fresh ginger

2 tablespoons Chicken Stock (page 59) or water

1 teaspoon salt

½ teaspoon freshly ground white pepper

2½ tablespoons Shaoxing rice wine or dry sherry

2 teaspoons sugar

2 teaspoons sesame oil

FOR THE GARNISH

3 tablespoons chopped spring onions

Sprinkle the fish fillets evenly on both sides with the salt. Cut the fish into strips 2.5 cm (1 inch) wide and let these sit for 20 minutes. Then dust them with the cornflour.

Heat a wok or large frying pan until it is very hot. Add the oil and when it is very hot and slightly smoking, add the ginger and, a few seconds later, the fish. Shallow-fry the fish strips until they are firm and partially cooked. Remove them with a slotted spoon and drain on kitchen paper.

Pour off all the oil and discard it. Wipe the wok or pan clean and add the rest of the ingredients. Bring them to the boil then return the fish slices to the wok or pan and coat them with the sauce. Turn the fish gently in the sauce for 1 minute, taking care not to break up the slices. Transfer to a warm serving platter, garnish with the spring onions and serve at once.

fried fish with garlic and spring onions

This is a simple dish, easy to make and it works especially well with any flat fish, such as sole or plaice. In coastal areas of China saltwater fish similar to sea bream or a type of red snapper would be used for this recipe. In this dish the wine, egg and spicy sauce nicely complement the taste and texture of the fish but do be careful not to overcook it. Serve with rice and a simple vegetable such as Stir-fried Chinese Greens (page 206).

Region: Fujian
Method: Shallow-frying

Serves 4

450 g (1 lb) sole or plaice fillets
1 teaspoon salt
¼ teaspoon freshly ground white pepper
50 g (2 oz) cornflour
2 eggs, lightly beaten
150 ml (5 fl oz) groundnut (peanut) oil
3 tablespoons finely sliced garlic
2 tablespoons finely chopped spring onions
2 tablespoons Shaoxing rice wine or dry sherry
1 teaspoon salt
2 teaspoons sesame oil

If you are using plaice, have your fishmonger remove the dark skin of the plaice or else remove it yourself with a small, sharp knife. Cut the fish fillets into 2.5 cm (1 inch) strips. Sprinkle the strips with salt and pepper and let them sit for 15 minutes. Dip the strips of fish into the cornflour and then into the beaten egg.

Heat a wok or large frying pan until it is very hot. Add the oil and when it is very hot and slightly smoking, turn the heat down to medium. Shallow-fry the fish strips on each side, in several batches, until they are golden brown. Drain them on kitchen paper. Pour off the oil and discard it. Wipe the wok or pan clean and add the rest of the ingredients. Simmer for 2 minutes. Put the fried fish fillets on a warm serving platter and pour over the hot sauce. Serve at once.

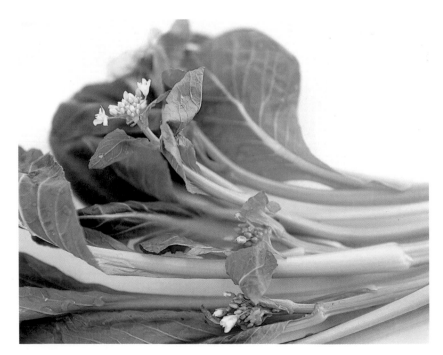

Right:
Chinese flowering cabbage
(*page 23*)

fish in hot sauce

A firm white fish such as cod, sea bass, halibut or haddock is most suitable for this recipe because they are meaty and hold their shape during the cooking process. Carp is a favourite fish for this recipe in China. Serve with plain rice and any stir-fried vegetable.

Region: Sichuan
Method: Shallow-frying

Serves 4

450 g (1 lb) fresh, firm white fish fillets, such as cod, sea bass or halibut
1 teaspoon salt
Cornflour for dusting
3 spring onions
150 ml (5 fl oz) groundnut (peanut) oil
1 tablespoon finely chopped garlic
2 teaspoons finely chopped fresh ginger

FOR THE SAUCE
150 ml (5 fl oz) Chicken Stock (page 59)
2 teaspoons whole yellow bean sauce
1 tablespoon chilli bean sauce
2 tablespoons Shaoxing rice wine or dry sherry
2 teaspoons dark soy sauce
2 teaspoons sesame oil
1/2 teaspoon salt
1/4 teaspoon freshly ground white pepper

Sprinkle the fish evenly on both sides with the salt. Cut into strips 5 cm (2 inches) wide and let them sit for 20 minutes. Then dust them with the cornflour.

Cut the spring onions into 5 cm (2 inch) slices. Heat a wok or large frying pan until it is very hot. Add the oil and when it is very hot and slightly smoking, turn the heat down. Shallow fry the fish strips until they are firm and partially cooked. Remove and drain the fish on kitchen paper. Pour off the oil, leaving about 1 tablespoon in the wok or pan.

Re-heat the wok or pan and add the spring onions, garlic and ginger. Stir-fry them for 30 seconds. Then add the sauce ingredients and bring the mixture to the boil. Turn the heat down to a simmer and return the fish to the wok or pan. Simmer for about 2 minutes, then turn the fish and sauce on to a warm serving platter and serve at once.

fish in hot and sour sauce

The combination of hot and sour is a popular one in the Sichuan region. A quick and simple dish, this is perfect for a light family meal. Stir-Fried Spinach with Garlic (page 216) is a suitable accompaniment.

Region: Sichuan
Method: Shallow-frying

Serves 4

450 g (1 lb) fresh, firm white fish fillets, such as sole or plaice

Cornflour for dusting

150 ml (5 fl oz) groundnut (peanut) oil

FOR THE HOT AND SOUR SAUCE

150 ml (5 fl oz) Chicken Stock (page 59)

2 tablespoons Shaoxing rice wine or dry sherry

1½ tablespoons dark soy sauce

1 tablespoon tomato purée

2 teaspoons chilli bean sauce

½ teaspoon freshly ground white pepper

2 tablespoons Chinese black rice vinegar or cider vinegar

2 teaspoons sugar

FOR THE GARNISH

3 tablespoons finely chopped spring onions

If you are using plaice, have your fishmonger remove the dark skin of the plaice or else remove it yourself using a small, sharp knife. Cut the fish fillets, across the width and at a slight diagonal, into 2.5 cm (1 inch) wide strips. Dust the pieces with cornflour, shaking off any excess.

Heat a wok or large frying pan until it is very hot. Add the oil and when it is very hot and slightly smoking, turn the heat down to medium. Fry the fish strips gently for 2 to 3 minutes until they are golden brown. (You may have to do this in several batches.) Drain the cooked fish strips on kitchen paper.

Pour off all the oil, wipe the wok or pan clean and re-heat it. Add all the hot and sour sauce ingredients. Bring the sauce to a boil, then lower the heat to a simmer. Add the fried fish strips and simmer them in the sauce for 2 minutes. Turn onto a warm serving platter and serve garnished with the spring onions.

steamed fish with garlic, spring onions and ginger

Steaming fish is a great southern Chinese tradition and it is my favourite method of cooking fish as it preserves the purest flavours of the fish. Because it is such a gentle cooking technique, nothing masks the fresh taste of the fish, which remains moist and tender at the same time, and you can savour the combination of the other ingredients. Always ask your fishmonger for the freshest possible fish.

Region: Canton
Method: Steaming

Serves 4

450 g (1 lb) fresh, firm white fish fillets, such as cod, sea bass or sole or a whole fish such as sole or turbot

1 teaspoon coarse sea salt or plain salt

1½ tablespoons finely shredded fresh ginger

FOR THE GARNISH

3 tablespoons finely shredded spring onions

1 tablespoon light soy sauce

2 teaspoons dark soy sauce

1 tablespoon groundnut (peanut) oil

2 teaspoons sesame oil

2 cloves garlic, peeled and thinly sliced

If you are using a whole fish, remove the gills. Pat the fish or fish fillets dry with kitchen paper. Rub with the salt on both sides, and let them sit for 30 minutes. (This helps the flesh to firm up and draws out any excess moisture.)

Set up a steamer or put a rack into a wok or deep pan and fill it with 5 cm (2 inches) of water. Bring the water to the boil over a high heat. Put the fish on a heatproof plate and scatter the ginger evenly over the top. Put the plate of fish into the steamer or on to the rack. Cover the pan tightly and gently steam the fish until it is just cooked. Flat fish will take about 5 minutes to cook. Thicker fish or fillets will take 12 to 14 minutes.

Remove the plate of cooked fish and sprinkle on the spring onions and light and dark soy sauces. Heat the two oils together in a small saucepan. When they are hot, add the garlic slices and brown them. Pour the garlic-oil mixture over the top of the fish. Serve at once.

braised fish

Onions in all forms are popular in Chinese cookery but shallots are especially prized for their distinctive flavour. I think they complement fish beautifully. If you can't get shallots for this recipe you can use spring onions instead. A firm white fish such as cod, haddock or bass will work better than delicate ones such as plaice or sole. Plain steamed rice and a fresh green vegetable would go well with this dish.

Region: Fujian
Methods: Shallow-frying and braising

Serves 4

450 g (1 lb) fresh, firm white fish fillets, such as cod or halibut

2 teaspoons salt

150 ml (5 fl oz) groundnut (peanut) oil

275 g (10 oz) small shallots, peeled and left whole or spring onions

2 tablespoons finely chopped fresh ginger

1 tablespoon light soy sauce

1 tablespoon dark soy sauce

2 teaspoons sugar

2 tablespoons Shaoxing rice wine or dry sherry

150 ml (5 fl oz) Chicken Stock (page 59)

2 teaspoons sesame oil

Pat the fish fillets dry using kitchen paper. Rub both sides with salt and then cut them into 3.5 cm (1½ inch) wide, diagonal strips. Let them sit for 20 minutes, then again pat them dry with kitchen paper. The salt will have extracted some of the excess moisture from the fish. If you are using spring onions, cut them into 7.5 cm (3 inch) pieces.

Heat a wok or large frying pan until it is very hot. Add the oil and when it is very hot and slightly smoking, turn the heat to medium. Shallow-fry the fish strips until they are firm and partially cooked. Remove and drain on kitchen paper. Pour off the oil, leaving about 1 tablespoon in the wok or pan.

Re-heat the wok or pan and add the shallots or spring onions and ginger. Stir-fry them for 1 minute, and then add the rest of the ingredients. Bring this mixture to the boil, then turn the heat down to a simmer and cook for 5 minutes or until the shallots are tender. Return the fish to the pan, cover it and re-heat the fish in the sauce for 2 minutes. Using a slotted spoon, gently remove the fish and shallots and arrange them on a warm serving platter. Then pour the sauce over the top and serve at once.

stir-fried fish with peas

This dish is a favourite in southern China, especially when made with grouper, a firm, white, fleshy fish. However, it works equally well with cod fillets. It is important to use a firm-textured fish which will not fall apart during the stir-frying process. Serve it with Deep-Fried Green Beans (page 193) and Ham and Marrow Soup (page 72).

Region: Canton
Methods: Stir-frying and
quick braising

Serves 4

450 g (1 lb) fresh, firm white fish fillets,
such as cod, halibut or sea bass

2 teaspoons salt

100 g (4 oz) fresh or frozen peas

2 tablespoons groundnut (peanut) oil

50 g (2 oz) Parma ham or lean smoked
bacon, shredded

FOR THE SAUCE

150 ml (5 fl oz) Chicken Stock (page 59)

1 tablespoon Shaoxing rice wine or
dry sherry

1 tablespoon light soy sauce

1 teaspoon salt

½ teaspoon freshly ground white pepper

2 teaspoons sugar

2 teaspoons cornflour blended with
2 teaspoons water

2 teaspoons sesame oil

Cut the fish fillets into strips 2.5 cm (1 inch) wide and sprinkle the salt evenly over them. Let them sit for 20 minutes. If you are using fresh peas, cook them for 5 minutes in a pan of boiling water and then drain them in a colander. If you are using frozen peas, simply thaw them.

Heat a wok or large frying pan until it is very hot. Add the oil and when it is very hot and slightly smoking add the fish strips. Stir-fly these gently, taking care not to break them up, for about 2 minutes. Add the ham or bacon, peas, stock, Shaoxing rice wine or dry sherry, soy sauce, salt, pepper and sugar. Bring the sauce to a boil, add the cornflour mixture and stir this in well. Cook for another 1 minute, stir in the sesame oil and then serve at once.

sweet and sour fish

A sweet and sour sauce is a perfect foil for fish. The sugar and vinegar in the sauce contrasts well with the distinctive flavour of the fish. The dish is at its most impressive when a whole fish is used but it can be just as successfully made with fish fillets. The best fish to use are cod, haddock or sea bass. The sauce can be made in advance and re-heated just before you are ready to serve.

Regions: Canton and Fujian
Method: Deep-frying

Serves 4

450 g (1 lb) whole firm white fish or fish fillets, such as cod, haddock or sea bass

2 teaspoons salt

1 teaspoon freshly ground white pepper

100 g (4 oz) carrots

100 g (4 oz) peas

100 g (4 oz) mangetout, trimmed

Cornflour for dusting

1 egg

1 teaspoon sesame oil

1.2 litres (2 pints) groundnut (peanut) oil (see Deep-Fat Fryers, page 40)

FOR THE SAUCE

2 tablespoons finely chopped spring onions

1½ tablespoons finely chopped fresh ginger

300 ml (10 fl oz) Chicken Stock (page 59)

1 tablespoon light soy sauce

2 tablespoons Shaoxing rice wine or dry sherry

1½ tablespoons tomato purée

2 tablespoons Chinese white rice vinegar or cider vinegar

2 tablespoons sugar

2 teaspoons cornflour blended with 2 teaspoons water

1 teaspoon salt

½ teaspoon freshly ground white pepper

If you are using fish fillets, select ones which are at least 2.5 cm (1 inch) or more thick and remove the skin. If you are using a whole fish it should be cleaned and gutted and the gills removed. Either leave the head on as the Chinese do or remove it if you prefer. Using a sharp knife or cleaver, make criss-cross slashes across the top of the fish or each fillet. Do not cut right through, but keep the fish or fillets intact. Rub the fish evenly with the salt and pepper and set aside.

Next prepare the vegetables. Peel and dice the carrots. Blanch the carrots, peas and mange tout in a pan of boiling water for about 4 minutes each. Then plunge them into cold water and drain them. Put all the blanched vegetables into a pan with all the sauce ingredients. Bring the mixture to a simmer, stir well and remove the pan from the heat.

Coat the fish or fish fillets well with cornflour, shaking off any excess. In a small bowl, combine the egg and sesame oil. Spread this over the fish and then dust again with cornflour, shaking off any excess. Heat the oil in a deep-fat fryer or large wok until it is slightly smoking then deep-fry one of the fish or fillets (one at a time) until crisp and brown. Drain on kitchen paper. Return the sauce to a simmer. Arrange the fish or fillets on a warm serving platter and pour the reheated sauce over the top. Serve at once.

steamed salmon with black beans

The virtues of fish and seafood most brilliantly shine forth against a backdrop of piquant flavours. In this case, we rely upon the pungent seasoning of black beans, which add zest and depth without overwhelming the subtle character of the fish. We use salmon here, which is not a Chinese fish although it is growing in popularity in cosmopolitan Hong Kong and Canton. It is a most delicious way to prepare fish. Serve it with plain rice and another stir-fry dish and you have a complete meal.

Region: Hong Kong
Method: Steaming

Serves 4

450 g (1 lb) salmon fillet, boneless, skinned and divided into 4 equal pieces
1 teaspoon salt
¼ teaspoon freshly ground white pepper
2 tablespoons black beans, rinsed and chopped
1½ tablespoons finely chopped garlic
1 tablespoon finely chopped fresh ginger
1½ tablespoons Shaoxing rice wine or dry sherry
1 tablespoon light soy sauce

FOR THE GARNISH
3 tablespoons finely chopped spring onions
Small handful of fresh coriander
1½ tablespoons groundnut (peanut) oil

Sprinkle the salmon pieces evenly with salt and pepper. Combine the black beans, garlic and ginger in a small bowl. Put the fillets on a deep heatproof plate and evenly scatter the black bean mixture over the top. Pour the Shaoxing rice wine or dry sherry and soy sauce over the fish.

Set up a steamer or put a rack into a wok or deep pan and fill it with 5 cm (2 inches) of water. Bring the water to the boil over a high heat. Carefully lower the fish and plate into the steamer or on to the rack. Turn the heat to low and cover the wok or pan tightly. Steam gently for 8 to 10 minutes, depending on the thickness of the fillets. Top up with boiling water from time to time. When the fish is cooked, remove the plate from the steamer or wok. Scatter the spring onions and coriander on top of the fish.

Heat a wok or large frying pan until it is very hot. Add the oil and when it is very hot and slightly smoking, pour this over the fillets. Serve at once.

fish balls with broccoli

We often made this dish in our family restaurant but usually just for the Chinese customers. My uncle thought that his non-Chinese diners would not enjoy it. I remember how laborious it was, mincing the fish until it was smooth and like a paste. Now, thanks to modern kitchen equipment, this dish can be easily prepared at home in minutes. And I eventually discovered how much my European friends love this dish! One touch of the proper spices makes the whole world kin. Serve this with plain steamed rice and Hot and Sour Soup (page 76).

Regions: Fujian and Canton
Methods: Poaching and stir-frying

Serves 4 to 6

450 g (1 lb) fresh, firm white fish fillets, such as cod, sea bass or halibut

1 egg white

2 teaspoons salt

1 teaspoon freshly ground white pepper

2 teaspoons cornflour

2 teaspoons sesame oil

450 g (1 lb) broccoli

1½ tablespoons groundnut (peanut) oil

3 tablespoons finely shredded fresh ginger

50 g (2 oz) Parma ham, or lean smoked bacon, finely shredded

1 tablespoon light soy sauce

2 tablespoons Shaoxing rice wine or dry sherry

300 ml (10 fl oz) Chicken Stock (page 59)

2 teaspoons cornflour blended with 2 teaspoons water

2 teaspoons sesame oil

Remove the skin from the fish fillets and then cut them into small pieces about 2.5 cm (1 inch) square. Combine the fish, egg white, salt, pepper, cornflour and sesame oil in a food processor and blend the mixture until you have a smooth paste. If you are using an electric blender, pulse by turning the blender on and off until the mixture is well mixed otherwise the paste will turn out rubbery.

Bring a large pan of salted water to simmering point. Take spoonfuls of the fish paste and form the mixture into balls about 2.5 cm (1 inch) in diameter. Poach the fish balls in the boiling water for about 3 to 4 minutes until they float to the top. Remove them with a slotted spoon and drain them on kitchen paper.

Divide the broccoli heads into small florets. Peel the skin off the stems as they are often fibrous and stringy, and then cut them into thin slices at a slight diagonal. This will ensure that the stems cook evenly with the florets. Bring a pan of water to the boil, add the broccoli florets and stems and cook for about 5 minutes. Then drain them, plunge into cold water, and drain again.

Heat a wok or large frying pan until it is very hot. Add the oil and when it is very hot and slightly smoking, add the ginger, ham or bacon and stir-fry for 30 seconds. Then add the light soy sauce, Shaoxing rice wine or dry sherry, stock and the cornflour mixture. Bring to the boil and then add the broccoli and poached fish balls. Stir over a high heat for 1 minute to mix. Add the sesame oil and then turn the mixture on to a warm serving platter. Serve at once.

fish in wine sauce

This is an elegant Shanghai fish dish served in many homes as well as in the best restaurants. Even though it calls for a rich wine sauce, it is surprisingly easy to make. The fish is coated with an egg white mixture and then gently cooked in oil (although you can use water); then it is drained and mixed with the sauce. The mushrooms add a rich smoky flavour, a nice accompaniment to the subtle taste of the fish fillets. Because it is so delicious and so easy to make, this is an excellent recipe for a special dinner party.

Serves 4

50 g (2 oz) Chinese dried mushrooms

450 g (1 lb) fresh, firm white fish, such as sea bass, halibut or cod

1 egg white

2 teaspoons cornflour

1 teaspoon salt

1/2 teaspoon freshly ground white pepper

600 ml (1 pint) groundnut (peanut) oil or water

FOR THE WINE SAUCE

3 tablespoons Shaoxing rice wine or dry sherry

2 teaspoons dark soy sauce

1 teaspoon light soy sauce

1 teaspoon salt

1 teaspoon freshly ground white pepper

1½ tablespoons rock sugar or granulated sugar

150 ml (5 fl oz) Chicken Stock (page 59)

2 teaspoons cornflour blended with 1 tablespoon water

Soak the mushrooms in warm water for 20 minutes. Drain them and squeeze out the excess liquid. Remove and discard the stems and finely shred the caps.

Cut the fish into 5 cm (2 inch) pieces and then combine them with the egg white, cornflour, salt and pepper in a medium-sized bowl. Mix well and refrigerate for 20 minutes.

Heat a wok until it is very hot. Add the oil and when it is very hot and slightly smoking, remove the wok from the heat. Immediately add the fish, stirring vigorously to prevent the pieces from sticking. After about 2 minutes when the fish pieces turn white, quickly drain the fish and all the oil in a stainless steel colander set in a bowl. Discard the oil.

(If you use water instead of oil, bring it to a boil in a saucepan. Remove the saucepan from the heat and immediately add the fish pieces, stirring vigorously to prevent them from sticking. After about 2 minutes when the fish pieces turn white, drain the fish and all the water in a stainless steel colander set in a bowl. Discard the water.)

Heat the sauce ingredients in a saucepan and bring to a simmer. Add the mushrooms and cook for about 2 minutes. Then add the fish pieces and heat through. Serve at once.

steamed fresh oysters

The Chinese in Hong Kong enjoy fresh oysters steamed; it brings out their subtle taste and wonderful texture. Although sometimes they are steamed with black beans, I enjoy them simply with ginger and spring onions. This is a Hong Kong variation on a traditional recipe and is quite delicious. You may substitute clams or mussels, but the cooking time will be shorter. Watch them carefully to prevent overcooking.

Region: Hong Kong
Method: Steaming

Serves 4

16 large fresh oysters

FOR THE SAUCE
2 teaspoons finely chopped garlic
1 tablespoon finely chopped fresh ginger
1 teaspoon chilli bean sauce
1 tablespoon Shaoxing rice wine or dry sherry
1 tablespoon light soy sauce
2 teaspoons dark soy sauce
2 fresh red chillies, seeded and chopped
3 tablespoons finely shredded spring onions
3 tablespoons groundnut (peanut) oil

FOR THE GARNISH
Fresh coriander sprigs

Scrub the oysters clean. Place them on two separate heatproof plates; you will have to steam them in 2 batches.

Next set up a steamer or put a rack into a wok or deep pan and fill it with 5 cm (2 inches) of water. Bring the water to the boil over a high heat. Put one of the plates with the oysters into the steamer or on to the rack Turn the heat to low and cover tightly. Steam gently for 5 minutes or until the oysters begin to open.

Meanwhile, combine all the sauce ingredients except the oil in a heatproof bowl. Heat a wok or large frying pan until it is very hot. Add the oil and when it is very hot and slightly smoking, pour over the sauce ingredients and stir well.

Remove the oysters from the steamer and cook the second batch. Remove the top shell of the oyster and spoon a little sauce over each oyster. Garnish with fresh coriander sprigs and serve. While you are serving the first batch, repeat the cooking procedure with the other batch.

deep-fried oysters

Oysters are a staple item among the Hong Kong Chinese. The variety found in the South China Sea is quite large and they are usually cut up, dipped in batter and deep-fried. The Chinese never eat oysters raw, believing them to be unhealthy when uncooked. This dish is based on a recipe given to me by a friend who is a chef in the fishing village of Lau Fau Shan in the New Territories in Hong Kong. I have added a Western touch to it by using breadcrumbs on top of the batter. This dish makes an excellent cocktail snack.

Region: Canton
Method: Deep-frying

Serves 4

450 g (1 lb) oysters, shelled

1 egg

2 tablespoons cornflour

1 tablespoon water

2 teaspoons baking powder

1 teaspoon salt

½ teaspoon freshly ground white pepper

2 teaspoons sesame oil

50 g (2 oz) breadcrumbs, toasted

600 ml (1 pint) groundnut (peanut) oil (see Deep-Fat Fryers, page 42)

FOR THE GARNISH

Lemon wedges

FOR THE DIPPING SAUCE

Roasted Salt and Pepper (page 39) or Five-Spice Salt (page 38)

Drain the oysters in a colander and then pat them dry with kitchen paper. Make a batter by mixing the egg, cornflour, water, baking powder, salt, pepper and sesame oil. Leave for about 20 minutes.

Dip the oysters, a few at a time into the batter and then into the breadcrumbs. Set them on a plate.

Heat a wok or large frying pan until it is very hot. Add the oil and when it is very hot and slightly smoking, turn the heat down to medium. Deep-fry the coated oysters for just a few minutes until they are golden brown. Drain them on kitchen paper and serve with lemon wedges and your choice of dipping sauce.

stir-fried scallops with pigs' kidneys

Be assured that scallops and kidneys go well together, even though they may seem an unlikely combination. If the kidneys are properly prepared their texture is quite similar to that of scallops, and their two different flavours blend deliciously together. The richness of this dish means that it is best for special occasions. It goes very well with plain steamed rice and Braised Cauliflower with Oyster Sauce (page 201).

Region: Fujian
Method: Stir-frying

Serves 4

450g (1 lb) pigs' kidneys

1 teaspoon bicarbonate of soda

1 teaspoon Chinese white rice vinegar or cider vinegar

1/2 teaspoon salt

225 g (8 oz) scallops, including the corals

2 tablespoons groundnut (peanut) oil

2 teaspoons finely chopped fresh ginger

2 tablespoons finely chopped spring onions

2 tablespoons Shaoxing rice wine or dry sherry

1 tablespoon light soy sauce

2 teaspoons dark soy sauce

1 teaspoon sugar

1/2 teaspoon salt

1/2 teaspoon freshly ground white pepper

1 teaspoon cornflour blended with 2 teaspoons of stock or water

2 teaspoons sesame oil

Using a sharp knife, remove the thin outer kidney membrane then split the kidney in half lengthways by cutting horizontally as described on page 120. Cut away the small knobs of fat and any tough membrane surrounding them. Score the top surface of the kidneys in a criss-cross pattern, then cut the halved kidneys into thin slices. Toss the kidney slices in the bicarbonate of soda and let them sit for about 20 minutes. Rinse them with cold water and toss them in the vinegar and salt. Put them into a colander and let them drain for 30 minutes.

Cut the scallops into thick slices horizontally and put them in a bowl. Blot the kidney dry with kitchen paper.

Heat a wok or large frying pan until it is very hot. Add 1 tablespoon of the oil and when it is very hot and slightly smoking, add the scallops. Stir-fry them for about 30 seconds and then add the ginger and spring onions and stir-fry for 30 seconds. Remove them from the pan.

Wipe the wok or pan clean then re-heat until it is very hot. Add the remaining oil and when it is very hot and slightly smoking, add the kidneys. Stir-fry them for 1 minute and add the rice wine or sherry, the soy sauces, sugar, salt and pepper. Stir-fry for 1 minute then return the scallops, add the cornflour mixture and stir for a minute or so. Stir in the sesame oil and serve.

sichuan-style scallops

Scallops are a favourite with the Chinese and stir-frying works especially well because if they are overcooked they become tough. Here they have a spicy Sichuan sauce which goes well with plain rice and Ham and Bean Sprout Soup (page 68).

Region: Sichuan
Method: Stir-frying

Serves 4

1½ tablespoons groundnut (peanut) oil

1 tablespoon finely chopped fresh ginger

1 tablespoon finely chopped garlic

2 tablespoons finely chopped spring onions

450 g (1 lb) scallops, including the corals

FOR THE SAUCE

1 tablespoon Shaoxing rice wine or dry sherry

2 teaspoons light soy sauce/ 2 teaspoons dark soy sauce

2 tablespoons chilli bean sauce/ 2 teaspoons tomato purée

1 teaspoon sugar

½ teaspoon salt/½ teaspoon freshly ground white pepper

2 teaspoons sesame oil

Heat a wok or large frying pan until it is very hot. Add the oil and when it is very hot and slightly smoking, add the ginger, garlic and spring onions and stir-fry for 10 seconds. Add the scallops and stir-fry for 1 minute. Add all the sauce ingredients except the sesame oil. Continue to stir-fry for 4 minutes until the scallops are firm and thoroughly coated with the sauce. Add the sesame oil and stir-fry for a further 1 minute. Serve at once.

prawns

Most prawns previously available in Britain were sold cooked, either peeled or unpeeled. However, large uncooked prawns, known as Pacific or king prawns, are becoming increasingly available and are usually found frozen. These are most suitable for Chinese cooking. Most Chinese grocers and many fishmongers and some supermarkets stock them frozen and in the shell and they are quite reasonably priced. Fresh prawns are occasionally available. In any case, the frozen uncooked prawns are preferable to cooked prawns which in most cases are already overcooked. Thus, any sauce you cook them in will not permeate to flavour the prawns.

To peel prawns First twist off the head and pull off the tail. It should then be quite easy to peel off the shell and with it the tiny legs. If you are using large, uncooked king prawns make a shallow cut down the back of each prawn and remove the fine digestive cord which runs the length of each prawn. Wash the prawns before you use them.

Chinese trick for frozen uncooked prawns After peeling and preparing the uncooked prawns as instructed above, rinse them three times in 1 tablespoon of salt and 1.2 litres (2 pints) of cold water, changing the mixture of salt and water each time. This process helps to firm the prawns and gives them a crystalline, clean taste as well as a crispy texture.

mango prawns

This exotic and unlikely combination is one of the best examples of how Chinese food practices evolve in Hong Kong, with the new and the foreign being joined to the venerable and the native. I have had this dish several times in Hong Kong and found it delicious every time. The rich sweetness and soft texture of the mango works extremely well with the fresh sea fragrance and delicate taste of the prawns. The mango is cooked for a short time, just enough to warm through. Mangoes are now very popular in Hong Kong. They are imported from Thailand and the Philippines. It is one of the most popular of all tropical fruits and, as this recipe indicates, mixes well with other distinctively flavoured foods.

Region: Hong Kong
Methods: Velveting and stir-frying

Serves 4

450 g (1 lb) uncooked prawns
1 egg white
2 teaspoons cornflour
1 teaspoon salt
1 teaspoon sesame oil
½ teaspoon freshly ground white pepper
450 g (1 lb) mangoes
450 ml (15 fl oz) groundnut (peanut) oil or water
1½ tablespoons groundnut (peanut) oil
1½ tablespoons finely chopped fresh ginger
2 teaspoons finely chopped garlic
1 tablespoon Shaoxing rice wine or dry sherry
1 teaspoon salt
½ teaspoon freshly ground white pepper
2 teaspoons sesame oil

FOR THE GARNISH
2 tablespoons finely chopped spring onions

Peel the prawns and, if you are using large, uncooked ones, cut them to remove the fine digestive cord (see opposite). Wash the prawns and pat them dry with kitchen paper. Combine the prawns with the egg white, cornflour, salt, sesame oil and pepper. Mix well and leave in the refrigerator for 20 minutes.

Peel the mangoes and remove the stones. Cut the flesh into cubes.

Heat a wok or large frying pan until it is very hot. Add the oil and when it is very hot, remove the wok from the heat. Immediately add the prawns, stirring vigorously to prevent them from sticking. After about 2 minutes when the prawns turn white, quickly drain the prawns and all the oil in a stainless steel colander set in a bowl. Discard the oil.

(If you use water instead of oil, bring it to a boil in a saucepan. Remove the saucepan from the heat and immediately add the prawns, stirring vigorously to prevent them from sticking. After about 2 minutes when the prawns turn white, quickly drain the prawns and all the water in a stainless steel colander set in a bowl. Discard the water.)

Heat the wok or large frying pan until it is very hot. Add the oil, and when it is very hot and slightly smoking, add the ginger and garlic and stir-fry for 10 seconds. Then return the prawns to the wok or pan, together with the Shaoxing rice wine or dry sherry, salt and pepper. Stir-fry the mixture for 1 minute. Add the mango pieces and stir gently for 1 minute to warm the mango. Stir in the sesame oil.

Turn on to a warm serving platter, garnish with spring onions and serve.

stir-fried prawns with egg

This dish is commonly known in the West as Egg Fuyung. It is popular because it is light and delicious, is easy to make and uses familiar ingredients. You can substitute crab, fish or even minced pork or beef for the prawns. However, I think it is at its best made with good quality prawns. This distinctive dish goes well with Hot and Sour Soup (page 76) and Stir-Fried Beef with Ginger (page 105).

Region: Canton
Method: Velveting and stir-frying

Serves 4

225 g (8 oz) uncooked prawns
1 egg white
1 teaspoon salt
½ teaspoon freshly ground white pepper
1 teaspoon sesame oil
2 teaspoons cornflour
6 large eggs, beaten
2 teaspoons sesame oil
3 tablespoons Chicken Stock (page 59) or water
1 tablespoon Shaoxing rice wine or dry sherry
1 teaspoon salt
½ teaspoon freshly ground black pepper
1 tablespoon light soy sauce
1 teaspoon sugar
2 tablespoons groundnut (peanut) oil

FOR THE GARNISH
3 tablespoons finely chopped spring onions, green part only

Peel the prawns and, if you are using large, uncooked ones, cut them to remove the fine digestive cord (see page 174). Wash the prawns and pat them dry with kitchen paper. Put the prawns into a bowl and mix in the egg white, salt, pepper, sesame oil and cornflour. Let the mixture sit in the refrigerator for 20 minutes. Combine the eggs, sesame oil and the rest of the ingredients except the cooking oil and garnish in a bowl.

Heat a wok or large frying pan until it is very hot. Add 1 tablespoon of oil and when it is very hot and slightly smoking, add the prawns and stir-fry for 2 minutes. Remove with a slotted spoon. Wipe the wok or pan clean, re-heat it over a high heat, then put the remaining tablespoon of oil into the pan. Quickly add the egg mixture and stir-fry for 1 minute until the egg begins to set. Return the prawns to the egg mixture and continue to stir-fry for 1 minute. Garnish with spring onions and serve at once.

braised prawns

In preparing seafood or fish, simplest is best and this is one of the simplest prawn recipes in Chinese cookery. It takes only a minute to prepare. If you are using cooked prawns reduce the cooking time so the prawns just heat through.

Serves 4

450 g (1 lb) uncooked prawns

FOR THE SAUCE
150 ml (5 fl oz) Chicken Stock (page 59)
1 tablespoon Shaoxing rice wine or dry sherry
1 teaspoon salt
1 tablespoon sugar
1 tablespoon dark soy sauce
1 teaspoon light soy sauce
2 teaspoons Chinese black rice vinegar or cider vinegar
2 tablespoons finely chopped spring onions
1 tablespoon finely chopped fresh ginger
2 teaspoons finely chopped garlic
1 teaspoon cornflour blended with 2 teaspoons water
2 teaspoons sesame oil

Peel the prawns and, if you are using large, uncooked ones, cut them to remove the fine digestive cord (see page 174). Wash the prawns and pat them dry with kitchen paper.

Combine the sauce ingredients in a wok or large frying pan. Bring it to a simmer and then add the prawns. Braise the prawns slowly over a low heat for 5 minutes. Serve at once.

sweet and sour prawns

A very popular Chinese dish in the West, the sweet and pungent flavours of the sauce combine well with the firm and succulent prawns. It is simple to make and can be served as part of a Chinese meal or on its own as a starter for a European meal.

Serves 4

450 g (1 lb) uncooked prawns

225 g (8 oz) water chestnuts, peeled if fresh, rinsed if canned (page 37)

100 g (4 oz) red or green pepper (about 1)

4 spring onions

1½ tablespoons groundnut (peanut) oil

1 tablespoon finely chopped garlic

2 teaspoons finely chopped ginger

FOR THE SAUCE

150 ml (5 fl oz) Chicken Stock (page 59)

2 tablespoons Shaoxing rice wine or dry sherry

3 tablespoons light soy sauce

2 teaspoons dark soy sauce

1½ tablespoons tomato purée

3 tablespoons Chinese white rice vinegar or cider vinegar

1 tablespoon sugar

1 tablespoon cornflour blended with 2 tablespoons water

Peel the prawns and, if you are using large, uncooked ones, cut them to remove the fine digestive cord (see page 174). Wash the prawns and pat them dry with kitchen paper. Slice the water chestnuts, dice the pepper into 2.5 cm (1 inch) squares, and slice the spring onions diagonally into 3.5 cm (1½ inch) pieces.

Heat a wok or large frying pan until it is very hot. Add the oil, and when it is very hot and slightly smoking, add the garlic, ginger and spring onions and stir-fry for 20 seconds. Then add the prawns and stir-fry for 10 more seconds. Add the pepper and water chestnuts and stir-fry for a further 30 seconds. Add all the sauce ingredients, bring to the boil, then turn down the heat and simmer for 4 minutes. Serve immediately with plain steamed rice.

peking prawns

This is my adaptation of a favourite northern Chinese prawn dish. The use of breadcrumbs is, of course, a Western touch but one which works perfectly for this recipe. It is so simple to make that it presents no problem even if you are serving it at a dinner party. The shallow-frying, however, must be done at the last minute.

Region: Beijing
Method: Shallow-frying

Serves 4

450 g (1 lb) uncooked prawns, unpeeled
50 g (2 oz) plain flour
50 g (2 oz) breadcrumbs, toasted
1 egg
2 teaspoons sesame oil
1 teaspoon salt
½ teaspoon freshly ground white pepper
300 ml (10 fl oz) groundnut (peanut) oil

FOR THE DIPPING SAUCE
2 tablespoons hoisin sauce
1 teaspoon sesame oil

Peel the prawns but leave the tail shell on. Using a sharp knife, split each prawn lengthways but leave it still attached at the back. Open the prawn out so that it splays out flat in a butterfly shape. If you are using large, uncooked prawns, remove the fine digestive cord (see page 174). Wash the prawns and pat them dry with kitchen paper.

Spread out the flour and breadcrumbs on separate plates. Beat the egg in another small bowl, add the sesame oil, salt and pepper and mix well.

Dip the prawns into the flour, then into the egg mixture, and finally into the breadcrumbs, shaking off any excess. Heat the oil in a wok or large frying pan until it is very hot and slightly smoking. Shallow-fry the prawns in two batches and drain on kitchen paper.

Mix the hoisin sauce with the sesame oil in a small, shallow dish and serve with the hot prawns.

sizzling rice prawns

This is a dramatic dish which is sure to earn you compliments. It is moderately easy to make but requires organization and some experience of Chinese cooking. Attempt this dish after you have cooked some of the simpler recipes in this book. I'm sure that once you have tried it, it will become a regular feature of your repertoire. The key to success is that the prawn sauce mixture and rice cake should both be fairly hot. You will then achieve a dramatic sizzle when the two are combined. Serve with Cold Marinated Bean Sprouts (page 198) and Stir-Fried Chinese Greens (page 206).

Region: Sichuan
Methods: Stir-frying and deep-frying

Serves 6

450 g (1 lb) uncooked prawns, unpeeled

2 tablespoons groundnut (peanut) oil

1 tablespoon finely chopped fresh ginger

1½ tablespoons finely chopped garlic

3 tablespoons finely chopped spring onions

1.2 litres (2 pints) groundnut (peanut) oil (see Deep-fat fryers, page 42)

1 rice cake, made according to the recipe on page 224, broken into pieces

FOR THE SAUCE

100 g (4 oz) green or red pepper (about 1), diced

1½ tablespoons cider vinegar or Chinese black rice vinegar

1 tablespoon dark soy sauce

2 teaspoons light soy sauce

1½ tablespoons chilli bean sauce

1½ tablespoons tomato purée

2 tablespoons Shaoxing rice wine or dry sherry

2 teaspoons sugar

300 ml (10 fl oz) Chicken Stock (page 59)

1 tablespoon cornflour blended with 2 tablespoons water

1 tablespoon sesame oil

Peel the prawns and discard the shells. Using a small sharp knife, split each prawn lengthways but leave it still attached at the back. Open the prawn out so that it splays out in a butterfly shape. If you are using large uncooked prawns, remove the fine digestive cord (see page 174). Wash the prawns and pat them dry with kitchen paper.

Heat a wok or large frying pan until it is very hot. Add the 2 tablespoons of oil and when it is very hot and slightly smoking, add the ginger and stir it quickly for a few seconds, then add the garlic and spring onions. A few seconds later add the prawns and stir-fry them quickly until they become firm. Then add all the sauce ingredients except the cornflour mixture and sesame oil. Bring the mixture to the boil, remove it from the heat and stir in the cornflour mixture. Bring back to the boil, stir in the sesame oil and then reduce the heat to a very slow simmer.

Now you are ready to fry the rice cake. Heat a wok or deep-fry fryer until it is very hot. Add the 1.2 litres (2 pints) of oil, and when it is very hot and slightly smoking, drop in a small piece of the dried rice cake to test the heat. It should bubble all over and immediately come up to the surface. Now deep-fry the pieces of rice cake for about 1 to 2 minutes until they puff up and brown slightly. Remove them immediately with a slotted spoon and set them to drain on a plate lined with kitchen paper. Then quickly transfer the pieces of hot rice cake to a warm platter and pour the hot prawn sauce mixture over them. It should sizzle dramatically. Once you are skilled at preparing this dish, you can attempt to perform this trick at the dinner table. (The oil used for deep-frying the rice cake can be saved and re-used once it has cooled. Filter it through coffee filter papers before storing it.)

crabs

Canned or frozen crabmeat If you are using frozen crabmeat, thaw it thoroughly before you use it. Canned crabmeat has a fishy odour. If you are forced to use it, rinse it carefully first in cold water. However, my advice is to avoid either the canned or frozen crabmeat.

Choosing a crab Where possible the Chinese prefer to buy crabs live and cook them when they are needed. In this country most crabs are sold already cooked, so take care to buy one which is fresh and does not have a fishy smell. The heavier the crab the better.

Cooking live crabs Bring a large pan of water to the boil, add 2 teaspoons of salt and then put in the crab. Cover the pan and cook the crab for about 5 to 7 minutes until it turns bright red. Remove with a slotted spoon and drain in a colander. Leave to cool.

Removing cooked crabmeat Extracting the crabmeat is not difficult but it takes a little time and patience. Follow the steps opposite:

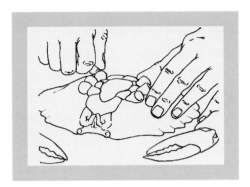

1 Place the crab upside down with the shell on the work top. Using your fingers, twist the claws from the body. Do the same with the rest of the legs. They should come off quite easily.

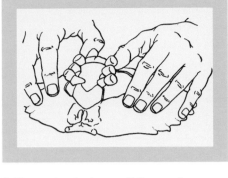

2 Now twist the bony tail flap on the underside of the crab and discard it. With your fingers, pry the body from the main shell.

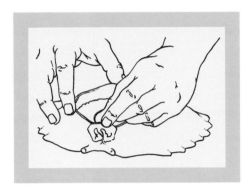

3 Remove and discard the small, bag-like stomach sac and its appendages which are located just behind the crab's mouth.

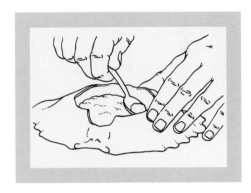

4 With a teaspoon, scoop out the brown crabmeat.

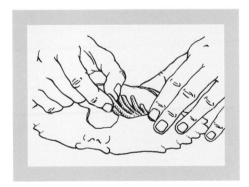

5 Pull the soft feathery gills, which look a little like fingers, away from the body and discard them.

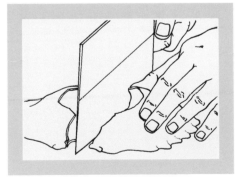

6 Using a cleaver or a heavy knife, split the crab body in half and, using a knife, fork or skewer, scrape out all the white crabmeat from the body and from the claws and legs.

7 Combine the brown and white crabmeat.

crab with black bean sauce

This recipe can only be made with fresh crabs in the shell since the shell has to protect the delicate crabmeat during the stir-frying process. If you can't get crab in the shell use prawns instead. I have added some minced pork, a Chinese trick which helps to stretch the crab, which can be expensive. (Of course you can always use just crab if you are feeling extravagant.) I love to eat this dish with plain steamed rice and Braised Spicy Aubergines (page 191).

Region: Canton
Method: Stir-frying

Serves 4 to 6

1.5 kg (3 lb) freshly cooked crab
in the shell

2 tablespoons groundnut (peanut) oil

3 tablespoons black beans, rinsed and
coarsely chopped

1½ tablespoons finely chopped garlic

1 tablespoon finely chopped fresh ginger

3 tablespoons finely chopped
spring onions

225 g (8 oz) minced pork

2 tablespoons light soy sauce

1 tablespoon dark soy sauce

2 tablespoons Shaoxing rice wine or
dry sherry

450 ml (15 fl oz) Chicken Stock (page 59)

2 eggs, beaten

2 teaspoons sesame oil

Remove the tail-flap, stomach sac and feathery gills from the crab (see page 183). Using a heavy knife or cleaver, cut the crab, shell included, into large pieces.

Heat a wok or large frying pan until it is very hot. Add the oil and when it is very hot and slightly smoking, add the black beans, garlic, ginger and spring onions and stir-fry for 20 seconds. Add the pork and stir-fry for 1 minute. Add the crab pieces and the rest of the ingredients except the eggs and sesame oil. Stir-fry the mixture over a high heat for about 10 minutes. Combine the eggs with sesame oil and then mix this into the crab mixture. Turn it on to a large, warm serving platter and serve.

It is perfectly good manners to eat the crab with your fingers, but I suggest that you have a large bowl of water decorated with lemon slices on the table so that your guests can rinse their fingers.

crab in egg custard

There are many delicious and meaty varieties of crab which are harvested off the coast of eastern China. A favourite way to prepare them is to steam them whole and then crack them at the table and dip them in vinegar and sugar. In this Shanghai-inspired dish, cooked crab is mixed with a light egg custard and then steamed. The result is a sort of savoury velvet- or satin-textured custard. I recommend using only the freshest cooked crabmeat you can find for this dish. It makes a satisfying main course with rice and Curried Sweetcorn Soup with Chicken (page 64).

Region: Shanghai
Method: Steaming

Serves 4

225 g (8 oz) freshly cooked
white crabmeat

FOR THE CUSTARD

4 eggs

300 ml (10 fl oz) Chicken Stock (page 59)

2 teaspoons finely chopped fresh ginger

3½ tablespoons finely chopped spring
onions, white part only

1½ tablespoons Shaoxing rice wine or
dry sherry

1 teaspoon freshly ground white pepper

1 teaspoon salt

FOR THE GARNISH

2 teaspoons dark soy sauce

2 tablespoons finely chopped
spring onions

1 tablespoon groundnut (peanut) oil

Mix the custard ingredients in a bowl and then add the cooked crabmeat. Mix well to blend all the ingredients together. Put the mixture into a deep heatproof dish.

Next set up a steamer or put a rack into a wok or deep pan and fill it with 5 cm (2 inches) of water. Bring the water to the boil over a high heat. Carefully lower the dish with the crab mixture into the steamer or on to the rack. Turn the heat to low and cover the wok or pan tightly. Steam gently for 20 to 25 minutes or until the custard has set. Remove the custard and pour the soy sauce over the top, then sprinkle with the spring onions. Meanwhile, heat the oil in a small pan until it is very hot and slightly smoking. Pour this over the custard and serve at once.

steamed crab with ginger vinegar sauce

Region: Shanghai
Method: Steaming

One of the great anticipated events in Shanghai during late autumn is the arrival of fresh river crabs. The crabs are heavy with roe and the flesh is sweet and delicate. They are cooked in the simplest method possible, gently steamed with medicinal herbs to balance the richness of the crab. They are then served with a ginger-vinegar dipping sauce. Here is my version of this delicious and easy crab dish. However, please remember that it must be made with freshest crab in the shell you can find. I make this dish when I want a special main course treat. Serve it with fried rice and a stir-fried vegetable dish for a tasty and light meal.

Serves 4–6

1.5 kg (3 lb) freshly cooked crab in the shell

4 tablespoons Shaoxing rice wine or dry sherry

2 tablespoons fresh ginger, finely shredded

3 spring onions, finely shredded

FOR THE DIPPING SAUCE

2 tablespoons light soy sauce

3 tablespoons red or black rice vinegar

2 teaspoons sugar

2 tablespoons fresh ginger, finely shredded

Remove the tail-flap, stomach sac and feathery gills from the crab (see page 183). Using a heavy knife or cleaver, cut the crab, shell included, into large pieces. Combine the pieces with the rice wine, ginger and spring onions and allow to marinate for 30 minutes.

Next set up a steamer or put a rack into a wok or deep pan and fill it with 5 cm (2 inches) of water. Bring the water to the boil over a high heat. Put the crab pieces with the marinade ingredients onto a heatproof plate and then carefully lower it into the steamer or onto the rack. Turn the heat to low and cover the wok or pan tightly. Steam gently for 15 minutes.

Meanwhile, prepare the ginger vinegar dipping sauce by mixing all the sauce ingredients in a small bowl. Set aside.

Remove the crab pieces, drain and discard the marinade ingredients. Turn it on to a large, warm serving platter and serve at once with the dipping sauce. It is perfectly good manners to eat crab with your fingers, but I suggest that you have a large bowl of water decorated with lemon slices on the table so that your guests can rinse their fingers.

stir-fried squid with vegetables

Squid cooked the Chinese way is both tender and tasty. The secret is to use very hot water for blanching it and then a minimum amount of cooking time – just enough for the squid to firm up slightly. Cooking it too long will make it tough, like chewing on rubber bands. This simple recipe can also be prepared with prawns if you find squid difficult to obtain. Serve with Hot and Sour Soup (page 76) and plain rice.

Regions: Canton and Fujian
Methods: Blanching and stir-frying

Serves 4

450 g (1 lb) squid, fresh or frozen
100 g (4 oz) red or green pepper (about 1)
1½ tablespoons groundnut (peanut) oil
2 tablespoons finely chopped garlic
1 tablespoon finely chopped fresh ginger
100 g (4 oz) mangetout, trimmed
85 ml (3 fl oz) Chicken Stock (page 59)
1 tablespoon Shaoxing rice wine or dry sherry
3 tablespoons oyster sauce
1 tablespoon light soy sauce/2 teaspoons dark soy sauce
2 teaspoons salt
2 teaspoons cornflour blended with 2 teaspoons water
2 teaspoons sesame oil

The edible parts of the squid are the tentacles and the body. Using a small sharp knife, split the body in half. Remove the transparent bony section. Wash the halves thoroughly under cold running water and then pull off and discard the skin. Cut the tentacles from the head. If you are using frozen squid make sure it is properly thawed before cooking it.

Cut the squid meat into 3.5 cm (1½ inch) strips. Blanch the strips and the tentacles in a large pan of boiling water for 15 seconds. The squid will firm up slightly and turn an opaque white colour. Remove and drain in a colander.

Cut the pepper into 3.5 cm (1½ inch) strips. Heat a wok or large frying pan until it is very hot. Add the oil and when it is very hot and slightly smoking, add the garlic and ginger and stir-fry for 15 seconds. Then add the pepper strips and mangetout and stir-fry for 1 minute. Finally, add the rest of the ingredients, except the squid and bring the mixture to the boil. Give it a quick stir, then add the squid and mix well. Cook for a further 30 seconds. Serve at once.

Nutritionists all agree that vegetables are an indispensable ingredient in a well balanced diet. Chinese cookery needs no encouragement in this regard. Even as a child I loved vegetables; in this predilection, I am thus very Chinese. As for my European friends, as children they despised vegetables and even as adults they often refuse to eat them. They have their reasons, of course. Many Western cooks simply overcook vegetables, draining them of their natural flavours and colours and rendering them limp and lifeless. In China, vegetables are never overcooked nor are they undercooked. The techniques of stir-frying, blanching, deep-frying and even braising all preserve the flavours of vegetables while retaining their crispness and texture. The trick is to know when to stop cooking. Simplicity is another factor. The Chinese rarely cover their vegetables with heavy sauces, preferring the natural tastes and textures. But vegetables are rarely eaten raw unless they are pickled; even lettuce is cooked and cold Chinese salads always consist of cooked or pickled vegetables, too. All Chinese meals include one or two vegetable dishes, since apart from being highly nutritious they add colour and texture to a well balanced meal.

Westerners generally agree that vegetables cooked in the Chinese fashion are delectable. This excellence in the preparation of vegetables is, of course, based on thousands of years of culinary experience. China is also fortunate in having a vast array of native edible plants, supplemented in recent centuries by foreign imports such as tomatoes, carrots, sweet potatoes and various types of marrow.

The Buddhist-Taoist tradition is one source of the Chinese people's expertise with vegetables. Buddhists avoid meat because they abhor killing any living animal since this contradicts their doctrine of reincarnation. Taoists are vegetarian because they believe that to kill animals is to shatter the essential unity of the universe. For the past 1500 years, therefore, these minority groups have promoted vegetarianism, and their chefs have made imaginative and creative use of vegetables. They have concocted imitations of meat, chicken, fish and seafood dishes which are so realistic and delicious that people are hard-put to distinguish the replica from the real thing. Because vegetables are not good sources of protein, the soya bean, that miracle protein food which is found everywhere in China, was pressed into service. Beancurd, soyabean milk and other beancurd products became staples in the vegetarian diet. Instead of poultry or meat broths, the liquid left from soaking dried Chinese black mushrooms provided the base for sauces and soups. All of these innovations slowly spread beyond the Buddhist and Taoist groups to the much larger society of non-vegetarian Chinese.

Many of the recipes in this chapter are true vegetarian recipes: these are marked with their titles in tinted boxes. Many of the other recipes can easily be made into vegetarian dishes by simply substituting a vegetarian stock, Shaoxing rice wine or water for the chicken stock. In recipes where meats are mixed with the vegetables, you can simply cut out the meat without losing the taste of the final dish.

vegetables

VEGETABLE COOKING TECHNIQUES

Technique is especially important in vegetable cookery. We cook with a minimum of water or oil to obtain the best results. The use of high heat and rapid cooking seals in the flavours and nutrients but retains texture and crispness. Blanching vegetables in hot water and then plunging them into cold water after brief cooking ensures than the natural flavour and colour of the vegetables is retained. This process is particularly important when stir-frying harder vegetables such as carrots or broccoli which need to be partly cooked before being stir-fried.

Deep-frying is another favourite method of cooking vegetables, since hot oil seals in the flavours and gives vegetables a crunchy texture. Whatever technique you use I hope you will discover the same pleasure that the Chinese have been deriving from vegetables for centuries. Most of the vegetables used in the following recipes are well known in this country. I have, however, included some which may be less familiar.

Left:
Cold sweet and sour chinese leaves
(*page 202*)

braised spicy aubergines

Aubergines are one of my favourite vegetables. For this dish, it's worth trying to get the small, long thin Chinese aubergines for their sweet taste. However, you can also use the larger European variety. I leave the skin on because it holds the aubergine together during the cooking and because the skins are tender, tasty and nutritious.

Two techniques are employed here: a quick stir-frying to blend the seasonings, and braising, which cooks the aubergines and makes a sauce in which to serve them.

Region: Sichuan
Method: Stir-frying and braising

Serves 4

450 g (1 lb) aubergines
2 teaspoons salt
1½ tablespoons groundnut (peanut) oil
2 tablespoons finely chopped garlic
1½ tablespoons finely chopped fresh ginger
3 tablespoons finely chopped spring onions, white part only
2 tablespoons dark soy sauce/1 tablespoon chilli bean sauce
1 tablespoon whole yellow bean sauce
1 tablespoon sugar
1 tablespoon Chinese black vinegar or cider vinegar
2 teaspoons Sichuan peppercorns, roasted and freshly ground (page 35)
300 ml (10 fl oz) Chicken Stock (page 59) or water

FOR THE GARNISH
2 tablespoons chopped spring onions, green tops only

Roll-cut the Chinese aubergines (see page 45), or if you are using the large variety, trim and cut them into 2.5 cm (1 inch) cubes. Sprinkle with salt and leave them in a colander to drain for 2 minutes. Then rinse them under cold water and pat them dry with kitchen paper.

Heat a wok or large frying pan until it is very hot. Add the oil and when it is very hot and slightly smoking, add the garlic, ginger and spring onions and stir-fry them for 30 seconds. Add the aubergines and continue to stir-fry for 1 minute. Add the rest of the ingredients and simmer, uncovered, for 10 to 15 minutes until the aubergine is tender.

Return the heat to high and stir until the liquid has been reduced and thickened. Garnish with the spring onions.

country-style aubergine

This dish is quite delicious because of its use of spices and seasonings: it is hot, sour, salty and sweet at the same time. It sounds (and tastes) very Sichuan and indeed it is. You can find this dish in countless homes in the countryside throughout China. Pork is used to stretch this homely dish. It is easy to make and re-heats quite well. In some parts of the world, aubergine is known as eggplant, a name no doubt derived from the ivory-coloured variety which in fact looks like a large egg. Aubergines, which originated in northern India and migrated to China hundreds of years ago, come in various sizes, shapes and colours: red, yellow, white, striped and purple-black.

Region: Sichuan
Methods: Deep-frying and stir-frying

Serves 4

450 g (1 lb) aubergines
2 teaspoons salt
450 ml (15 fl oz) groundnut (peanut) oil
4S0 g (1 lb) minced pork
2 tablespoons finely chopped garlic
2 tablespoons finely chopped fresh ginger
3 tablespoons finely chopped spring onions
2 tablespoons dark soy sauce
3 tablespoons Shaoxing rice wine or dry sherry
3 tablespoons Chinese black vinegar
2 tablespoons sugar
1 tablespoon Sichuan peppercorns, roasted and freshly ground (page 35)
2 teaspoons chilli bean sauce
1/2 teaspoon freshly ground black pepper
120 ml (4 fl oz) Chicken Stock (page 59)
2 teaspoons sesame oil

Roll-cut the Chinese aubergines (see page 45), or if you are using the large variety, trim and cut them into 2.5 cm (1 inch) cubes. Sprinkle the cubes with salt and leave them in a sieve to drain for 20 minutes. Then rinse them under cold running water and pat them dry with kitchen paper.

Heat a wok or large frying pan until it is very hot. Add the oil and when it is very hot and slightly smoking, deep-fry the aubergine for 3 minutes or until soft, in 2 batches. Drain well in a colander and then on kitchen paper.

Wipe the wok or pan clean and re-heat. When it is hot, return 1 tablespoon of the drained oil to it. Add the pork and stir-fry for 3 minutes. Add the garlic, ginger and spring onions and stir-fry for 2 minutes. Add the rest of the ingredients except the sesame oil. Bring to the boil, return the aubergines to the wok or pan and continue to cook over high heat until they are tender and most of the liquid has evaporated. Stir in the sesame oil. Serve at once or cool to room temperature.

deep-fried green beans

While the traditional recipe calls for Chinese asparagus or long beans, I have found runner beans equally suitable. The beans are deep-fried to transform their texture but they should remain green and not be overcooked. After deep-frying, the beans are stir-fried in an array of spices to create a delectable dish. They should be slightly oily but if they are too oily you can blot them with kitchen paper before stir-frying.

Region: Sichuan
Methods: Deep-frying and stir-frying

Serves 4

600 ml (1 pint) groundnut (peanut) oil (see Deep-fat fryers, page 42)

450 g (1 lb) runner beans, trimmed and sliced if long, whole otherwise

1½ tablespoons finely chopped garlic

1½ tablespoons finely chopped fresh ginger

3 tablespoons finely chopped spring onions, white part only

1½ tablespoons chilli bean sauce

1 tablespoon whole yellow bean sauce

2 tablespoons Shaoxing rice wine or dry sherry

1 tablespoon dark soy sauce

2 teaspoons sugar/1 tablespoon water

2 teaspoons chilli oil

Heat a wok or large frying pan until it is very hot. Add the oil and when it is very hot and slightly smoking, deep-fry half the beans until they are slightly wrinkled, about 3 to 4 minutes. Remove the beans and drain them. Deep-fry the second batch in the same way.

Transfer about 1 tablespoon of the oil in which you have cooked the beans to a clean wok or frying pan. Reheat the wok or pan, add the garlic, ginger and spring onions and stir-fry for about 30 seconds. Then add the rest of the ingredients. Stir-fry the mixture for 30 seconds, then add the cooked, drained beans. Mix well until all the beans are thoroughly coated with the spicy mixture. Serve as soon as the beans have heated through.

braised beancurd with mushrooms

Beancurd, which is also known as *doufu* or, in Japanese, *tofu* (see page 20), is a versatile and nutritious food. It is derived from the soyabean, which is exceedingly rich in protein. Beancurd is rather bland, but this is easily remedied by recipes such as this one, in which it is deep-fried, which alters its texture and then braised, which makes it tasty. The result is a delicious and unusual vegetable dish. An additional bonus is that it re-heats well.

Region: Sichuan
Methods: Deep-frying and braising

Serves 4

450 g (1 lb) fresh bean curd

50 g (2 oz) spring onions

450 ml (15 fl oz) groundnut oil (see Deep-fat fryers, page 42)

1 tablespoon groundnut (peanut) oil

1½ tablespoons finely chopped garlic

2 teaspoons finely chopped fresh ginger

100 g (4 oz) small, whole, button mushrooms, washed

2 teaspoons chilli bean sauce

1½ tablespoons Shaoxing rice wine or dry sherry

1 tablespoon dark soy sauce

1 teaspoon salt

½ teaspoon freshly ground black pepper

2 tablespoons Chicken Stock (page 59) or water

2 teaspoons Sichuan peppercorn, roasted and freshly ground (page 35)

Cut the beancurd into 2.5 cm (1 inch) cubes. Trim the spring onions and cut them into 2.5 cm (1 inch) pieces.

Heat the 450 ml (15 fl oz) of oil in a deep-fat fryer or large wok until it is very hot and slightly smoking. Deep-fry the beancurd cubes in two batches. When each batch of beancurd cubes is lightly browned, remove and drain well on kitchen paper. Let the cooking oil cool and then discard it.

Heat a wok or large frying pan until it is very hot. Add 1 tablespoon of oil and then add the garlic, ginger and spring onions. Stir-fry for a few seconds and then add the mushrooms. Stir-fry for 30 seconds, then add all the other ingredients. Reduce the heat to very low and then add the beancurd cubes. Cover the pan and slowly simmer for 8 minutes.

beancurd with vegetables

When it is shallow-fried, beancurd changes its texture from a slippery, soft one to one which is light and spongy. In this way the beancurd does not absorb the oil but forms a sort of skin which helps to hold it together during stir-frying.

Region: Canton
Methods: Shallow-frying and stir-frying

Serves 4

450 g (1 lb) fresh beancurd

50 g (2 oz) water chestnuts, peeled if fresh, rinsed if canned (page 37)

50 g (2 oz) canned bamboo shoots

50 g (2 oz) mangetout, trimmed

150 ml (5 fl oz) groundnut (peanut) oil

FOR THE SAUCE

1½ tablespoons Shaoxing rice wine or dry sherry

3 tablespoons oyster sauce

2 teaspoons dark soy sauce/2 teaspoons light soy sauce

2 teaspoons sugar

1 teaspoon salt

½ teaspoon freshly ground black pepper

50 ml (2 fl oz) Chicken Stock (page 59) or water

1 teaspoon cornflour blended with 1 teaspoon water

2 teaspoons sesame oil

Drain and rinse the beancurd in cold water. Blot dry with kitchen paper and cut into 1 cm (½ inch) cubes. If you are using fresh water chestnuts, peel and slice them. If using canned ones, rinse and slice them. Slice the bamboo shoots diagonally into 2.5 cm (1 inch) pieces.

Heat a wok or large frying pan until it is very hot. Add the oil and when it is very hot and slightly smoking, add the beancurd cubes and shallow-fry until they are lightly brown. Drain with a slotted spoon and dry on kitchen paper.

Pour off most of the oil, leaving about 1 tablespoon in the pan. Re-heat the oil, add the vegetables and stir-fry them for about 2 minutes. Then add all the sauce ingredients except the cornflour mixture and sesame oil. Bring the mixture to the boil, remove from the heat and then add the cornflour mixture. Return the pan to the heat and bring it back to the boil. Return the beancurd to the pan and add the sesame oil. Give the mixture a few stirs and turn on to a warm serving platter. Serve at once.

braised beancurd casserole family-style

Beancurd is ideal for braising as it readily absorbs flavours and colours and Chinese beancurd seems to me to be the best in the world; smooth and satiny in texture and invariably perfectly prepared. (Three thousand years of experience counts for something.) This recipe is a good one to try if you haven't cooked beancurd before. Here is a particularly tasty and easy-to-prepare recipe which re-heats extremely well. One of the ingredients, hoisin sauce, adds a rich reddish colour and a slightly sweet flavour to the beancurd. Hence dishes like this are often called red-cooked.

Region: Canton
Methods: Deep-frying and braising

Serves 4

450 g (1 lb) beancurd
8 spring onions
450 ml (15 fl oz) groundnut (peanut) oil
1½ tablespoons groundnut (peanut) oil
2 tablespoons coarsely chopped garlic
2 tablespoons Shaoxing rice wine or dry sherry
3 tablespoons hoisin sauce
1 tablespoon light soy sauce
2 teaspoons dark soy sauce
1 teaspoon sugar
250 ml (8 fl oz) Chicken Stock (page 58-9) or water
1 tablespoon sesame oil

Cut the beancurd into 2.5 cm (1 inch) cubes and drain it on kitchen paper. Trim the spring onions and cut them into 2.5 cm (1 inch) pieces.

Heat the 450 ml (15 fl oz) of oil in a deep-fat fryer or large wok until it is very hot and slightly smoking. Deep-fry the beancurd cubes in two batches. When each batch is lightly browned, remove and drain well on kitchen paper. Let the cooking oil cool and then discard it.

Wipe the wok clean and re-heat it over high heat until it is hot. Add the 1½ tablespoons of oil and when it is very hot and slightly smoking, add the garlic and spring onions. Stir-fry for a few seconds and then add the drained beancurd. Stir-fry for 30 seconds, then add all the other ingredients, except the sesame oil. Reduce the heat to low and simmer the mixture gently for 8 minutes. Turn the heat to high and cook until most of the liquid has evaporated. Stir in the sesame oil and serve at once.

salt and pepper beancurd

This is a vegetarian version of the popular salt and pepper dish which one can find in Hong Kong made with prawns or spareribs. It is a savoury way to enjoy beancurd and is easy to make. The beancurd is deep-fried first, then it is stir-fried with salt, aromatics and chillies. I think it makes a delicious starter for any meal.

Regions: Hong Kong and Canton
Methods: Deep-frying and stir-frying

Serves 4

450 g (1 lb) beancurd
2 teaspoons salt
2 teaspoons Sichuan peppercorns, roasted and freshly ground (page 35)
1 teaspoon freshly ground black pepper
1 teaspoon sugar
300 ml (10 fl oz) groundnut (peanut) oil
2 tablespoons finely chopped garlic
2 teaspoons finely chopped fresh ginger
3 fresh red or green chillies, coarsely chopped

FOR THE GARNISH
3 tablespoons finely chopped spring onions

Drain and rinse the beancurd in cold water. Blot it dry with kitchen paper, cut into 1 cm (½ inch) cubes and drain it further on kitchen paper. In a small bowl, combine the salt, Sichuan peppercorns, pepper and sugar.

Heat a wok or large frying pan until it is very hot. Add the oil and when it is very hot and slightly smoking, add the beancurd cubes and deep-fry them until they are lightly brown on all sides. Remove with a slotted spoon and drain well on kitchen paper.

Pour off most of the oil, leaving about 1 tablespoon in the wok or pan. Re-heat the wok or pan, and when it is hot, add the garlic, ginger and chillies and stir-fry them for 20 seconds. Then return the beancurd to the wok or pan and continue to stir-fry for 1 minute. Add the salt and pepper mixture and continue to stir-fry for another 2 minutes. Turn the mixture on to a warm serving platter, garnish with the spring onions and serve at once.

Right:
Fresh beancurd
(*page 20*)

cold marinated bean sprouts

This is a nutritious salad, easy to make and perfect either as an appetizer or as a salad course with grilled meat or fish. Always use fresh bean sprouts – never tinned ones which are soggy and tasteless. Fresh ones are widely available and are also very easy to grow. I prefer to trim the sprouts at both ends. Although this is a bit laborious, it is well worth the effort as it makes the finished dish look more elegant. This dish may be prepared up to 4 hours in advance and may be served cold or at room temperature. It is perfect for warm summer days.

Region: Beijing
Method: Marinating

Serves 4

450 g (1 lb) fresh bean sprouts

2 fresh red or green chillies

3 tablespoons Chinese white rice vinegar or cider vinegar

2 tablespoons light soy sauce

2 tablespoons finely chopped fresh coriander

2 teaspoons finely chopped garlic

Trim and discard both ends of the bean sprouts and put the trimmed sprouts into a glass bowl. Split the chillies in half and carefully remove and discard the seeds. Shred the chilli as finely as possible. Add it, together with all the other ingredients, to the trimmed bean sprouts. Mix well. Let the mixture marinate for at least 2 to 3 hours, turning the bean sprouts in the marinade from time to time. When you are ready to serve the salad, drain the bean sprouts and discard the marinade.

stir-fried ginger broccoli

Broccoli is a colourful and extraordinarily nutritious vegetable. The type known in the West is different from the Chinese variety. The Western variety is often considered to combine the best features of cauliflower and asparagus and its distinctive flavour is milder than the Chinese type. It goes well with many seasonings but ginger is one of its most congenial companions. After stir-frying this dish, I let it cool and serve it at room temperature, so it is particularly suitable for summertime.

Region: Canton
Method: Stir-frying

Serves 4

450 g (1 lb) fresh broccoli
1½ tablespoons groundnut (peanut) oil
2 tablespoons finely shredded fresh ginger
1 teaspoon salt
½ teaspoon freshly ground black pepper
4–5 tablespoons water
2 teaspoons sesame oil

Separate the broccoli heads into small florets, and peel and slice the stems. Blanch the broccoli pieces in a large pan of boiling salted water for 5 minutes, and then plunge them into cold water. Drain thoroughly in a colander.

Heat a wok or large frying pan until it is very hot. Add the oil and when it is very hot and slightly smoking, add the ginger shreds, salt and pepper. Stir-fry for a few seconds, then add the blanched broccoli. Add a few tablespoons of water. Stir-fry at a moderate to high heat for 4 minutes until the broccoli is thoroughly heated through. Add the sesame oil and continue to stir-fry for 30 seconds, then the broccoli is ready to serve.

cold sesame broccoli

This dish makes a good garnish for meats or a wonderful vegetable dish for summer picnics. For a tangy alternative, you could substitute finely chopped fresh ginger for the sesame seeds (using roughly the same amount). It can be prepared a day in advance and actually tastes even better if you do this.

Region: Beijing
Method: Blanching

Serves 4 to 6

450–750 g (1–1½ lb) broccoli
1 tablespoon sesame seeds
1 tablespoon groundnut (peanut) oil
2 teaspoons sesame oil
1 teaspoon finely chopped garlic
1½ tablespoons light soy sauce
2 tablespoons finely chopped spring onions

Separate the broccoli heads into small florets. Peel and slice the stems. Blanch the broccoli pieces in a large pan of boiling, salted water for 5 minutes, drain then plunge them into cold water. Drain thoroughly in a colander and put them into a clean bowl.

Roast the sesame seeds in a pre-heated oven, gas mark 5, 375°F (190°C), or under a grill, until they are brown. In a small glass bowl combine the roasted sesame seeds with all the rest of the ingredients and mix them together well. Then pour the mixture into the bowl of broccoli and toss well. (If you are using this dish the next day, tightly cover the bowl with cling film and keep it in the refrigerator until it is needed.)

stir-fried broccoli with hoisin sauce

The flavour of broccoli blends perfectly with the rich taste of hoisin sauce, which has a good colour and fragrance, but a little goes a long way. Served hot, it makes a perfect vegetable accompaniment. Carrots or courgettes can be used instead of broccoli.

Region: Beijing
Method: Stir-frying

Serves 4

450 g (1 lb) fresh broccoli
1½ tablespoons groundnut (peanut) oil
1 tablespoon finely chopped garlic
2 teaspoons salt
1 teaspoon freshly ground black pepper
2 tablespoons hoisin sauce
2 tablespoons Shaoxing rice wine or dry sherry
3 tablespoons water

Separate the broccoli heads into florets, and peel and slice the stems. Blanch the broccoli pieces in a large pan of boiling, salted water for 5 minutes. Drain and plunge them into cold water. Drain thoroughly in a colander.

Heat a wok or large frying pan until it is very hot. Add the oil and when it is very hot and slightly smoking, add the garlic, salt, pepper and broccoli pieces. Stir-fry them for about 1 minute, and then add the hoisin sauce, Shaoxing rice wine or dry sherry and water. Continue to stir-fry at a moderately high heat for about 5 minutes or until the broccoli is thoroughly cooked. Serve at once.

braised cauliflower with oyster sauce

Cauliflower is a versatile vegetable which is both delicious and easy to prepare. It needs a longish cooking time so stir-frying is not the most appropriate cooking technique. I prefer to braise it in oyster sauce which goes well with its mild taste.

Region: Canton
Methods: Stir-frying and braising

Serves 4

750 g (1½ lb) cauliflower
1 tablespoon groundnut (peanut) oil
4 cloves garlic, crushed
2 tablespoons finely shredded fresh ginger
1 teaspoon light soy sauce
1 teaspoon dark soy sauce
3½ tablespoons oyster sauce
450 ml (15 fl oz) Chicken Stock (page 59) or water
2 teaspoons sesame oil

FOR THE GARNISH
2 tablespoons finely chopped spring onions

Cut the cauliflower into small florets about 4 cm (1½ inches) wide.

Heat a wok or large frying pan until it is very hot. Add the oil and when it is very hot and slightly smoking add the garlic and ginger. Stir-fry for about 20 seconds to flavour the oil. Quickly add the cauliflower florets and stir-fry them for a few seconds. Next add the two soy sauces, the oyster sauce and the stock or water. Turn the heat down and simmer for 8 minutes or until the cauliflower is tender. Stir in the sesame oil, turn on to a warm serving platter and sprinkle with the spring onions. Serve at once.

cold sweet and sour chinese leaves

In northern China, with its short growing season and long cold winters, fresh vegetables are available for only a few months of the year. In the absence of modern refrigeration, other means of preserving foods are necessary. Some of the most common methods are pickling in brine, in salt and wine, in a mixture of sugar and salt, or by inducing fermentation. In this recipe, Chinese leaves (or cabbage) undergo a sweet and sour pickling process. They can be eaten at once or stored for later use. Dishes like this are served at room temperature at the beginning of a meal and their sweet and sour flavours are designed to stimulate the palate and whet the appetite.

Region: Beijing
Methods: Blanching and pickling

Serves 4 to 6

750 g (1½ lb) Chinese leaves or white cabbage, cut into 5 cm (2 inch) strips

85 ml (3 fl oz) groundnut (peanut) oil

1 tablespoon sesame oil

5 dried red chillies

2 tablespoons whole Sichuan peppercorns, roasted (page 35)

100 g (4 oz) sugar

150 ml (5 fl oz) Chinese white rice vinegar or cider vinegar

2 tablespoons salt

1½ tablespoons finely chopped fresh ginger

3 tablespoons finely chopped garlic

3 tablespoons coarsely chopped fresh red chillies

Blanch the Chinese leaves or cabbage strips in hot water for a few seconds until they wilt. Drain them and put them to one side in a glass bowl. Heat the two oils in a wok or pan until they are hot. Add the chillies and whole roasted peppercorns. When the chillies and peppercorns turn dark, turn the heat off. Pour the flavoured oil through a strainer and then over the leaves or cabbage strips. Wrap the chillies and peppercorns in cheesecloth and tie into a bag like a bouquet garni, so that it can be removed later. Place it among the vegetable strips.

Now add the sugar and vinegar to the leaves and mix well. Add the salt, ginger, garlic and fresh chillies and make sure that everything is mixed in well. Let the mixture sit at room temperature for several hours and refrigerate overnight. This dish will keep for up to 1 week in the refrigerator. Before you serve it, drain off all the marinade and remove the chilli/peppercorn bouquet garni.

spiced chinese leaves

Unlike the more familiar green and red cabbage, Peking cabbage ('Chinese leaves') has a sweet flavour which is delicate, rather like lettuce. Cooking is needed to make it palatable, and because it is so light, it calls for a robust sauce. I like to serve it with this spicy sauce. For a variation you might substitute curry powder for the chilli.

Region: Sichuan
Methods: Stir-frying and braising

Serves 2 to 4

750 g (1¹⁄₂ lb) Chinese leaves
1 tablespoon groundnut (peanut) oil
1 tablespoon finely chopped fresh ginger
1¹⁄₂ tablespoons finely chopped garlic
2 dried red chillies, split in half
1¹⁄₂ tablespoons Shaoxing rice wine or dry sherry
1 tablespoon dark soy sauce
1 teaspoon light soy sauce
2 teaspoons chilli bean sauce
¹⁄₂ teaspoon freshly ground black pepper
2 teaspoons sugar
50 ml (2 fl oz) Chicken Stock (page 59) or water
1 tablespoon sesame oil

Separate the Chinese leaves and wash them well. Cut them into 2.5 cm (1 inch) strips.

Heat a wok or large frying pan until it is very hot. Add the oil and when it is very hot and slightly smoking, add the ginger, garlic and chillies. Stir-fry them for a few seconds. Add the Chinese leaves and stir-fry for a few seconds and then add the Shaoxing rice wine or dry sherry, soy sauces, chilli bean sauce, pepper, sugar and stock or water. Turn the heat down and simmer for 8 minutes until the leaves are tender. (At this point, you can, if you wish, remove the dried chillies.) Add the sesame oil and stir in well. Serve at once.

braised peking cabbage in cream sauce

Region: Beijing
Methods: Stir-frying and braising

Vegetarian dishes are common throughout China. Historic and religious influences and rituals played a part, but the availability of so many different vegetables, especially soya beans, had a practical influence. Peking cabbage (commonly known here as Chinese leaves), for example, was enjoyed pickled as well as fresh. One of the best versions is this traditional dish. Here the cabbage was first stir-fried, then slowly braised in chicken stock, with the stock reduced, thickened and enriched with chicken fat. I omit the last step here; in any case I think the dish is tasty enough without it. To make the dish pure vegetarian, I would substitute plain water for the chicken stock and thicken it with cornflour rather than the chicken fat to make the cream sauce. A humble dish, but one worthy of the Imperial banquet hall.

Serves 4

450 g (1 lb) Chinese leaves
(Peking cabbage)
1½ tablespoons groundnut (peanut) oil
3 cloves garlic, peeled and finely sliced
450 ml (15 fl oz) water or Chicken Stock
(page 59)
2 teaspoons salt
1 teaspoon freshly ground white pepper
2 teaspoons cornflour blended with
1 tablespoon water

Cut the Chinese leaves into 5 cm (2 inch) thick strips.

Heat a wok or large frying pan until it is very hot. Add the oil and when it is very hot and slightly smoking, add the garlic and stir-fry for 15 seconds. Then add the Chinese leaves and stir-fry for 2 minutes. Add the water or stock, salt and pepper. Turn the heat to low, cover and cook for 10 minutes or until the cabbage is very tender. Remove the cabbage with a slotted spoon.

Boil to reduce the liquid in the wok or pan by half, add the cornflour mixture and continue to reduce by half again until the sauce is thick. Arrange the cabbage on a warm serving platter, pour the sauce over the cabbage and serve at once.

stir-fried chinese greens

Chinese greens are also known by their Cantonese name, bok choy. They were a staple food in my childhood as they were inexpensive, nutritious and readily available. Even today I look forward to this simple stir-fried dish. Sometimes the greens are merely blanched but I think they are delicious stir-fried with oil and garlic or with a little soy sauce and stock. They make a delicious dish to serve with meat and fish and are excellent in vegetarian menus. You can get Chinese greens at Chinese grocers, but Swiss chard or mangetout work equally well.

Region: Canton
Method: Stir-frying

Serves 4

1 tablespoon groundnut (peanut) oil
3 cloves garlic, peeled and finely sliced
2 teaspoons salt
750 g (1½ lb) Chinese greens, such as Chinese flowering cabbage or bok choy
2 tablespoons Chicken Stock (page 59) or water

Heat a wok or large frying pan until it is very hot. Add the oil and when it is very hot and slightly smoking, add the garlic and salt. Stir-fry for 15 seconds, then add the Chinese greens. Stir-fry for 3 to 4 minutes until the greens have wilted a little. Then add the chicken stock or water and continue to stir-fry for a few more minutes until the greens are tender but are still slightly crisp.

chinese leaves in soy sauce

This simple dish is one of my favourite ways of preparing Chinese leaves. The blanching preserves the sweetness while the hot oil imparts a rich, nutty flavour to the vegetable. It is quick and easy to make. You can also use white cabbage or any other leafy green vegetable for this dish.

Region: Canton
Method: Blanching

Serves 2

450 g (1 lb) Chinese leaves
1 tablespoon light soy sauce
2 teaspoons dark soy sauce
3 tablespoons finely chopped spring onions
1 tablespoon groundnut (peanut) oil

Cut the Chinese leaves into 4 cm (1½ inch) strips and blanch them in a pan of boiling, salted water for about 5 minutes. Drain thoroughly, then arrange the blanched leaves on a warm serving platter. Dribble the light and dark soy sauces and spring onions over them.

Heat the oil in a wok or frying pan until it is very hot and slightly smoking and then pour the hot oil over the leaves. Serve at once. For a spicy taste, try using Chilli Oil (page 23) instead of groundnut (peanut) oil. This is a perfect dish for a cold winter's night. Plain steamed rice makes a delicious accompaniment.

crispy 'seaweed'

This is one of the most popular dishes among frequent Chinese restaurant diners in Britain. I am not sure who was the first to bring this unique eastern-northern Chinese dish to Britain; suffice it to say, however, that not 'seaweed' but cabbage is being used. A special type of seaweed, which is indeed used in China, is unfortunately not yet available in the UK. The adaptability of Chinese cuisine is once again demonstrated in this dish: if the original ingredients are not available, then technique and ingenuity will overcome the deficiency. This dish is delicious and easy to make and, speaking of adaptability, this recipe can also be tried with spinach leaves.

Serves 4

1.24 kg (2½ lb) bok choy
900 ml (1½ pints) groundnut (peanut) or vegetable oil
1 teaspoon salt
2 teaspoons sugar
50 g (2 oz) pine kernels, lightly roasted

Pre-heat the oven to gas mark ½, 120°C (250°F).

Separate the stalks from the stem of the bok choy and cut the green leaves from the white stalks. (Save the stalks, you can use them for soup.) Wash the green leaves through several changes of cold water. Drain them thoroughly in a colander and spin them dry in a salad spinner. Take the leaves and roll them tightly and then finely shred them. Lay them out to dry on a baking sheet and put them in the oven for 10 minutes to dry slightly. They should not be completely dried, as they will burn when fried. Remove from the oven and allow to cool. This can be done the day before.

Heat a wok or deep fat fryer until it is very hot. Add the oil and when it it is very hot and slightly smoking, deep-fry the greens in 2 or 3 batches. When they turn deep green, in about 30 seconds, remove them immediately, drain well on kitchen paper and allow to cool.

Toss the crispy greens in salt and sugar. Garnish with the pine kernels and serve.

stir-fried cucumbers with hot spices

As a child, it always surprised me to see Americans eating cucumbers raw. We Chinese rarely eat them like this. If they are not pickled then they must be cooked. We prefer them when they are in season: young, tender and bursting with juice. This is a simple stir-fried cucumber dish from western China. Once the ingredients are assembled, it is very quick to cook. The chilli and garlic contrast well with the cool, crisp cucumber. Once you get into the habit of cooking cucumbers, you will be delighted by their transformation into a true vegetable.

Region: Sichuan
Method: Stir-frying

Serves 4

750g (1½ lb) cucumbers (about 1½)

2 teaspoons salt

1 tablespoon groundnut (peanut) oil

1½ tablespoons finely chopped garlic

1½ tablespoons black beans, rinsed and coarsely chopped

1 tablespoon finely chopped fresh ginger

2 tablespoons finely chopped spring onions

2 teaspoons chilli bean sauce

1 teaspoon salt

½ teaspoon freshly ground black pepper

2 teaspoons sugar

120 ml (4 fl oz) water

2 teaspoons sesame oil

Peel the cucumbers, slice them in half lengthways and, using a teaspoon, remove the seeds. Then cut the cucumber halves into 2.5 cm (1 inch) cubes. Sprinkle them with the salt and mix well. Put the mixture into a colander and let it sit for 20 minutes to drain. This rids the cucumber of any excess liquid. When the cubes have drained, rinse them in water and then blot them dry with kitchen paper.

Heat a wok or large frying pan until it is very hot. Add the oil and when it is very hot and slightly smoking, add the garlic, black beans, ginger and spring onions and stir-fry for about 30 seconds. Then add the cucumbers, chilli bean sauce, salt, pepper and sugar and stir for another 30 seconds until they are well coated with the spices and flavourings. Add the water and continue to stir-fry over a high heat for 3 to 4 minutes until most of the water has evaporated and the cucumbers are cooked. Add the sesame oil and serve at once.

fried stuffed cucumbers

There are countless Chinese recipes for all kinds of stuffed vegetables. Even beancurd can be filled. Cucumbers, in particular, lend themselves to stuffing because their tender, succulent flesh is complemented by a savoury filling – this recipe uses seasoned minced pork. Thick cucumber slices are stuffed and then shallow-fried; this seals in the flavours of the stuffing. Then they are simmered to create the sauce.

Region: Fujian
Method: Shallow-frying

Serves 4

750 g (1½ lb) cucumbers (about 1½)

2 tablespoons cornflour

3 tablespoons groundnut (peanut) oil

FOR THE STUFFING MIXTURE

225 g (8 oz) fatty pork, finely minced

1 egg white

1½ tablespoons finely chopped spring onions

1 tablespoon finely chopped fresh ginger

2 teaspoons Shaoxing rice wine or dry sherry

2 teaspoons light soy sauce

2 teaspoons sugar

1 teaspoon salt

1 teaspoon freshly ground black pepper

1 teaspoon sesame oil

FOR THE SAUCE

300 ml (10 fl oz) Chicken Stock (page 59)

2 tablespoons Shaoxing rice wine or dry sherry

2 tablespoons light soy sauce

1 tablespoon oyster sauce

2 teaspoons sugar

1 teaspoon cornflour blended with 2 teaspoons water

FOR THE GARNISH

2 teaspoons sesame oil

2 tablespoons finely chopped fresh coriander

Cut the cucumbers into 2.5 cm (1 inch) slices without peeling them. Remove the seeds and pulp from the centre of each cucumber slice using a small sharp knife. Hollow the cucumber so that you have at least a 5 mm (¼ inch) shell. Lightly dust the hollow interior of the cucumber slices with a little cornflour. Mix all the stuffing ingredients together in a large bowl. Then stuff each cucumber ring with this mixture.

Heat a wok or large frying pan and add the oil. When it is moderately hot, add some of the stuffed cucumber rings and cook them slowly until they are slightly browned. Turn them over and brown the other side. You may have to do this in several batches adding more oil if necessary. When the cucumber rings are brown, remove them from the oil with a slotted spoon and put them on a plate. When you have fried all the cucumber rings, wipe the wok or pan clean.

Re-heat the wok or pan, add the sauce ingredients and bring the liquid to a simmer. Add the stuffed cucumber rings. Cover the pan with a lid and simmer slowly for 7 minutes or until the cucumbers are completely cooked. Transfer them to a warm serving platter, lifting them out of the sauce with a slotted spoon.

Reduce the sauce by a third over a high heat. Then add the sesame oil and fresh coriander. Pour the sauce over the stuffed cucumbers and serve at once.

lettuce with oyster sauce

Here is lettuce prepared in a very familiar Chinese way – blanched and served with oyster sauce. Lettuce prepared like this retains a crispy texture and its delicate flavour. The combination makes a simple, quickly prepared, tasty vegetable dish.

Regions: Canton and Hong Kong
Method: Blanching

Serves 2 to 4

750 g (1½ lb) Cos or Iceberg lettuce

3 tablespoons oyster sauce

1 tablespoon groundnut (peanut) oil

Separate the lettuce leaves and blanch them in a pan of boiling, salted water for about 30 seconds or until they have wilted slightly. Remove them and drain well. Mix the oyster sauce with the oil. Arrange the lettuce leaves on a warm serving dish, pour the oyster sauce mixture over it and serve immediately.

stir-fried mangetout with water chestnuts

In China, fresh water chestnuts are cultivated between rows of rice plants. They are a favourite delicacy. It is worth trying to get the fresh ones either in your supermarket or at the Chinese grocers. Fresh water chestnuts are often dipped into a sugar syrup and eaten as a snack. Cooked, they have a sweet taste and crunchy texture. This is a straightforward recipe which should be made with the freshest mangetout you can find. Asparagus, when in season, makes a delightful alternative.

Regions: Canton and Fujian
Method: Stir-frying

Serves 4

225 g (8 oz) water chestnuts, peeled if fresh, rinsed if canned (page 37)

1 tablespoon groundnut (peanut) oil

3 tablespoons finely chopped spring onions

225 g (8 oz) mangetout, trimmed

1 tablespoon light soy sauce

2 tablespoons water

1 teaspoon salt

½ teaspoon freshly ground black pepper

1 teaspoon sugar

2 teaspoons sesame oil

Thinly slice the water chestnuts.

Heat a wok or large frying pan until it is very hot. Add the oil and when it is very hot and slightly smoking, add the spring onions and stir-fry for 10 seconds. Add the mangetout and fresh water chestnuts if you are using them, and stir-fry for 1 minute, making sure you coat them thoroughly with the oil. Then add the rest of the ingredients, except the sesame oil and continue to stir-fry for another 3 minutes. If you are using canned water chestnuts, add these now and cook for a further 2 minutes or until the vegetables are cooked. Stir in the sesame oil and serve at once.

spicy stir-fried mushrooms

Although button mushrooms are common in Europe and America they were virtually unknown in China until quite recently. They are now increasingly popular there. Their mild, subtle flavour makes them perfect for stir-frying with Chinese spices. This dish is simple to make and re-heats well. Serve it with Braised Duck (page 145) and plain steamed rice. It also goes perfectly with English grills.

Region: Sichuan
Method: Stir-frying

Serves 4

1 tablespoon groundnut (peanut) oil
2 teaspoons finely chopped garlic
2 teaspoons finely chopped fresh ginger
1 tablespoon finely chopped spring onions
450 g (1 lb) small, whole, button mushrooms
2 teaspoons chilli bean sauce
1 tablespoon Shaoxing rice wine or dry sherry
2 teaspoons dark soy sauce
1 teaspoon salt
1/2 teaspoon freshly ground black pepper
1 tablespoon Chicken Stock (page 59) or water
2 teaspoons sugar
2 teaspoons sesame oil

Heat a wok or large frying pan until it is very hot. Add the oil and when it is very hot and slightly smoking, add the garlic, ginger, and spring onions and stir-fry for about 20 seconds. Add the mushrooms and stir-fry them for about 30 seconds. Quickly add the rest of the ingredients except the sesame oil. Continue to stir-fry for about 5 minutes or until the mushrooms are cooked through and have absorbed all the spices and seasonings. Just before serving, add the sesame oil and give the mixture a couple of quick stirs. Turn it on to a warm serving dish and serve at once as the mushrooms are particularly delicious when hot.

Right:
Mushrooms
(*page 28*)

cold peppers with black beans

Peppers, both mild and hot, are enjoyed throughout China. This is a recipe inspired by a Sichuan one using fresh mild, whole chillies. Here they are combined with zesty and spicy aromatics from Sichuan province. The black beans add a pungent aroma, as well as a delectable touch to this savoury vegetarian dish. It is easy to prepare, and tastes even better if you let the beans sit for two hours before serving. Use them as a summer dish which can be served at room temperature or serve as a vegetable dish.

Region: Sichuan
Method: Stir-frying

Serves 4

1½ tablespoons groundnut (peanut) or vegetable oil

3 tablespoons finely chopped shallots

2 tablespoons black beans, rinsed and coarsely chopped

1½ tablespoons finely chopped garlic

1 tablespoon finely chopped fresh ginger

175 g (6 oz) red peppers, de-seeded and cut into 2.5 cm (1 inch) squares

175 g (6 oz) yellow peppers, de-seeded and cut into 2.5 cm (1 inch) squares

175 g (6 oz) green peppers, de-seeded and cut into 2.5 cm (1 inch) squares

2 tablespoons Shaoxing rice wine or dry sherry

1 tablespoon chilli bean sauce

1 tablespoon light soy sauce

2 tablespoons dark soy sauce

2 teaspoons sugar

150 ml (¼ pint) Chicken Stock (page 59) or water

2 teaspoons sesame oil

Heat a wok or large frying pan until it is very hot. Add the oil and when it is hot and slightly smoking, add the shallots, black beans, garlic and ginger and stir-fry for 1 minute. Then add the peppers and stir-fry for 1 minute. Finally, add the Shaoxing rice wine or dry sherry, chilli bean sauce, soy sauces, sugar and chicken stock. Cook over high heat for 5 minutes or until the peppers are soft and most of the liquid has evaporated. Then stir in the sesame oil and mix well. Turn on to a platter and let cool. Serve at room temperature.

three mushroom braise

Mushrooms are very popular in China, especially in the south where the warm, moist climate is ideal for fungi. The varieties of mushrooms are endless. The three used in this recipe have very different characteristics: Straw mushrooms have a musky scent and meaty texture; Chinese dried mushrooms are smoky-flavoured and densely textured; button mushrooms are mild and soft. Combining all three in a substantial and rich sauce transforms the mushrooms from a supporting ingredient to a vegetable dish in its own right. Straw and dried mushrooms can be bought at Chinese grocers and some supermarkets, but if you can't get them, this recipe is nearly as delicious made entirely with button ones. (Use 350 g [12 oz] button mushrooms.)

Regions: Canton and Fujian
Methods: Stir-frying and braising

Serves 4

25 g (1 oz) Chinese dried mushrooms

1 x 227 g (8 oz) can Chinese straw mushrooms

75 g (3 oz) button mushrooms

1 tablespoon groundnut (peanut) oil

3 cloves garlic, peeled and thinly sliced

1 tablespoon light soy sauce

2 tablespoons Shaoxing rice wine or dry sherry

3 tablespoons oyster sauce

2 teaspoons sugar

65 ml (2½ fl oz) Chicken Stock (page 59) or water

2 tablespoons finely chopped spring onions

If you are using Chinese dried mushrooms, soak them in warm water for 20 minutes, and then drain them. Rinse them well and squeeze out any excess liquid. Discard the tough stem, then shred the caps and put them side. If you are using tinned straw mushrooms, drain and rinse them but leave them whole. Wash and slice the button mushrooms.

Heat a wok or large frying pan until it is very hot. Add the oil and when it is very hot and slightly smoking, add the garlic and stir-fry for 15 seconds. Add all the mushrooms and stir-fry them, mixing them well, for a few seconds. Then quickly add the soy sauce, Shaoxing rice wine or dry sherry, oyster sauce, sugar and chicken stock. Turn the heat down and cook for about 7 minutes, stirring continually, until the fresh mushrooms are thoroughly cooked. Turn the heat back to high and continue to cook until most of the liquid has been reduced. Mix in the spring onions and serve.

buddhist casserole

This is my adaptation of a famous Buddhist dish. The original recipe calls for many obscure, dried Chinese vegetables but my version uses vegetables which are readily available. I like to add a little coriander which Buddhists do not eat. A deeply satisfying dish, this casserole is suitable for both summer and winter. I prefer to cook it in a Chinese clay pot (see page 43) but you can also use a good, small cast-iron pot. Take care not to overcook the vegetables. The casserole may be made in advance and re-heated very slowly. It is delicious with rice, noodles or fresh bread.

Region: Fujian
Methods: Deep-frying and braising

Serves 4

225 g (8 oz) fresh beancurd

100 g (4 oz) broccoli

100 g (4 oz) Chinese leaves or white cabbage

100 g (4 oz) small courgettes

100 g (4 oz) red pepper (about 1)

100 g (4 oz) mangetout

450 ml (15 fl oz) groundnut (peanut) oil (see Deep-fat fryers, page 42)

600 ml (1 pint) Chicken Stock (page 59) or water

2 tablespoons light soy sauce

3 tablespoons hoisin sauce

2 tablespoons whole yellow bean sauce

1 tablespoon finely chopped fresh coriander

1 teaspoon salt

½ teaspoon freshly ground black pepper

1 tablespoon sesame oil

Cut the beancurd into 2.5 cm (1 inch) cubes. Drain it on kitchen paper. Next, prepare all the vegetables. Break the broccoli heads into small florets. Peel and slice the broccoli stems. Cut the Chinese leaves or cabbage into 2.5 cm (1 inch) chunks. Slice the courgettes into rounds 5 mm (¼ inch) thick or roll cut them (see page 45). Thinly slice the pepper. Trim the mangetout.

Heat a wok or deep-fat fryer until it is very hot. Add the oil and when it is very hot and slightly smoking, deep-fry the beancurd cubes in 2 batches. Drain each batch on kitchen paper.

Put the chicken stock or water, soy sauce, hoisin sauce and whole yellow bean sauce into a large, cast-iron enamel pot or Chinese clay pot and bring it to the boil. Add the broccoli and stir in the Chinese leaves or cabbage. Boil for 2 minutes. Add the courgettes and pepper and cook for another 2 minutes. Finally add the mangetout and beancurd cubes and cook for a further 1 minute. Stir in the fresh coriander and season with salt and pepper. Finally stir in the sesame oil and the dish is ready to serve. To re-heat, bring to a simmer on a very low heat until all the vegetables are hot.

spinach with fermented beancurd

Throughout south and south-west China, in both restaurants and homes, Chinese water spinach is a very popular vegetable. Chinese water spinach differs from the European variety in that it has hollow stems and arrowhead-shaped leaves. When properly prepared, it offers a nice contrast between the soft leaf and the still crunchy stem. The fermented beancurd seasoning provides a zesty dimension. It makes a fine accompaniment to any meat dish and is perfect with rice.

Region: Canton
Method: Stir-frying

Serves 4

1 kg (2 lb) fresh Chinese water spinach or European spinach

2 tablespoons groundnut (peanut) oil

4 cloves garlic, peeled and thinly sliced

3 tablespoons chilli-fermented beancurd or plain fermented beancurd

2 tablespoons Shaoxing rice wine or dry sherry

3 tablespoons water

Wash the spinach thoroughly and drain. Cut off 5 cm (2 inches) from the bottom of the stem, which tends to be tough. Cut the rest of the spinach into 7.5 cm (3 inch) segments. If you are using ordinary spinach, wash it thoroughly and remove all the stems, leaving just the leaves.

Heat a wok or large frying an until it is very hot. Add the oil and when it is very hot and slightly smoking, add the garlic and stir-fry for 15 seconds. Then add the fermented beancurd and crush it with a spatula, breaking it into small pieces. Add the spinach and stir-fry for 3 minutes. Pour in the rice wine and water and continue to cook for another 3 minutes. Put on to a warm serving platter and serve at once.

stir-fried spinach with garlic

Spinach has often been regarded with disdain in the West, probably because it is usually overcooked. This is a delicious, time-honoured, southern Chinese recipe. The spinach is quickly stir-fried and then seasoned. It is very simple to prepare.

Region: Canton
Method: Stir-frying

Serves 4

750 g (1½ lb) fresh spinach

1 tablespoon groundnut (peanut) oil

1 tablespoon finely chopped garlic

1 teaspoon salt

1 teaspoon sugar

Wash the spinach thoroughly. Remove all the stems, leaving just the leaves. Heat a wok or large frying pan until it is very hot. Add the oil and when it is very hot and slightly smoking, add the garlic and salt and stir-fry for 10 seconds. Then add the spinach and stir-fry for about 2 minutes to coat the spinach leaves thoroughly with the oil, garlic and salt. When the spinach has wilted to about one-third of its original size, add the sugar and continue to stir-fry for another 4 minutes. Transfer to a plate and pour off any excess liquid. Serve hot or cold.

deep-fried milk

One of the most interesting dishes I have encountered in Hong Kong is this dish of so-called deep-fried milk. It has become quite popular in Chinese restaurants in the West. The cooking process allows the milk to be digested by people who ordinarily cannot take milk. Milk custard is lightly battered and deep-fried. The result is a crispy exterior with a creamy custardy interior, a combination of textures that appeals to the Chinese taste. How milk made its way into Hong Kong cuisine is an intriguing question. I suspect it is a northern dish that perhaps made its way into southern cooking. The contrast between the slightly salty custard and sugar is also striking. In Hong Kong, deep-fried milk is served with spareribs or simply dipped in sugar, as in this recipe. Either way, I think you will discover, as I have, that it is a delicious dish.

Region: Hong Kong
Method: Deep-frying

Serves 4

350 ml (12 fl oz) milk
175 ml (6 fl oz) evaporated milk
2 teaspoons salt
1 teaspoon freshly ground white pepper
6 tablespoons cornflour
1 tablespoon groundnut (peanut) oil
450 ml (15 fl oz) groundnut (peanut) oil

FOR THE BATTER
75 g (3 oz) plain flour
4 tablespoons cornflour
2 teaspoons baking powder
175 ml (6 fl oz) water
Sugar, for dipping

In a medium-sized bowl, combine the two milks, salt, pepper and cornflour. Beat the mixture until it is smooth and pour this into a saucepan. Simmer the mixture over low heat for about 10 minutes or until the mixture has thickened. Oil a 15 cm (6 inch) square cake tin, pour in the mixture and allow it to cool thoroughly. Cover with cling film and refrigerate. This can be done the night before.

In a medium-sized bowl, mix the batter ingredients and allow to sit at room temperature for 30 minutes. Cut the milk curd into 5 cm (2 inch) squares.

Heat a wok or large frying pan over high heat until it is very hot. Add the oil and when it is very hot and slightly smoking, dip several of the milk cubes into the batter with chopsticks or a slotted spoon and deep-fry them for 3 minutes or until golden and crispy. Drain them on kitchen paper and repeat the process until you have fried all the milk cubes. Serve them with a dish of sugar for dipping.

All authentic Chinese meals include two main food types. The first is the so-called (in Chinese) *cai*, which consists of meat, poultry, fish and vegetable dishes. The other is the *fan* and includes rice, wheat, sorghum, millet and other grains which form the staple food of the diet. I should point out that, contrary to popular depictions, most Chinese rely upon grains other than rice as their staple food, especially in the drier, colder, northern areas where rice cannot be cultivated. Rice *fan* is eaten in its basic form. Grains are consumed mainly in the form of noodles, including rice noodles and doughs; that is dumplings, buns and pancakes.

Both *fan* and *cai* are integral to Chinese cookery but in China itself and as with 'staples' everywhere, the *fan* is fundamental: as one Chinese sage put it, 'Without *cai* the food is less tasteful, but without the *fan*, one's hunger cannot be satisfied.' This chapter is divided into three sections, rice, noodles and doughs. I offer detailed information on the different types of rice and noodles and on the various flours or doughs. You will, I trust, become a fan of *fan*.

rice, noodles and doughs

rice

Rice includes long-grain, short-grain and glutinous varieties and all are made into flour, noodles, wines and vinegars as well as being used directly in cooking. Brown rice, which is a popular wholefood in the West, is not used by the Chinese who dislike its texture. Plain white rice – boiled or steamed – is eaten with meals. Fried rice, now popular in Chinese restaurants all over the world, is served in China as a snack or as the last course at a banquet and never with other cai dishes.

Long-grain rice This is the most popular rice for cooking in southern China and it is my favourite, too. It needs to be washed before it is cooked. Do not confuse it with the 'easy-cook' and pre-cooked varieties which are now widely available as these are unsuitable for Chinese cooking. They lack the starchy flavour, texture and clean white colour which is so essential to Chinese cuisine.

Short-grain rice This rice is not to be confused with pudding rice. Short-grain rice is usually used in Chinese cooking for making congee and is more popular outside southern China. Varieties known as 'American Rose' or 'Japanese Rose' can be found in many Chinese grocers. If you cannot find short-grain rice, use long-grain instead.

Glutinous rice Glutinous rice is also known as sweet rice or sticky rice. It is short, round and pearl-like and is not to be confused with regular short-grain rice or pudding rice. It has more gluten than ordinary rice and when cooked is sticker and sweeter. It is used mainly for stuffings and desserts and for making Chinese rice wine and vinegar. Most Chinese grocers stock it. Glutinous rice must be washed and soaked for at least 2 hours before cooking. You may cook it in the same way as long-grain rice or by steaming. If you want to steam it, soak the rice for at least 8 hours or overnight. Then line a bamboo steamer with cheesecloth and spread the rice over it. Steam it for about 40 minutes or until the rice is cooked.

To wash rice Put the required amount of rice into a large bowl. Fill the bowl with cold water and swish the rice around with a spoon or with your hands. Carefully pour off the cloudy water, keeping the rice in the bowl. Repeat this process several times until the water is clear.

steamed rice

Steaming rice the Chinese way is one of the most simple and efficient techniques in rice cookery. I prefer to use long-grain white rice which is drier and fluffier when cooked. Don't use pre-cooked or 'easy-cook' rice for Chinese cookery as both these types of rice have insufficient flavour and lack the texture and starchy taste which is fundamental to Chinese rice.

The secret of preparing rice without it being sticky is to cook it first in an uncovered pan at a high heat until most of the water has evaporated. Then the heat should be turned very low, the pan covered and the rice cooked slowly in the remaining steam. As a child I was always instructed never to peek into the rice pot during this stage or else precious steam would escape and the rice would not be cooked properly, thus bringing bad luck. Here is a good trick to remember: if you make sure that you cover the rice with about 2.5 cm (1 inch) of water it should always cook properly without sticking. Many packet recipes for rice use too much water and result in a gluey mess. Follow my method and you will have perfect steamed rice, the easy Chinese way.

Most Chinese eat quite large quantities of rice (about 150 g (5 oz) per head, which is more than many Westerners are able to manage). This recipe and that for Fried Rice allows about 375 g dried weight (13 oz) of rice for 4 people. If you want more than that just increase the quantity of rice, but remember to add enough water so that the level of water is about 2.5 cm (1 inch) above the top of the rice.

For the most authentic *Chinese* cooking, the required rice is simple long-grain rice, of which there are many varieties. There are a few rules that are worth repeating in regard to long-grain rice.

The water should be at a level 2.5 cm (1 inch) above the surface of the rice; too much water means gummy rice. Recipes on commercial packages generally recommend too much water.

Never uncover the pan once the simmering process has begun; time the process and wait.

Follow the directions overleaf and you are on your way to perfect rice.

Serves 4

Enough long-grain rice to fill a glass
measuring jug to 400 ml (14 fl oz) level
600 ml (1 pint) water

Put the rice into a large bowl and wash it in several changes of water until the water becomes completely clear. Drain the rice and put it into a heavy pan with 600 ml (1 pint) of water and bring it to the boil. Continue boiling until most of the surface liquid has evaporated. This should take about 15 minutes. The surface of the rice should have small indentations like a pitted crater. At this point, cover the pan with a very tight-fitting lid, turn the heat as low as possible and let the rice cook undisturbed for 15 minutes. There is no need to 'fluff' the rice. Remove the pan from the heat and let it rest for 5 minutes before serving it.

fried rice

In China, fried rice is eaten as a 'filler' at the end of a dinner party. It is not eaten with other dishes in place of steamed rice, although many Westerners do so. Fried rice is common in Chinese restaurants, but it is frequently incorrectly cooked. Here are a few important points to remember when making authentic fried rice.

Regions: Fujian and Canton
Method: Stir-frying

The cooked long-grain rice should be thoroughly cool, preferably cold before you start preparing Fried Rice. Once cooled, much of the moisture in the rice evaporates, allowing the oil to coat the dry grains and prevent them from sticking. Store the cooked rice in the refrigerator until you are ready to use it.

Never put any soy sauce into Fried Rice. This not only colours the rice unnaturally but makes it too salty. Any moisture will also make the rice gummy. Fried rice should be quite dry and the grains quite separate.

Always be sure the oil is hot enough to avoid saturating the boiled or steamed plain rice. Saturated rice is greasy and heavy. The finished fried rice should have a wonderful smoky taste and flavour.

If you follow these simple guidelines, you will be rewarded with perfect fried rice as it should be. Fried rice goes with almost any dish, but in China it is usually served at the end of a dinner to clean the palate and fill up hungry guests.

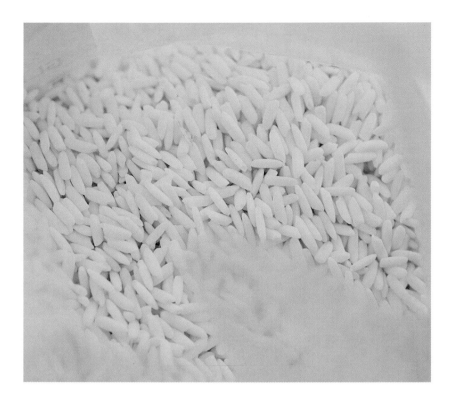

Serves 4

100 g (4 oz) fresh or frozen peas

2 eggs, beaten

2 teaspoons sesame oil

2 tablespoons groundnut (peanut) oil

Long-grain rice measured to the 400 ml (14 fl oz) level in a measuring jug and cooked according to the method given on page 222

50 g (2 oz) cooked ham, finely diced

2 teaspoons salt

½ teaspoon freshly ground black pepper

3 tablespoons finely chopped spring onions, white part only

100 g (4 oz) fresh bean sprouts

FOR THE GARNISH

2 tablespoons finely chopped spring onions

Blanch the peas in a pan of boiling water for about 5 minutes if they are fresh; if they are frozen, simply thaw them. Drain. Mix the egg and sesame oil in a small bowl and set aside.

Heat a wok or large frying pan until it is very hot. Add the oil and when it is very hot and slightly smoking, add the cooked rice and stir-fry it for 3 minutes. Add the ham, peas, salt and pepper. Stir-fry the mixture for 5 minutes over a high heat. Add the egg mixture and stir-fry for another 1 minute. Add the spring onions and bean sprouts and stir-fry for 2 minutes or until the eggs have set. Turn the mixture on to a plate and garnish it with the spring onions. Serve hot or cool for a cold rice salad.

rice cake

Regions: All
Method: Steaming

Rice cakes were probably invented by a thrifty Chinese cook centuries ago in order to make use of that thin layer of rice which sometimes gets stuck at the bottom of the pan. This crispy left-over has evolved into an accompaniment to many dishes. Its taste and crunchy texture go deliciously with Sizzling Rice Prawns (page 181), for example. After trying it you will never discard your left-over rice crust again.

Do not use 'easy-cook' rice for this dish because it does not have enough starch to form any crust; use long-grain white rice. Once it has been cooked, it can be left out at room temperature for several days. Do not cover it, or moisture will make the cake mouldy or soggy. Let it dry out and it is ready to be deep-fried or used to make a soup. As a simple snack, break it into chunks and eat it hot with a sprinkling of salt.

Makes 1 x 23 cm (9 inch) rice cake

225 g (8 oz) long-grain rice
600 ml (1 pint) water
2 teaspoons groundnut (peanut) oil

Wash the rice and put it, with the water, in a 23–24 cm (9–9½ inch) wide, heavy pan. Bring to the boil over a high heat, then turn the heat down as low as possible, cover and cook for about 45 minutes. The rice should form a heavy crust on the bottom. Remove all the loose rice – it can be used for making Fried Rice (page 222-3).

Drizzle the oil evenly over the top of the crust and let it cook over a very low heat for 5 minutes. The crust should lift off easily. If it is still sticky, add another teaspoon of oil and continue to cook until it comes loose. It is now ready for use.

rice congee

Rice congee is what many Chinese eat for breakfast; it is simply a boiled rice porridge. In various areas of China, fried bread dough, fermented beancurd, pickles, preserved salt or spicy mustard greens may be added to the congee. In the south, meat, chicken, roast duck, peanuts or fermented eggs are added. Interestingly enough, the word congee is a Hindi word and this perhaps indicates its origin.

The technique used in making congee is to boil the rice and then simmer it slowly. The starch is released gradually, thickening the porridge without the rice grains disintegrating. I find short-grain rice best for making congee, but you may use long-grain. In this recipe the rice needs no washing as all the starch is needed to thicken the porridge.

Region: Canton
Method: Simmering

Serves 4

225 g (8 oz) Chinese sausages (or any flavouring of your choice, such as Sichuan preserved vegetable, or diced cooked chicken or duck or left-over meats, fish, etc.)

1.5 litres (2½ pints) water

Short-grain or long-grain rice to fill a glass measuring jug to the 150 ml (5 fl oz) level, unwashed

2 teaspoons salt

3 tablespoons finely chopped spring onions

2 tablespoons finely chopped fresh coriander

Cut the Chinese sausages, or whatever flavouring you are using, into fine dice and set aside.

Bring the water to the boil in a large pan and add the rice and salt. Let the mixture come back to the boil and give it several good stirs. Then turn the heat down to low and cover the pan. Let the mixture simmer for about 1 hour, stirring occasionally. Then add the Chinese sausages or your chosen flavouring and simmer for a further 5 minutes with the pan uncovered. Just before serving, add the spring onions and fresh coriander. Serve it at once. If you like, congee can be made in advance. In this case re-heat it slowly, and simply add some more water if the porridge is too thick.

chicken, sausage and rice casserole

I have many pleasant memories of this dish. Even though I grew up in America, I often went to school with a typically Chinese lunch. Very early in the morning, my mother would steam chicken and sausage with rice and put it in a thermos flask to keep it warm. I would often exchange bits of my hot lunch for portions of my classmates' sandwiches! This dish is easy to make and is a simple but fully satisfying meal in itself. It is well worth the effort to obtain authentic Chinese sausages from a Chinese grocer. There is no adequate substitute for this unique, delicious sausage. An added bonus is that this dish is easy to re-heat. You might serve this with Braised Spicy Aubergines (page 191) or Spiced Chinese Leaves (page 204).

Region: Canton
Method: Steaming

Serves 4

400 g (14 oz) glutinous rice

750 g (1½ lb) boneless chicken pieces, skinned

1 tablespoon Shaoxing rice wine or dry sherry

2 tablespoons light soy sauce

2 teaspoons dark soy sauce

2 teaspoons sugar

1 teaspoon salt

1 teaspoon freshly ground black pepper

1 teaspoon sesame oil

25 g (1 oz) Chinese dried mushrooms

175 g (6 oz) Chinese sausages or pork sausages

900 ml (1½ pints) Chicken Stock (page 59) or water

1½ tablespoons finely chopped fresh ginger

3 tablespoons finely chopped spring onions

Soak the glutinous rice in cold water for at least 8 hours.

Cut the chicken into 5 cm (2 inch) pieces. Put these into a bowl and combine them with the Shaoxing rice wine or dry sherry, soy sauces, sugar, salt and pepper and sesame oil. Leave the mixture to marinate for at least 20 minutes.

Soak the mushrooms in warm water for 20 minutes. Then drain them and squeeze out the excess liquid. Remove and discard the stems and chop the caps. Slice the sausages thinly on a slight diagonal into 5 cm (2 inch) long pieces.

Bring the chicken stock to a boil in a large pan. Drain the soaking rice and add it to the pan and turn the heat to low. Cover and let cook for 2 minutes.

Add the chicken, mushrooms, sausages, ginger and spring onions. Stir the mixture into the rice and continue to cook for about 25 minutes until the rice, chicken and sausages are cooked. Serve at once.

rainbow rice

Rice is so basic that it is usually taken for granted. This recipe gives a touch of glamour to the prosaic staple. It is a popular rice dish in the south. At first glance the recipe may seem similar to that of Fried Rice (page 222-3) but it is really quite different since the rice and the other ingredients all have to be cooked separately, and then combined. It is a substantial dish, beautifully coloured and ideal for a special dinner.

Region: Canton
Method: Stir-frying

Serves 4

Long-grain rice measured to the 400 ml (14 fl oz) level in a measuring jug and cooked according to the method on page 222

50 g (2 oz) Chinese dried mushrooms

50 g (2 oz) red pepper (about ½)

50 g (2 oz) carrot

100 g (4 oz) Chinese sausages or cooked ham

50 g (2 oz) fresh or frozen peas

2 tablespoons groundnut (peanut) oil

3 tablespoons finely chopped spring onions

1 tablespoon light soy sauce

1 teaspoon salt

½ teaspoon freshly ground black pepper

2 teaspoons sesame oil

Prepare the rice as instructed in the recipe on page 222. Soak the dried mushrooms in warm water for about 20 minutes until they are soft. Meanwhile cut the red pepper, carrot and sausages or ham into small dice. Squeeze the excess liquid from the mushrooms and remove and discard their stems. Cut the caps into small dice. If you are using frozen peas make sure they are thoroughly thawed.

Heat a wok or large frying pan. Add the oil and spring onions and stir-fry for about 30 seconds. Then add all the vegetables and the sausages or ham. Stir-fry the mixture for about 2 minutes and then add the soy sauce, salt and pepper. Give the mixture a few stirs and then add the sesame oil. Remove the pan from the heat and let the mixture cool.

When the rice is almost ready, pour the cooked mixture over it to cover the rice. Let it cook for a further 5 minutes. Then stir to mix well. Turn on to a warm serving platter and serve at once.

fried rice with beef

Dependable but bland rice is easily enlivened with a small amount of beef which adds body and flavour. Traditionally served as a finish to a banquet or dinner – for those gourmands who might still be hungry – today, it is more and more served as a rice dish to accompany the entrée. It is very easy to make and always enjoyable.

Serves 4

2 tablespoons groundnut (peanut) oil

225 g (8 oz) minced beef

2 teaspoons light soy sauce

1 teaspoon dark soy sauce

1 teaspoon salt

½ teaspoon freshly ground black pepper

1 tablespoon finely chopped fresh ginger

3 tablespoons finely chopped spring onions

Long-grain rice measured to the 400 ml (14 fl oz) level in a measuring jug and cooked according to the method on page 222

2 teaspoons sesame oil

Heat a wok or large frying pan until it is very hot. Add the oil and when it is very hot and slightly smoking, add the beef and stir-fry for 2 minutes. Add the soy sauces, salt, pepper, ginger and spring onions and stir-fry for 2 minutes. Add the rice, mix well and continue to stir-fry the mixture for another 5 minutes until the rice is heated through. Stir in the sesame oil, mix well and serve at once.

noodles

There has always been an argument about whether the Chinese invented noodles before the Italians discovered spaghetti. Marco Polo professed amazement at Chinese pasta but Italians claim he was only being polite. It remains true, however, that Chinese noodles are more varied than Italian ones. They come in all shapes and sizes and are made from a variety of flours. They are most commonly made from wheat or rice flour and water and, in the south, from wheat flour, water and eggs. There is also a type which is made from mung beans although this is strictly speaking not a noodle but a vegetable.

To see an expert noodlemaker at work is a real treat. Hand-made noodles are formed by an elaborate but rapid process of kneading, pulling, tossing and twisting of the dough into a cascade of fine long noodles. This spectacular skill takes four to five years to acquire and is a delight to watch.

Noodles play an important part in Chinese tradition since they are a symbol of longevity. For this reason they are often served at Chinese New Year and at birthday dinners and it is considered bad luck to cut them since this might shorten one's life! Noodles can be boiled and eaten plain instead of rice, with sauces; cold as salads; or in soups. Alternatively, fried with meat and vegetables they make a delicious and sustaining light meal.

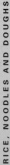

cold spicy noodles

These savoury noodles are perfect for summertime, and I enjoy making them because much of the work can be done in advance. Most people enjoy the fragrance of the sesame paste in this recipe, but if you can't get it you can use peanut butter instead. Cold Spicy Noodles can be served with that very British dish – a mixed grill.

Region: Sichuan
Method: Blanching

Serves 4

450 g (1 lb) dried or fresh egg noodles
2 tablespoons sesame oil

FOR THE SAUCE

3 tablespoons sesame paste or smooth peanut butter
1 tablespoon chilli bean sauce
1¹/₂ tablespoons finely chopped garlic
2 teaspoons Chilli Oil (page 23)
2 tablespoons Chinese white vinegar or cider vinegar
2 tablespoons light soy sauce
2 teaspoons dark soy sauce
1 teaspoon salt
1 teaspoon freshly ground black pepper
2 teaspoons sugar
2 teaspoons Sichuan peppercorns, roasted and freshly ground (page 35)
1 tablespoon groundnut (peanut) oil
1¹/₂ tablespoons sesame oil

FOR THE GARNISH

3 tablespoons finely chopped spring onions

Cook the noodles by boiling them for 3 to 5 minutes in a pan of boiling water. Drain and plunge them into cold water. Drain thoroughly and toss in the sesame oil. Arrange them on a platter or in a bowl.

Mix the sauce ingredients together in a bowl or in an electric blender. This can be done in advance and kept refrigerated, as the sauce is meant to be cold. Pour the sauce over the top and sprinkle on the spring onions. Toss the noodles well with the sauce before serving.

Note: If you wish to make this dish in advance, please keep the sauce and noodles separate, tossing them only at the last possible moment.

Right:
Fresh egg noodles
(*page 29*)

bean sauce noodles

Noodles are so popular in northern China that they are even eaten for breakfast, usually in soup. They are a common snack for the millions of patrons of the food stalls throughout capital city of Beijing (Peking). This recipe is an adaptation of a common noodle dish, of which there are hundreds of variations. Once you have mastered it you can add your own touches, just as the Chinese do. Serve with snacks such as Spring Rolls (page 256-7) and Steamed Open Dumplings (page 261).

Region: Beijing
Methods: Stir-frying and simmering

Serves 4

450 g (1 lb) dried or fresh egg noodles
1½ tablespoons sesame oil

FOR THE SAUCE
1½ tablespoons groundnut (peanut) oil
1½ tablespoons finely chopped garlic
1 tablespoon finely chopped fresh ginger
3 tablespoons finely chopped
spring onions
450 g (1 lb) minced pork
3 tablespoons whole yellow bean sauce
1 tablespoon chilli bean sauce
1½ tablespoons Shaoxing rice wine or
dry sherry
2 tablespoons dark soy sauce
2 teaspoons salt
½ teaspoon freshly ground black pepper
2 teaspoons Chilli Oil (page 23), optional
2 teaspoons sugar
300 ml (10 fl oz) Chicken Stock (page 59)
or water

FOR THE GARNISH
3 tablespoons coarsely chopped
spring onions

Cook the noodles by boiling them for 3 minutes in a pan of boiling water. Drain and plunge them into cold water. Drain thoroughly and toss in the sesame oil. (They can be kept in this state, if tightly covered with cling film, for up to 2 hours in the refrigerator.)

Heat a wok or large frying pan until it is very hot. Add the oil and when it is very hot and slightly smoking, add the garlic, ginger and spring onions and stir-fry for 15 seconds. Add the pork, stir well to break up all the pieces and continue to stir-fry for about 2 minutes or more until the pork loses its pink colour. Add the rest of the sauce ingredients, stirring all the time. Bring the mixture to the boil, turn the heat down to low and simmer for 5 minutes. Plunge the noodles into boiling water for 30 seconds or until they are just heated through and then drain them well in a colander or sieve. Then quickly tip the noodles into a large bowl and pour the hot sauce over the top. Sprinkle on the spring onions, mix everything well and serve at once.

beef noodle soup

This is a warming, satisfying dish, rich in beefy flavour – one of my favourite northern Chinese dishes. It re-heats wonderfully and is especially delicious on cold wintery nights. Don't use an expensive cut of meat for this recipe. Even stewing steak is too extravagant as it has insufficient flavour and will be too dry. Use a coarse, gristly cut of beef, such as chuck or shin. I find that oxtails make for a delicious soup.

Region: Beijing
Methods: Blanching and braising

Serves 4 to 6

900 g (2 lb) boneless shin or chuck beef or oxtails

2 Chinese cinnamon bark or whole cinnamon stick

3 whole star anise

2 tablespoons fennel seeds

1 tablespoon cumin seeds

3 tablespoons Shaoxing rice wine or dry sherry

2 tablespoons light soy sauce

1 tablespoon dark soy sauce

6 dried red chillies, split in half

2 dried citrus peels, soaked and left whole (page 25)

2 teaspoons salt

1 teaspoon freshly ground black pepper

1.2 litres (2 pints) Chicken Stock (page 59)

350 g (12 oz) dried or fresh egg noodles

Cut the meat into 5 cm (2 inch) cubes. Blanch the meat for 10 minutes in a large pan of boiling water.

Place the cinnamon, star anise, fennel seeds and cumin seeds in a piece of muslin and tie it like a bouquet garni. Then combine the meat with all the other ingredients except the noodles in a large pan. Bring the mixture to the boil and then lower the heat to a simmer. Skim any scum or fat off the surface for the first 15 minutes. Cover the pan and simmer gently for 2½ to 3 hours until the meat is tender.

Cook the noodles by boiling them for 3 to 5 minutes in a pan of boiling water. Drain and place the noodles either in individual bowls or a large soup tureen.

When the meat is tender, skim off any surface fat. Ladle some meat and broth over the noodles and serve at once.

chow mein

Chow Mein literally means 'stir-fried noodles' and this dish is as popular outside China as it is in southern China. It is a quick and delicious way to prepare egg noodles. Almost any ingredient you like, such as fish, meat, poultry or vegetables, can be added to it. It is a popular lunch dish, either served at the end of the meal or eaten by itself. It also makes a tasty noodle salad if served cold.

Region: Canton
Method: Stir-frying

Serves 4

225 g (8 oz) dried or fresh egg noodles

1 tablespoon sesame oil

100 g (4 oz) chicken breasts, skinned

2 teaspoons light soy sauce

2 teaspoons Shaoxing rice wine or dry sherry

1 teaspoon sesame oil

1/2 teaspoon salt

1/2 teaspoon freshly ground white pepper

2 1/2 tablespoons groundnut (peanut) oil

1 tablespoon finely chopped garlic

50 g (2 oz) mangetout, trimmed

50 g (2 oz) Parma ham or cooked ham, finely shredded

2 teaspoons light soy sauce

2 teaspoons dark soy sauce

1 tablespoon Shaoxing rice wine or dry sherry

1 teaspoon salt

1/2 teaspoon freshly ground white pepper

1/2 teaspoon sugar

3 tablespoons finely chopped spring onions

2 teaspoons sesame oil

Cook the noodles by boiling them for 3 to 5 minutes in a pan of boiling water. Drain and plunge them into cold water. Drain thoroughly and toss in the sesame oil.

Using a cleaver or sharp knife, slice the chicken breasts into fine shreds 5 cm (2 inches) long. Combine the chicken shreds with the light soy, Shaoxing rice wine or dry sherry, sesame oil, salt and pepper in a small bowl. Mix well and leave the chicken to marinate for about 20 minutes.

Heat a wok or large frying pan until it is very hot. Add 1 tablespoon of oil and when it is very hot and slightly smoking, add the chicken shreds. Stir-fry the mixture for about 2 minutes and then transfer to a plate. Wipe the wok or pan clean.

Re-heat the wok or pan until it is very hot, then add the remaining oil. When it is slightly smoking, add the garlic and stir-fry for 10 seconds. Add the mangetout and ham and stir-fry for about 1 minute. Add the noodles, soy sauces, Shaoxing rice wine or dry sherry, salt, pepper, sugar and spring onions and continue to stir-fry for about 2 minutes. Return the chicken and any juice to the noodle mixture. Continue to stir-fry for about 3 to 4 minutes or until the chicken is cooked. Stir in the sesame oil and give the mixture a few final stirs. Turn it on to a warm serving platter and serve at once.

chicken on crispy noodles

This noodle dish is a great favourite of many *dim sum* diners in Hong Kong and Canton. Pan-fried, so that thin, crispy fresh egg noodles are browned on both sides, and then served with a shredded chicken sauce, it makes a wonderful finale to any *dim sum* meal. As with noodles in general, this dish is enjoyable any time and one can see people eating it throughout the day, not just after *dim sum*. It combines a crispy texture of the noodles with the softness and blandness of the chicken breasts; in this recipe the chicken is velveted, that is, coated with egg white and cornflour, to keep the meat moist and tender. The result is a homely dish elevated to a simple culinary delight. It makes a satisfying luncheon dish.

Regions: Hong Kong and Canton
Methods: Shallow-frying and stir-frying

Serves 4

225 g (8 oz) boneless chicken breasts, skinned and finely shredded
1 egg white
2 teaspoons cornflour
1 teaspoon salt
½ teaspoon freshly ground white pepper
225 g (8 oz) fresh, thin Chinese egg noodles
3 tablespoons groundnut (peanut) oil
300 ml (10 fl oz) groundnut (peanut) oil or water
2 tablespoons Shaoxing rice wine or dry sherry
1½ tablespoons oyster sauce
1 tablespoon light soy sauce
300 ml (10 fl oz) Chicken Stock (page 59)
1 teaspoon salt
½ teaspoon freshly ground black pepper
1 tablespoon cornflour blended with 1½ tablespoons water

FOR THE GARNISH
3 tablespoons finely chopped spring onions

Combine the chicken, egg white, cornflour, salt and pepper in a small bowl. Mix well and leave in the refrigerator for at least 20 minutes.

Blanch the noodles for 2 minutes in a large pan of salted, boiling water. Drain them well.

Heat a frying pan until it is hot and add 1½ tablespoons of oil. Spread the noodles evenly over the surface, turn the heat to low and allow the noodles to brown slowly. This should take about 5 minutes. When the noodles are brown, gently flip them over and brown the other side, adding more oil if needed. When both sides are browned, remove the noodles to a platter and keep them warm.

Heat a wok or large frying pan until it is very hot. Add the oil and when it is very hot and slightly smoking, remove from the heat. Immediately add the chicken, stirring vigorously to prevent it from sticking. After about 2 minutes when the chicken pieces turn white, drain the chicken and all the oil in a stainless steel colander set in a bowl. Discard the oil.

(If you use water instead of oil, bring it to a boil in a saucepan. Remove from the heat and immediately add the chicken pieces, stirring vigorously to prevent them from sticking. After about 2 minutes when the chicken pieces turn white, quickly drain the chicken and all of the water in a colander set in a bowl. Discard the water.)

Clean the wok or pan and re-heat it over high heat. Add the Shaoxing rice wine or dry sherry, oyster sauce, soy sauce, chicken stock, salt and pepper and bring the mixture to a boil. Add the cornflour mixture and return to a simmer again. Return the chicken to the sauce and give the mixture a few stirs. Pour this over the noodles, garnish with the spring onions and serve at once.

stir-fried rice noodles with vegetables

My mother often used to cook rice noodles as an alternative to egg noodles. I like the drier texture of the rice noodles. I think my mother liked them because they needed less cooking! Rice noodles can be found in Chinese grocers and some supermarkets. But if you can't get them, this recipe can be made with egg noodles. As with most noodles, this dish is best served either alone or with snacks such as Steamed Spareribs with Black Beans (page 254) or Sesame Prawn Toast (page 255).

Regions: Fujian and Canton
Method: Stir-frying

Serves 4

225 g (8 oz) rice noodles, rice vermicelli or rice sticks

225 g (8 oz) fresh bean sprouts

100 g (4 oz) red or green chillies

225 g (8 oz) water chestnuts, peeled if fresh, rinsed if canned (page 37)

2 tablespoons groundnut (peanut) oil

1½ tablespoons finely chopped garlic

2 teaspoons finely chopped fresh ginger

6 spring onions, shredded

1 teaspoon salt

½ teaspoon freshly ground white pepper

2 tablespoons light soy sauce

1 tablespoon dark soy sauce

2 teaspoons whole yellow bean sauce

2 tablespoons Shaoxing rice wine or dry sherry

5 tablespoons Chicken Stock (page 59) or water

Soak the rice noodles in a bowl of warm water for 25 minutes. Then drain them in a colander or sieve.

Trim the bean sprouts at both ends. Finely shred the chillies and the water chestnuts.

Heat a wok or large frying pan until it is very hot. Add the oil and when it is very hot and slightly smoking, add the garlic, ginger and spring onions and stir-fry for 15 seconds. Then add the bean sprouts, shredded chillies and shredded water chestnuts and stir-fry for about 1 minute. Then add the rest of the ingredients and the drained noodles. Stir-fry for about 3 minutes until it is well mixed and heated through. Serve at once.

singapore noodles

Curry is not original to Chinese cuisine. It was introduced to China centuries ago by immigrants returning home from sojourns in south-east Asia, especially from the east coast of India. This is why, even today, curry continues to be popular in south and eastern China, the regions which had the most returning immigrants from faraway Singapore. Chinese cuisine readily adopts new foods and ingredients when their virtues are recognized, as in the case of curry. These light and subtle rice noodles are an ideal foil for the spicy sauce. A bonus is that it is easy to make.

For a vegetarian version, just eliminate the meat and use more coconut milk – another adopted food – in place of chicken stock.

Serve them with a fish or meat dish, or they are delicious just by themselves. If rice noodles are unavailable, substitute Chinese egg noodles. This dish is also wonderful cold and would make a lovely and unusual picnic offering.

Regions: Hong Kong, Fujian and Canton
Method: Stir-frying

Serves 4 to 6

225 g (8 oz) thin rice noodles

50 g (2 oz) Chinese black mushrooms

175 g (6 oz) frozen small garden peas or
petit pois

4 eggs, beaten

1 tablespoon sesame oil

1 teaspoon salt

1/2 teaspoon freshly ground white pepper

3 tablespoons groundnut (peanut) oil

1 1/2 tablespoons finely chopped garlic

1 tablespoon finely chopped fresh ginger

6 fresh red or green chillies, de-seeded
and finely shredded

6 water chestnuts, peeled if fresh, rinsed
if canned (page 37)

100 g (4 oz) Chinese barbecue pork or
cooked ham, finely shredded

3 spring onions, finely shredded

100 g (4 oz) small cooked prawns, peeled

FOR THE CURRY SAUCE

2 tablespoons light soy sauce

3 tablespoons Indian Madras curry paste
or 2 tablespoons powder

2 tablespoons Shaoxing rice wine or
dry sherry

1 tablespoon sugar/1 teaspoon salt

1 teaspoon freshly ground black pepper

250 ml (8 fl oz) canned coconut milk

175 ml (6 fl oz) Chicken Stock (page 59)

FOR THE GARNISH

Fresh coriander leaves

Soak the rice noodles in a bowl of warm water for 25 minutes then drain them in a colander or sieve. (If you are using dried egg noodles, cook them by boiling them for 3 to 5 minutes in a pan of boiling water. Drain and plunge them into cold water. Drain thoroughly and toss them in the groundnut (peanut) oil.) Set them aside until you are ready to use them. Soak the mushrooms in warm water for 20 minutes. Then drain them and squeeze out the excess liquid. Remove and discard the stems and finely shred the caps into thin strips. Put the peas in a small bowl and let them thaw. Combine the eggs with sesame oil, salt and pepper and set aside.

Heat a wok or large frying pan until it is very hot. Add the oil, and when it is very hot and slightly smoking, add the garlic, ginger and chillies and stir-fry the mixture for 30 seconds. Add the water chestnuts, mushrooms, pork or ham and spring onions then stir-fry for 1 minute. Then add the rice noodles, prawns and peas and continue to stir-fry for 2 minutes. Now add all the sauce ingredients and continue to cook over high heat for another 5 minutes or until most of the liquid has evaporated. Now add the egg mixture, stir-frying constantly until the egg has set. Turn on to a large, warm serving platter, garnish with the coriander leaves and serve at once.

hot bean thread noodles

Bean thread, or cellophane, noodles are delightfully light. They are very fine, white and almost transparent and can be easily obtained from Chinese grocers and supermarkets. They are quite easy to prepare and go well with almost any kind of sauce. Unlike other types of noodle, bean thread noodles can be successfully re-heated. This spicy sauce gives the noodles body and character – delicious with plain rice.

Region: Sichuan
Method: Stir-frying

Serves 4

100 g (4 oz) bean thread (transparent) noodles
1 tablespoon groundnut (peanut) oil
3 tablespoons finely chopped spring onions
2 tablespoons finely chopped garlic
450 g (1 lb) minced beef

FOR THE SAUCE
450 ml (15 fl oz) Chicken Stock (page 59)
1½ tablespoons chilli bean sauce
1 tablespoon whole yellow bean sauce
2 tablespoons light soy sauce
2 teaspoons dark soy sauce
½ teaspoon salt
½ teaspoon freshly ground black pepper
2 teaspoons sesame oil

FOR THE GARNISH
2 teaspoons coarsely chopped spring onions

Soak the noodles in a large bowl of warm water for 15 minutes. When soft, drain and discard the water. Cut into 7.5 cm (3 inch) lengths using scissors or a knife.

Heat a wok or large frying pan until it is very hot. Add the oil and when it is very hot and slightly smoking, add the spring onions and garlic and stir-fry for 15 seconds. Add the meat and stir-fry it for 8 minutes or until it is cooked. Add all the sauce ingredients except the sesame oil and cook over a gentle heat for about 5 minutes. Now add the drained noodles and sesame oil and cook for a further 5 minutes or until most of the liquid has evaporated. Ladle the noodles into individual bowls, garnish with the spring onions and serve at once.

spicy sichuan noodles

This is a typical Sichuan dish. Although it is spicy and pungent, it is nevertheless popular throughout China, especially in the north. Such noodle dishes – *xiao chi*, or 'small eats' – are found in hole-in-the-wall restaurants, food stalls, and other commercial spots offering snacks. There are many versions of the dish and they are all easy to make, tasty and quite filling. This is my version of this delightful noodle dish.

Region: Sichuan
Method: Stir-frying

Serves 4

225 g (8 oz) minced fatty pork
1 tablespoon dark soy sauce
2 teaspoons Shaoxing rice wine or dry sherry
1 teaspoon salt
½ teaspoon freshly ground black pepper
450 g (1 lb) dried or fresh Chinese egg noodles
1 tablespoon sesame oil
2 tablespoons groundnut (peanut) oil
2 tablespoons finely chopped garlic
2 tablespoons finely chopped fresh ginger
5 tablespoons finely chopped spring onions
2 tablespoons sesame paste or smooth peanut butter
2 tablespoons dark soy sauce
2 teaspoons light soy sauce
2 teaspoons chilli bean sauce
2 tablespoons Chilli Oil (page 23)
1 teaspoon salt
1 teaspoon freshly ground black pepper
250 ml (8 fl oz) Chicken Stock (page 59)

FOR THE GARNISH
2 teaspoons Sichuan peppercorns, roasted and freshly ground (page 35)

Combine the pork, soy sauce, Shaoxing rice wine or dry sherry, salt and pepper in a bowl and mix well. Allow it to marinate for 20 minutes.

Cook the noodles by boiling them for 3 to 5 minutes in a pan of boiling water. Drain and plunge them into cold water. Drain thoroughly and toss in the sesame oil. (They can be kept in this state, if tightly covered with cling film, for up to 2 hours in the refrigerator.)

Heat a wok or large frying pan until it is very hot. Add the oil and when it is very hot and slightly smoking, add the garlic, ginger and spring onions and stir-fry for 30 seconds. Then add the pork mixture and continue to stir-fry until the pork loses its pink colour. Add the rest of the ingredients except the Sichuan peppercorns and cook for 2 minutes. Now add the noodles, mixing well. Turn the noodles on to a warm serving platter, garnish with the peppercorns and serve at once.

dumplings, buns and pancakes

Many types of flour are used in China to make dough for buns, pancakes and dumplings. Rice flour, especially that made from glutinous rice, is particularly favoured for desserts and pastries. I have used two types of flour in the recipes in this book – neither Chinese – but both very satisfactory, easy to handle and easy to obtain.

Plain white flour Plain white wheat flour is a soft flour which is ideal for making Chinese pancakes. It contains relatively little gluten and can be quickly mixed and rolled out. Wholewheat flour is not suitable for Chinese cookery.

Self-raising flour This is not at all Chinese but I find it works well for buns and dumplings and it is easier and quicker to use since it avoids the need for yeast. (Of course your buns will be slightly heavier than the authentic Chinese ones.)

potsticker dumplings

This is a popular and rather substantial snack from northern China where, during the harsh cold winter, the dumplings are often kept frozen outside until they are needed. At Chinese New Year whole families gather round and stuff the dumplings together. The dumplings can be shallow-fried, boiled or steamed, but I find shallow-frying to be the tastiest way of cooking them. Shallow-fried dumplings are called potstickers because once they have been fried they are covered with liquid and cooked until they literally stick to the pan. They should be crispy on the bottom, soft on the top, and juicy inside. A dipping sauce made from Chilli Oil (page 23), vinegar and soy sauce is generally served with the potstickers. Potsticker dumplings can be prepared in advance and then frozen, uncooked. If you do this you don't need to thaw them before cooking them, but you will need to cook them for a little longer.

Region: Beijing
Method: Shallow-frying

Makes about 18 dumplings

275 g (10 oz) plain flour
250 ml (8 fl oz) very hot water

FOR THE STUFFING
100 g (4 oz) minced fatty pork
85 g (3 oz) Chinese leaves or spinach, finely chopped
1 teaspoon finely chopped fresh ginger
1/2 tablespoon Shaoxing rice wine or dry sherry
1/2 tablespoon dark soy sauce
1/2 teaspoon light soy sauce
1/2 teaspoon salt
1/4 teaspoon freshly ground black pepper
1 1/2 tablespoons finely chopped spring onions
1 teaspoon sesame oil
1/2 teaspoon sugar
1 tablespoon cold Chicken Stock (page 59) or water

First make the dough. Put the flour into a large bowl and stir the hot water gradually into it, mixing it all the time with a fork or with chopsticks until most of the water is incorporated. Add more water if the mixture seems dry. Then remove the mixture from the bowl and knead it with your hands, dusting the dough with a little flour if it is sticky and continue kneading until it is smooth. This should take about 8 minutes. Put the dough back into the bowl, cover it with a clean damp towel and let it rest for about 20 minutes. While the dough is resting, combine the stuffing ingredients in a large bowl and mix them together thoroughly.

After the resting period, take the dough out of the bowl and knead it again for about 5 minutes, dusting with a little flour if it is sticky. Once the dough is smooth, form it into a roll about 23 cm (9 inches) long and about 2.5 cm (1 inch) in diameter. Take a knife and cut the roll into 18 equal segments.

Roll each of the dough segments into a small ball. Then roll each ball into a small, round, flat 'pancake' about 6 cm (2½ inches) in diameter. Arrange the round skins on a lightly floured tray and cover them with a damp kitchen towel to prevent them from drying out until you are ready to use them.

1 tablespoon groundnut (peanut) oil

75 ml (2½ fl oz) water

Put about 2 teaspoons of filling in the centre of each 'pancake' and moisten the edges with water. Then fold the dough in half and pinch together with your fingers. Pleat around the edge, pinching to seal well. (The dumpling should look like a small Cornish pasty with a flat base and a rounded top.) Transfer the finished dumpling to the floured tray and keep it covered until you have stuffed all the dumplings in this way.

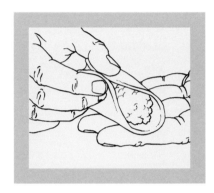
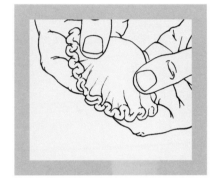

Heat a large frying pan (preferably a non-stick pan) until it is very hot. Add 1 tablespoon of oil, or more if necessary, and place the dumplings flat-side down into the pan. Turn down the heat and cook for about 2 minutes until they are lightly browned. Add the water, cover the pan tightly and simmer gently for about 12 minutes or until most of the liquid is absorbed. (Check the water half-way through and add more if necessary.) Uncover the pan and continue to cook for a further 2 minutes. Remove the dumplings and serve.

Provide each person with three small bowls each containing some Chinese white rice vinegar, Chilli oil (page 23), and light soy sauce. The idea is to concoct your own dipping sauce by mixing these three ingredients exactly to your taste.

steamed buns

Steamed buns are popular throughout China. Being steamed, they have no crust. Their texture is soft and light, fluffy yet firm. They make a pleasing foil for savoury dishes. In the south they are often stuffed with savoury meats or sweet bean paste and served as dim sum snacks. In the north and west they are served with Smoked Tea Duck or Crispy Sichuan Duck (page 144). Following the Chinese tradition, here I use plain flour and yeast to make these buns. Steamed buns re-heat well and can be frozen and, once thawed, re-steamed. They make a satisfying alternative to rice.

Regions: All
Method: Steaming

Makes about 18 buns

175 ml (6 fl oz) warm water
1 x 7 g package dried yeast
1 tablespoon sugar
2 tablespoons groundnut (peanut) oil
375 g (13 oz) plain flour

Parchment or greaseproof paper

Combine the warm water and yeast. Allow it to sit in a very warm place or turned off oven for 2 minutes. The mixture should be slightly foamy. Add the sugar and groundnut oil. Now combine the yeast mixture with the flour in a large bowl or alternatively, you can mix this in a food processor. Continue to mix until the mixture forms a smooth dough. Meanwhile, cut the sheets of parchment or greaseproof paper into 18 pieces, 6 cm (2½ inches) square.

Take the dough out of the bowl and knead it for a few minutes on a floured board. If it is still sticky, dust lightly with a few tablespoons of flour. Then form it into a roll about 46 cm (18 inches) long and about 5 cm (2 inches) in diameter. Take a sharp knife and cut the roll into equal segments. There should be about 18 pieces. Take a segment of dough and work it in the palm of your hand until it forms a smooth ball. Put the ball on to a paper square. Do the same with all the rest of the pieces and put them, together with their paper bases, on to a heatproof plate. Cover the buns with a large sheet of parchment or greaseproof paper and then a damp tea-towel and let it rest for about 30 minutes in a warm place or a turned off oven. After this period the buns should have doubled in size.

Next set up a steamer or put a rack into a wok or deep pan and fill it with 5 cm (2 inches) of water. Bring the water to the boil over a high heat, then turn the heat to very low. Now carefully lower one plate of buns into the steamer or on to the rack. Turn the heat to low and cover the wok or pan tightly. Steam gently over low heat for 20 minutes.

The steamed buns are now ready to be served with Crispy Sichuan Duck or Peking Duck. Alternatively you can let them cool and then pack them into a plastic bag and freeze them. Be sure to thaw them completely before re-heating. The best way of re-heating them is by resteaming, as above, for 10 to 15 minutes, until they are thoroughly hot.

chinese pancakes

These pancakes are the classic accompaniment to Peking Duck (page 142-3) and reflect the northern Chinese use of wheat instead of rice. The pancakes are easy to make once you get the knack, which comes with practice. The unusual method of rolling 'double' pancakes is designed to ensure thin, moist pancakes with less risk of overcooking them. Since they can be frozen it is possible to make them weeks ahead. They can also be used with other dishes, such as Stir-fried Minced Pork (page 84) or instead of the lettuce leaves in Rainbow Beef in Lettuce Leaves (page 100-1).

Region: Beijing
Method: Frying

Makes 18 pancakes

275 g (10 oz) plain flour
250 ml (8 fl oz) very hot water
2 tablespoons sesame oil

Put the flour into a large bowl. Stir the hot water gradually into the flour, mixing all the time with chopsticks or a fork until the water is fully incorporated. Add more water if the mixture seems dry. Then remove the mixture from the bowl and knead it with your hand until it is smooth. This should take about 8 minutes. Put the dough back into the bowl, cover it with a clean, damp towel and let it rest for about 30 minutes.

After the resting period take the dough out of the bowl and knead it again for about 5 minutes, dusting with a little flour if it is sticky. Once the dough is smooth, form it into a roll about 46 cm (18 inches) long and cut the roll into 18 equal segments. Roll each into a ball.

Take two of the dough balls. Dip one side of one ball into the sesame oil and place the oiled side on top of the other ball. Take a rolling pin, and roll the two simultaneously into a circle about 15 cm (6 inches) in diameter. It is important to do this because the resulting dough will remain moist inside and you will be able to roll them thinner but avoid the risk of overcooking them later.

Heat a frying pan or wok over a very low flame. Put the double pancake into the wok or pan and cook it until it has dried on one side. Flip it over and cook the other side. Remove from the pan, peel the 2 pancakes apart and set them aside. Repeat until all have been cooked.

Steam the pancakes to re-heat them, or alternatively you could wrap them tightly in a double sheet of foil and put them into a pan containing 2.5 cm (1 inch) of boiling water. Cover the pan, turn the heat down very low and simmer until they are re-heated. Don't be tempted to reheat them in the oven as this will dry them out. If you want to freeze the cooked pancakes, wrap them tightly in cling film first. When using pancakes which have been frozen, let them thaw in the refrigerator first before re-heating.

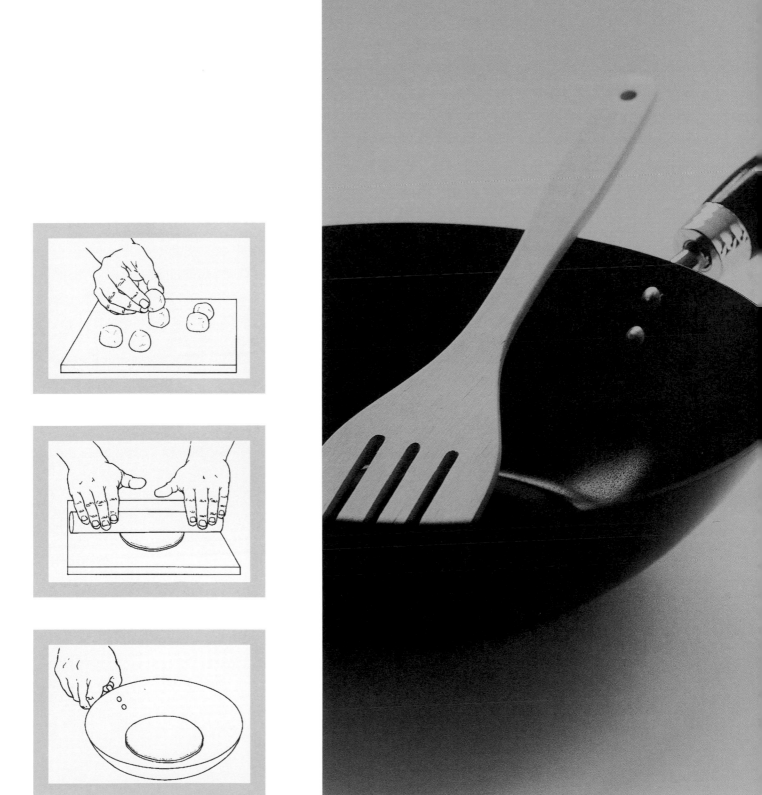

There is an enormous variety of Chinese savoury and sweet snacks which are eaten between meals and during banquets. Such treats have been enjoyed by the Chinese for hundreds of years. Originally they were consumed only by members of the Imperial household whose chefs concocted savoury delicacies such as minced pheasant dumplings and sweet ones made from steamed milk and sweet bean sauce. Over the centuries these and many less expensive versions, have found their way into the diet of the ordinary Chinese. By 1900, Cantonese restaurants were the acknowledged masters of this speciality. Appropriately, the Cantonese term for such snacks is *dim sum*, which literally means 'eating snacks for pleasures' or 'order what you fancy'. Today, Hong Kong's and southern China's Cantonese restaurants are some of the best places to enjoy *dim sum* because there, the range of snacks is both wide and adventurous. In northern China, these types of snacks are known as *dian xin*, a mandarin form of *dim sum*, the name referring more to sweet dessert snacks than to the savoury ones of the south.

Dim sum are eaten between mid-morning and late afternoon and most usually as a light, inexpensive lunch. Many *dim sum* restaurants in Hong Kong, as well as ones in Canton, are enormous places, consisting of a number of cavernous rooms which are jam-packed at lunchtime as family and friends meet to gossip or discuss business. The convivial noise can be deafening.

In many restaurants no menu is presented. Diners are provided with a pot of tea, cups, small plates and chopsticks. Waiters and waitresses circulate around the huge rooms pushing trollies containing various *dim sum*. Diners stop the trollies and select whatever appeals to them, sometimes accumulating as many as three dozen different small dishes. Tea is drunk throughout the meal, which is why *dim sum* is sometimes referred to as *yam cha* – the Cantonese words for drinking tea. At the end of the meal the bill is calculated by counting up the number of small plates or steamers on the table. It is all great fun.

snacks and sweets

Dim sum come in all flavours and can be hot, sour, sweet or spicy. They are prepared in many different ways, although some of the most popular are cooked in attractive little round bamboo steamers which are then transported in stacks on *dim sum* trolleys.

Some of the most popular dim sum *snacks are*:

Spring roll (*chun guen*): the familiar deep-fried pastry filled with vegetables and meat.

Barbecued pork bun (*cha siu bao*): steamed or baked buns filled with delicious pieces of roasted pork.

Pork dumplings (*siu mai*): dumplings filled with minced pork and steamed.

Steamed spareribs (*pai gwat*): spareribs cut into short pieces and steamed with black bean sauce.

Prawn or shrimp dumplings (*har gau*): delicate light dumplings filled with prawn and pork, and steamed.

Fried taro dumplings (*woo kok*): mashed taro root filled with pork and deep-fried.

There are dozens of other simple and exotic varieties. In this chapter I have included recipes for some of the simpler *dim sum* which can be successfully made at home. If you have never tried *dim sum*, do seek out a Chinese restaurant which serves them. You will find not every Chinese restaurant offers them as they require the expertise of several *dim sum* chefs.

As for desserts, I knew nothing of them as a child. In authentic Chinese tradition my mother served fresh fruit at the end of a family meal, usually oranges cut into wedges. Puddings, ice-cream and sweets were unknown to me until I ventured out into the non-Chinese world. Of course, Chinese desserts do exist although they are not a feature of the cuisine as they are in the West and are often served only at banquets or on special occasions. They usually come in the form of cloyingly sugared rice pudding or very rich moon cake snacks, but I find most of them overpoweringly sweet. I have therefore included recipes for some of the simpler and less sickly sweet Chinese desserts. Of course, one may serve European-style desserts at the end of a Chinese meal, but my experience is that the subtle and complex tastes and flavours of Chinese dishes are best appreciated when followed by a simple dessert of refreshing fresh fruit.

prawn crackers

I have always had a fondness for crispy snacks, especially prawn crackers. They are made from a combination of prawn meat, starch, salt and sometimes, sugar which is pounded into a paste and then dried into hard, round crisps. They are sold in many supermarkets and Chinese grocers and need only to be deep-fried. They are marvellous with drinks or you may use them as a colourful and crispy garnish for Chinese dishes. They come in many different shapes and colours. I prefer the natural pink-coloured ones.

Regions: Fujian and Canton
Method: Deep-frying

Serves 4

600 ml (1 pint) groundnut (peanut) or vegetable oil
125 g (4 oz) dried prawn crackers

Heat a wok or large frying pan until it is very hot. Add the oil and when it is very hot and slightly smoking, drop one prawn cracker in the oil. It should puff up and float to the top immediately.

When the oil is hot, drop a handful of the crackers in and scoop them out immediately with a slotted spoon. Drain on kitchen paper and repeat.

The oil can be saved and used with fish or prawn dishes. Do not use the oil for any other dishes.

cold marinated peanuts

Peanuts were only introduced into China in the sixteenth century, but they quickly won an important place in Chinese agriculture. The peanut plant replenishes the soil as it grows and the nuts themselves are a nutritious supplement to the diet both in their natural form and as groundnut (peanut) oil. This dish may be made a day or two in advance and can be served cold or at room temperature.

Region: Beijing
Method: Marinating

Serves 6 to 8

450 g (1 lb) raw peanuts, shelled
3 tablespoons light soy sauce
3 tablespoons dark soy sauce
1 tablespoon finely chopped garlic
2 teaspoons salt
1 teaspoon freshly ground black pepper
150 ml (5 fl oz) Chinese white rice vinegar or cider vinegar
85 ml (3 fl oz) Shaoxing rice wine or dry sherry

First blanch the peanuts by immersing them in a pan of boiling water for about 2 minutes. Drain them, let them cool and rub the skins off between your fingers.

Put the blanched peanuts in a bowl. Mix in all the other ingredients. Let the peanuts marinate in this mixture for at least 2 or 3 hours, stirring from time to time to ensure an even distribution of the marinade. Most of it will be absorbed by the peanuts. Serve with pickled vegetables (page 35) as snacks or appetizers. We Chinese eat them one by one using chopsticks!

steamed spareribs with black beans

This is a popular *dim sum* snack. The spareribs are steamed until the meat is so tender it melts in your mouth. The steaming process ensures that the meat is permeated by the pungent flavour and aroma of the black beans.

Region: Canton
Method: Steaming

Serves 4 (as snack or starter)

750 g (1½ lb) pork spareribs
2 teaspoons salt
120 ml (4 fl oz) Chicken Stock (page 59)
1½ tablespoons light soy sauce
2 teaspoons dark soy sauce
2 teaspoons sesame oil
1 tablespoon finely chopped fresh ginger
3 tablespoons black beans, rinsed and coarsely chopped
2 tablespoons finely chopped garlic
2 tablespoons fresh red or green chillies, de-seeded and coarsely chopped
1 teaspoon salt
1 teaspoon freshly ground black pepper
2 teaspoons sugar
1½ tablespoons Shaoxing rice wine or dry sherry

If possible, ask your butcher to cut the spareribs into individual ribs and then into 5 cm (2 inch) segments. Otherwise you can do this yourself with a Chinese cleaver or a sharp, heavy knife (see page 42). Rub them with salt and let them sit in a bowl for about 20 to 25 minutes. Fill a large saucepan with water and bring it to the boil. Turn the heat to low, add the spareribs and simmer them for 10 minutes. Drain them and discard the water.

Mix the other ingredients together in a large bowl and stir in the spareribs, coating them well with the mixture. Transfer to a deep plate or dish.

Next set up a steamer or put a rack into a wok or deep pan and fill it with 5 cm (2 inches) of water. Bring the water to the boil over a high heat. Carefully lower the dish with the spareribs into the steamer or on to the rack. Turn the heat to low and cover the wok or pan tightly. Steam gently for 1 hour or until the spareribs are very tender. Remember to keep a careful watch on the water level, and top it up with boiling water when necessary. Skim off any surface fat and serve.

You can make this dish in advance and re-heat the ribs by steaming for 20 minutes or until they are hot.

sesame prawn toast

This is a savoury snack often served in *dim sum* restaurants outside China. Its origins are rather obscure, but I suspect it is a variation on the prawn paste used widely in southern China for stuffings or for deep-frying into crispy balls. The paste can be kept, covered, in the fridge for several hours and it is best to use day-old bread because it absorbs less oil. If the bread is fresh, place it in a warm oven to dry out.

Region: Fujian and Canton
Method: Deep-frying

Makes about 30 pieces

10 slices bread, very thinly sliced

3 tablespoons white sesame seeds

450 ml (15 fl oz) groundnut (peanut) oil
(see Deep-fat fryers, page 40)

FOR THE PRAWN PASTE MIXTURE

100 g (4 oz) water chestnuts, peeled if
fresh, rinsed if canned (page 37)

450 g (1 lb) uncooked prawns, peeled and
finely chopped

100 g (4 oz) minced pork

1 teaspoon salt

½ teaspoon freshly ground white pepper

1 egg white

2 tablespoons finely chopped spring
onions, white part only

1 tablespoon finely chopped fresh ginger

2 teaspoons light soy sauce

2 teaspoons sesame oil

2 teaspoons sugar

Finely chop the water chestnuts and place in a bowl with the rest of the ingredients for the prawn paste and mix well until it is a spreading consistency. (You could do this in a food processor.)

Remove the crusts and cut the bread into rectangles about 7.5 x 2.5 cm (3 x 1 inch). Spread the prawn paste onto the pieces of bread. It should form a mound about 3 mm (⅛ inch) deep on each, although you can spread it more thinly if you prefer. Sprinkle the toasts with the sesame seeds.

Heat the oil in a deep-fat fryer or wok to a moderate heat. Deep-fry several prawn toasts at a time, paste-side down, for 2 to 3 minutes. Then turn them over and deep-fry for about 2 minutes or until they are golden brown. Remove with a slotted spoon, drain on kitchen paper. (You will have to do this in several batches.) Serve at once.

spring rolls

Spring rolls are among the best-known Chinese snacks. They are not difficult to make and are a perfect starter for any meal. Spring rolls should be crisp, light and delicate. Avoid the greasy, bulky imitations which are sometimes called egg rolls. The skins for spring rolls can be obtained fresh or frozen from Chinese grocers. Be sure to let them thaw thoroughly if they are frozen.

These nutritious snacks, as their name suggests, symbolize and commemorate the coming of the spring season. They are one of the traditional foods eaten in China on New Year's Eve which, by the Chinese lunar calendar, marks the end of the winter season; such foods as spring rolls and *jiaozi* (a popular northern Chinese dumpling) are always at hand then for family and for visitors.

But spring rolls are also enjoyed all year round. And wrappers, now commercially available, make them even easier to make. There are two types of wrappers: the Cantonese style which is a smooth, heavier noodle-type dough, and the Shanghai style which is transparent, lighter and more like rice paper. I prefer the Shanghai type.

Regions: Shanghai and Canton
Method: Deep-frying

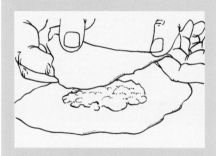

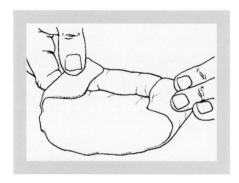

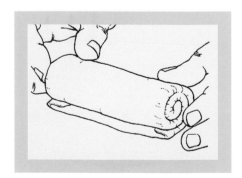

Makes about 15 to 18 spring rolls

1 packet spring roll skins, preferably the
Shanghai type

25 g (1 oz) Chinese black mushrooms

100 g (4 oz) uncooked prawns, peeled and
very finely chopped

100 g (4 oz) minced pork

1 teaspoon light soy sauce

1 teaspoon Shaoxing rice wine or
dry sherry

½ teaspoon cornflour

½ teaspoon sesame oil

½ teaspoon salt

¼ teaspoon freshly ground black pepper

1½ tablespoons groundnut (peanut) oil

2 tablespoons finely chopped garlic

1 tablespoon finely chopped fresh ginger

1½ tablespoons light soy sauce

1 tablespoon Shaoxing rice wine or
dry sherry

3 tablespoons finely chopped spring onion

1 teaspoon salt

1 teaspoon freshly ground black pepper

250 g (9 oz) Chinese leaves,
finely shredded

FOR THE EGG SEAL

1 egg, beaten

FOR DEEP-FRYING

1.2 litres (2 pints) groundnut (peanut) oil

FOR THE DIPPING SAUCE

Sweet and Sour Sauce (page 39)

If the spring roll skins are frozen, make sure they are thawed thoroughly. Soak the mushrooms in warm water for 20 minutes. Then drain them and squeeze out the excess liquid. Remove and discard the stems and finely shred the caps.

Combine the prawns and pork with the soy sauce, Shaoxing rice wine or dry sherry, cornflour, sesame oil, salt and pepper in a small bowl.

Heat a wok or large frying pan until it is very hot. Add the oil and when it is very hot and slightly smoking, add the garlic and ginger and stir-fry for 20 seconds. Then add the rest of the ingredients, the prawn mixture and mushrooms and stir-fry for 5 minutes. Place the mixture in a colander to drain and allow it to cool thoroughly.

Place 3 to 4 tablespoons of filling near the corner of each spring roll skin, fold in each side and roll up tightly. Use the beaten egg mixture to seal the open end by brushing a small amount on the edge. Then press the edge on to the roll. You should have a roll about 10 cm (4 inches) long, a little like an over-sized cigar.

Wash the wok or pan and re-heat it until it is very hot. Add the oil for deep-frying and when it is hot and slightly smoking, gently drop in as many spring rolls as will fit easily in one layer. Carefully fry them for about 4 minutes until the spring rolls are golden brown on the outside and cooked inside. Adjust the heat as necessary. Take the spring rolls out with a slotted spoon and drain on kitchen paper. (You will have to do this in several batches.) Serve them at once, with the sauce on the side for dipping.

marbled tea eggs

This unique method of cooking eggs in spiced tea derives its name from the marbled texture and web of cracks which appear on the surface of the eggs when they are shelled. Traditionally, tea eggs are served cold and they make a wonderful and easy garnish for cold platters. Not only are they delicious but they are also beautiful to look at. Once the eggs have cooled they can be kept in the tea liquid and stored in the refrigerator for up to 2 days. Eggs are rarely eaten as a plain dish by themselves in Chinese cuisine. However, they do lend themselves to imaginative combinations. These marbled eggs are one such unusual and delicious treat. Traditionally, these eggs are served cold as garnishes for cold platters. They are best left overnight in the liquid, so that the flavours can permeate the eggs. They are also wonderful to take along on picnics.

Regions: All
Method: Simmering

Serves 4 to 6 as starter

6 eggs, at room temperature
1.75 litres (3 pints) water

FOR THE TEA MIXTURE
6 tablespoons black tea, preferably Chinese
3 tablespoons dark soy sauce
1½ tablespoons light soy sauce
1 tablespoon five-spice powder
2 teaspoons Sichuan peppercorn, roasted and freshly ground (page 35)
2 teaspoons salt
3 Chinese cinnamon bark or cinnamon sticks
3 whole star anise
900 ml (1½ pints) water

Bring the water to the boil in a large pan and cook the eggs for 5 minutes. Remove the eggs and immediately plunge them in cold water, then gently crack the shells with a large spoon under cold running water until the entire shell is a network of cracks. Let them sit in the cold running water for at least 10 minutes. Drain.

Bring the tea-liquid mixture to a simmer in the pan and return the cracked eggs. Simmer them in this mixture for 10 minutes, making sure the liquid covers the eggs completely. Remove the pan from the heat and let it cool with the eggs left in the liquid.

Leave the cooked eggs in the liquid overnight in the refrigerator. When you are ready to serve the eggs, remove them from the cooled liquid and gently peel off the cracked shells. You should have a beautiful marble-like web on each hard-boiled egg. Serve them cut in half or quarters – marbled-side up – as a snack with other cold dishes or use them as garnish on cold platters. They are also a glamorous dish to take on a picnic.

fried wonton

Region: Canton
Method: Deep-frying

Prosaic wontons become savoury treats when dipped in a sweet and sour sauce. They make a great snack or starter for any meal. The sweet and sour sauce can be made a day in advance, refrigerated, and brought to room temperature before serving. Although I have rarely seen fried wonton in China, they are common in Chinese restaurants in the West. This is perhaps because they are easily prepared and their crisp, dry texture goes well with drinks. Wonton skins can be bought fresh or frozen from Chinese grocers. (Be sure to thaw them thoroughly if they are frozen.)

Serves 6

350 g (12 oz) uncooked prawns, peeled and coarsely chopped

100 g (4 oz) minced pork

2 teaspoons salt

1 teaspoon freshly ground black pepper

4 tablespoons finely chopped spring onions

2 teaspoons Shaoxing rice wine or dry sherry

1 teaspoon sugar

2 teaspoons sesame oil

1 egg white, lightly beaten

225 g (8 oz) wonton skins

FOR THE SWEET AND SOUR DIPPING SAUCE

150 ml (5 fl oz) water

2 tablespoons sugar

3 tablespoons Chinese white rice vinegar or cider vinegar

3 tablespoons tomato purée or tomato ketchup

1 teaspoon salt

1/2 teaspoon freshly ground white pepper

1 teaspoon cornflour blended with 2 teaspoons water

FOR DEEP-FRYING

600 ml (1 pint) groundnut (peanut) or vegetable oil

Put the prawns and pork in a large bowl, add the salt and pepper and mix well. Then add the rest of the ingredients and stir them well into the mixture. Wrap the bowl with cling film and chill it for at least 20 minutes.

In a small pan, combine all the ingredients for the sweet and sour sauce, except the cornflour mixture. Bring this mixture to a boil, stir in the cornflour mixture and cook for 1 minute. Allow to cool and set aside.

When you are ready to stuff the wontons, put 1 tablespoon of the filling in the centre of the first wonton skin. Dampen the edges with a little water and bring up the sides of the skin around the filling. Pinch the edges together at the top so that the wonton is sealed, it should look like a small filled bag.

Heat a wok or large frying pan until it is very hot. Add the oil and when it is very hot and slightly smoking, add a handful of wontons and deep-fry for 3 minutes until golden and crispy. If the oil gets too hot, turn it down slightly. Drain them well on kitchen paper. Continue to fry the wontons until they are all prepared then serve them immediately with the sweet and sour sauce.

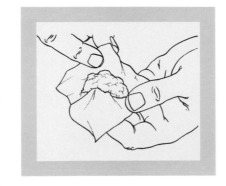 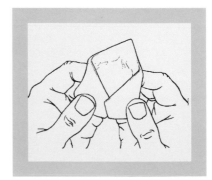

steamed open dumplings

This is a favourite snack in many *dim sum* teahouses throughout southern China. It is merely a wonton or egg dough dumpling which is filled and steamed instead of being poached and deep-fried. The steamed dumpling has a character wholly different from pan-fried or boiled dumplings. The texture and taste of the steamed dumpling filling is more pronounced, yet delicate and subtle at the same time. The skin, once steamed, retains a slightly chewy texture. Wonton skins can bc obtained fresh or frozen from Chinese grocers. This dish can be made in advance and reheated by steaming when you are ready to serve it.

Region: Canton
Method: Steaming

Serves 4 to 6

1 packet wonton skins (about 40 skins)

FOR THE FILLING
100 g (4 oz) water chestnuts, peeled if fresh, rinsed if canned (page 37)
350 g (12 oz) minced pork
100 g (4 oz) uncooked prawns, peeled and coarsely chopped
2 tablespoons Parma ham or lean smoked bacon, finely chopped
1 tablespoon light soy sauce
1 teaspoon dark soy sauce
1 tablespoon Shaoxing rice wine or dry sherry
3 tablespoons finely chopped spring onions
2 teaspoons finely chapped fresh ginger
2 teaspoons sesame oil
1 egg white, beaten
1 teaspoon salt
1/2 teaspoon freshly ground black pepper
2 teaspoons sugar

Start by preparing the filling. Finely chop the water chestnuts. Put them into a bowl with the rest of the filling ingredients and mix well together.

Place a portion of filling on to each wonton skin. Bring up the sides and press them around the filling mixture. Tap the dumpling on the bottom to make a flat base. The top should be wide open, exposing the meat filling.

Set up a steamer or put a rack inside a wok or large, deep pan. Pour in about 5 cm (2 inches) of water and bring it to the boil. Put the dumplings on a plate and place this into the steamer or on to the rack.

Cover the pan tightly, turn the heat low, and steam gently for about 20 minutes. (You may have to do this in several batches.) Serve the dumplings hot with your choice of dipping sauce (see pages 38-9). Keep the first batch warm by covering them with foil and place them in a warm but turned-off oven until all the dumplings are ready to serve.

stuffed peppers

Red or green peppers are especially delicious when they are stuffed and these snacks are featured on many *dim sum* menus in southern China. Easy to make, they also re-heat well. The quick pan-frying before serving gives the snacks a crusty, brownish top. They make an attractive dish for a light lunch.

Regions: Fujian and Canton
Methods: Steaming and shallow-frying

Serves 6 as a snack or starter

750 g–1 kg (1¹⁄₂ lb) red, yellow or green peppers or a mixture of the three

3 tablespoons cornflower

1¹⁄₂ tablespoons groundnut (peanut) oil

FOR THE FILLING

100 g (4 oz) water chestnuts, peeled if fresh, rinsed if canned (page 37)

225 g (8 oz) uncooked prawns, peeled and coarsely chopped

225 g (8 oz) minced pork

1 egg white

2 teaspoons cornflour

2 teaspoons salt

1 teaspoon freshly ground black pepper

1¹⁄₂ tablespoons light soy sauce

2 teaspoons dark soy sauce

2 teaspoons sesame oil

1 tablespoon Shaoxing rice wine or dry sherry

1 teaspoon sugar

3 tablespoons finely chopped spring onions

Halve the peppers and remove the seeds and pulp. Next prepare the filling. Finely chop the water chestnuts. Put the water chestnuts and prawns into a bowl with the rest of the filling ingredients and mix them well together. Dust the pepper halves with cornflour and stuff them with the filling. Cut each pepper half into 2 or 4 chunks and arrange them on a heatproof plate.

Next set up a steamer or put a rack into a wok or deep pan and fill it with 5 cm (2 inches) of water. Bring the water to the boil over a high heat. Carefully lower the plate into the steamer or on to the rack. Turn the heat to low and cover the wok or pan tightly. Steam gently for 12 minutes. (You may have to do this in two batches.) The snacks may be prepared in advance up to this point.

When you are ready to serve the peppers, heat a wok or large frying-pan until it is very hot. Add the oil and when it is very hot and slightly smoking, fry the peppers, stuffing side down, until they are lightly browned and heated enough. Serve at once.

caramel walnuts

The first time I had this delicious snack was at a Beijing-style restaurant in Hong Kong and I was determined to learn how to make them. They are surprisingly easy. The shelled walnuts must be blanched first to rid them of any bitterness. They are then rolled in sugar, left to dry for several hours, then deep-fried to caramelize the sugar coating. Finally they are rolled in sesame seeds. The result is a classic contrast of tastes and textures. They can be served cold or hot and are perfect with drinks.

Region: Beijing
Method: Deep-frying

Serves 4

225 g (8 oz) walnuts, shelled halves
100 g (4 oz) sugar
450 ml (15 fl oz) groundnut (peanut) oil
(see Deep-fat fryers, page 42)
3 tablespoons sesame seeds

Bring a pan of water to the boil. Add the walnuts and cook for about 10 minutes to blanch them. Drain the nuts in a colander or sieve. Pat dry with kitchen paper and spread them on a baking tray. Sprinkle the sugar over the walnuts and roll them around in the sugar to cover them completely. Place the tray in a cool draughty place. Let them dry for at least 2 hours, preferably overnight.

Heat the oil in a deep-fat fryer or wok to a moderate heat. Fry a batch of the walnuts for about 2 minutes or until the sugar melts and the walnuts turn golden. (Watch the heat to prevent burning.) Remove the walnuts from the oil with a slotted spoon or strainer. Sprinkle them with some of the sesame seeds and lay them on a cake rack to cool. (Do not drain them on kitchen paper as the sugar will stick when it dries.) Deep-fry and drain the rest of the walnuts in the same way. Once cooled, the caramel walnuts can be kept in a sealed glass jar for about 2 weeks. Serve them warm or cold.

almond jelly with fresh oranges

This is my version of a classic Chinese dessert. In the original version, agar-agar (a type of seaweed) is used instead of gelatine, ground almond juice is used instead of almond essence, and a sugar syrup is served with it instead of orange juice. The original version involves a long and laborious process which requires obscure ingredients. I think this recipe, although it departs from the original, is nevertheless a delicious and refreshing variation.

Region: Canton

Serves 4

1 tablespoon gelatine
300 ml (10 fl oz) water
300 ml (10 fl oz) milk
5 tablespoons sugar
1½ teaspoons almond essence
2 oranges
300 ml (10 fl oz) fresh orange juice

Put the gelatine into a small bowl. Add half the water to dissolve the gelatine and bring the other half to a boil in a small pan. Pour the hot water into the gelatine and cold water and stir until the gelatine has completely dissolved. Combine this with the milk, sugar and almond essence in a large bowl. Pour the mixture into a pyrex dish or square baking tin about 18 cm (7 inches) square and 4 cm (1½ inches) deep. Put it in the refrigerator for about 2 hours or until it has completely set.

Cut the peel and white pith from the oranges and cut them into segments. When the almond jelly is ready, cut it into 2.5 cm (1 inch) cubes. Put some orange segments into individual bowls. Add some almond jelly cubes and then pour a little orange juice over each portion.

fresh fruit

Our family meals usually ended with a plate of fresh oranges sliced into wedges. Occasionally during the summer we had special treats such as wedges of watermelon or honeydew melon instead. It has always struck me how appropriate simple fresh fruits are after a Chinese meal. They are invariably refreshing, cleansing the palate and adding a final sweet note to the end of a meal. I think it is probably the most pleasing and sensible dessert for a Chinese or any other meal — and it is so easy!

fruit compote

Region: Canton

Southern China is fortunate in having a bountiful supply of fruits, some of which are very exotic such as lychees, loquats and kumquats. Lychees were so sought after by the Imperial Court that, once picked, they were rushed to the Court by special fast horse relays. Some of these special fruits are now available in tins. They are acceptable but should be served without their overly sweet syrup. A mixed compote of fresh and tinned fruits is a delicious and most appropriate dessert for any dinner party.

Serves 4 to 6

2 apples
2 oranges
175 g (6 oz) cantaloupe melon
400 g (14 oz) tinned lychees, drained

Using a sharp knife, peel, core and slice the apples into thin wedges. Peel and slice the oranges into segments. Cut the melon in half, scoop out and discard the pulp and seeds. Cut the melon flesh into 2.5 cm (1 inch) cubes. Combine all the fruits together in a large bowl. Mix them gently together. Wrap the bowl tightly in cling film until you are ready to serve the compote.

peaches in honey syrup

Regions: Sichuan and Beijing
Method: Simmering

Any list of the classical fruits of China should begin with the peach, which figures prominently in folklore, traditional religion, literature and popular affection. New exotic varieties were introduced into China from Central Asia during the Tang dynasty (AD 618–907). In this recipe, peaches are poached in a sugar syrup and then the liquid reduced to honey-like consistency. The dish can be served warm or cold and makes a simple, light, sweet dessert.

Serves 4

2 large firm peaches
4 tablespoons Chinese rock sugar or ordinary sugar
150 ml (5 fl oz) water

Bring a pan of water to the boil and quickly blanch the peaches in it for a few seconds. Remove them with a slotted spoon. With a sharp knife, peel the skin off the peaches and split each one in half, discarding the stone.
Combine the sugar and water in a small pan and boil the mixture together until the sugar dissolves. Then add the peach halves and turn the heat down to a low simmer. Simmer the peach mixture for about 15 minutes or until the peaches are tender. Gently remove them with a slotted spoon. Turn the heat to high and reduce the liquid to about half the amount – it should become a sweet syrup. If you are serving the dish hot, pour the liquid over the peaches and serve at once. Otherwise let the liquid cool, pour it over the peaches and chill until you are ready.

steamed pears

Pears are a northern Chinese fruit which are eaten fresh, cooked in soups, deep-fried and are especially delicious when steamed. The steaming process cooks the pears without drying them out. The Chinese traditionally serve this dish hot, but I find it equally good cold.

Region: Beijing
Method: Steaming

Serves 4

4 firm pears
3 tablespoons Chinese rock sugar or ordinary sugar
85 ml (3 fl oz) water
2 Chinese cinnamon bark or cinnamon sticks

Peel the pears and cut them in half. Remove the core and seeds. Combine the sugar and water together in a small pan and boil it until the sugar has completely dissolved. Allow it to cool slightly.

Put the pears, sugar-water and cinnamon together in a heatproof shallow bowl. Next set up a steamer or put a rack into a wok or deep pan and fill it with 5 cm (2 inches) of water. Bring the water to the boil over a high heat. Carefully lower the dish of pears into the steamer or on to the rack. Turn the heat to low and cover the wok or pan tightly. Steam gently for 15 to 25 minutes until the pears are tender. (The cooking time will depend on the ripeness of the pears.)

When the pears are cooked, drain all the liquid and cinnamon stick or bark into a small pan and reduce the liquid to a syrup by boiling it vigorously. Remove and discard the cinnamon stick. Pour the syrup over the pears and serve at once. Alternatively, you can let the mixture cool, cover it with cling film and refrigerate until you are ready to serve it.

toffee apples and bananas

Although apples and bananas are most often associated with southern China, they are eaten as snacks throughout the country. The dish requires some dexterity which will come with experience. Try it out yourself before you attempt it for guests.

Region: Beijing
Method: Deep-frying

Serves 4

2 large firm apples/2 firm bananas

FOR THE BATTER
75 g (3 oz) plain flour
4 tablespoons cornflour
2 teaspoons baking powder
175 ml (6 fl oz) water
1 teaspoon sesame oil

300 ml (10 fl oz) groundnut (peanut) oil (see Deep-fat fryers, page 42)
2 teaspoons sesame oil
175 g (6 oz) sugar
2 tablespoons white sesame seeds

Peel and core the apples and cut each into 8 large thick wedges. Peel the bananas, split them in half lengthways, and cut them into 4 cm (1½ inch) chunks. In a medium-sized bowl, mix the batter ingredients together and set aside.

Combine the groundnut (peanut) oil and 2 teaspoons of sesame oil in a deep-fat fryer or wok and heat until moderately hot. Dip the fruit into the batter mixture using a slotted spoon and drain off any excess batter. Deep-fry for about 2 minutes until golden. Remove with a slotted spoon and drain on kitchen paper. Repeat the process until you have fried all the fruit.

Just before serving, prepare a bowl of iced water filled with ice-cubes. Re-heat the oil to a moderate heat and deep-fry the fruit again for about 2 minutes. Drain on kitchen paper. Put the sugar, sesame seeds and 2 tablespoons of oil from the deep-frying oil into a pan. Heat until the sugar melts and begins to caramelize. (Watch the heat to prevent it from burning.) When the caramel is light brown, add a few pieces of fruit and stir gently to coat them. Take them out and quickly plunge them into the iced water to make the caramel harden. Remove them from the water and serve at once. Repeat with the remaining fruit.

walnut biscuits

Although baking is not a common Chinese method of cooking, biscuits of all kinds are quite popular in the south. The most famous is the almond biscuit, but walnut biscuits are equally delicious. They can be served alone or with fresh fruit.

Region: Canton
Method: Baking

Makes about 12 biscuits

12 walnut halves
50 g (2 oz) lard
100 g (4 oz) plain flour
2 teaspoons baking powder
100 g (4 oz) sugar
2 eggs, beaten

Bring a pan of water to the boil. Add the walnut halves and simmer for about 5 minutes to blanch them. Drain the walnuts in a colander or sieve, then pat dry with kitchen paper and set aside.

Pre-heat the oven to gas mark 6, 200°C (400°F).

In a large bowl, rub the lard into the flour and baking powder until it is well mixed. Next mix in the sugar and half the egg to form a thick paste. Divide the mixture into 12 balls of dough and press them into flattish rounds about 5 cm (2 inches) in diameter. Put them on a non-stick baking tray or brush a baking sheet with 1 teaspoon of oil. Press a walnut half on the top of each biscuit. Using a pastry brush, glaze the tops with the remaining beaten egg. Put them in the oven and bake them for about 20 minutes. Remove the cooked biscuits and set them on a cooling rack. Once cooled, the biscuits can be stored in a tightly covered jar for about a week.

index

v denotes vegetarian recipes
Page numbers in *italic* indicate pictures

almond jelly with fresh oranges 264
apples, toffee, and bananas 268-9, *269*
asparagus, and minced chicken soup 78-9, *79*
aubergines 19-20
    braised spicy **v** 191
    country-style 192

bamboo shoots 20
bamboo steamer in wok 48
bananas, toffee apples and 268-9, *269*
barbecuing 49
bean sauce noodles 232-3, *233*
bean sprouts 20
    cold marinated **v** 198
    and ham soup 68
bean thread noodles 30
    hot *17, 240,* 240-1
beancurd 20, *21*
    braised beancurd casserole family-style
        v 196
    braised with mushrooms **v** 194
    and kidney soup 70
    pork braised with 94
    salt and pepper **v** 197
    spinach with fermented **v** 216
    spinach soup 71
    with vegetables **v** 195
beans
    bean sauce noodles 232-3, *233*
    Chinese long 24
    green *18*
    green, deep-fried **v** 193, *193*
    see also black beans
beef 82
    beef noodle soup 234
    fried rice with 229
    minced with scrambled eggs 108
    in oyster sauce 103
    rainbow beef in lettuce leaves *100,* 100-1
    steamed meatballs 107
    stewed northern-style 102

    stir-fried with ginger 105
    stir-fried with orange 104
    stir-fried pepper beef with mangetout 106,
birds' nest 20
biscuits, walnut 270
bitter melon 21
black beans 21, *21*
    chicken pieccs in black bean sauce 119
    cold peppers with **v** 212, *212*
    crab with black bean sauce 184, *184*
    pork with black bean sauce 83
    steamed salmon with 164-5, *165*
    steamed spareribs with 254
black rice vinegar 37
blanching 46
bok choy 24
    crispy 'seaweed' **v** 207
    stir-fried **v** 206
braised
    beancurd casserole family-style **v** 196
    beancurd with mushrooms **v** 194
    cauliflower with oyster sauce **v** 201
    chicken with leeks 134
    duck 145
    fish 161
    five-spiced red braised pigeons 148-9, *149*
    Peking braised lamb 112
    Peking cabbage in cream sauce **v** 205
    pork belly 99
    prawns 177
    spicy aubergines **v** 191
    three-mushroom braise **v** 213
braising and red-braising 48
broccoli
    cold sesame **v** 200
    fish balls with 166-7, *167*
    stir-fried ginger **v** 199
    stir-fried with hoisin sauce **v** 200
Buddhist casserole **v** *16,* 214-15, *215*
Buddhist-Taoist tradition 16, 188
buns, steamed 246-*7*

cabbage
    Chinese flowering 23, *23, 156*

    Chinese white 24
    Peking *see* Chinese leaves (Peking cabbage)
    and pork soup 73
cai and *fan* 16, 218
Cantonese roast duck 146
caramel walnuts 263
carrot flowers 50
cashew chicken 130
casserole
    Buddhist **v** *16,* 214-15, *215*
    chicken, sausage and rice *226,* 226-7
    lionhead pork meatball 86
caul fat 21
cauliflower, braised with oyster sauce **v** 201
cayenne pepper *see* chilli: powder
chicken 116
    asparagus and minced chicken soup 78-9, *79*
    braised with leeks 134
    cashew 130
    Chinese chicken salad 141
    crispy 140
    on crispy noodles 236
    curried with peppers 121
    curried sweetcorn soup with 64
    drunken chicken 129
    garlic chicken with cucumber 120
    with garlic vinegar sauce *124,* 124-5
    hot spiced 131
    lemon 127
    mango 138-9, *139*
    and mushroom soup 65
    paper-wrapped 132-3, *133*
    pieces in black bean sauce 119
    pork and chicken stock 60
    sausage and rice casserole *226,* 226-7
    shredded with sesame seeds 128
    soy sauce 136
    spicy with peanuts 122
    and spinach soup 61
    steeped 137
    stir-fried chicken shreds 123
    stock 58-9
    twice-cooked 135
    walnut chicken 126

Chicken, duck and game 116-51

chilli
  powder 22
  sauce 32

chillies 22
  bean sauce 32
  chilli oil/dipping sauce 22-3
  chilli pork sparerib 96-7
  fresh chilli flowers 51
  oil, extra hot 38

Chinese
  broccoli 23
  chicken salad 141
  dried mushrooms *28*, 28
  flowering cabbage (choi sum) 23, *23*, *156*
  greens, stir-fried **v** 206
  leaves *see* Chinese leaves (Peking cabbage)
  long beans 24
  okra (silk squash) 35
  pancakes 248-9, *249*
  parsley (coriander) 25, *25*
  sausages 33, *33*
  tea 36, 54
  tree fungus 29
  water spinach 36
  white cabbage *see bok choy*
  white radish (mooli) 24, *25*
  wood ear fungus 29

Chinese cooking 10-17
  Eastern school 12
  how to eat Chinese food 52-3
  Northern school 12
  outside China 14-17
  Southern school 10-11
  Western school 13

Chinese leaves (Peking cabbage) 24
  braised in cream sauce **v** 205
  cabbage and pork soup 73
  Chinese cabbage soup 77
  cold sweet and sour **v** *190*, 202-3, *203*
  in soy sauce **v** 206
  spiced **v** 204

Chinese restaurant syndrome 19

choi sum 23

chopping 46
  board 42

chopsticks 43, 53

chow mein 235

cinnamon sticks or bark 24, *25*

citrus peel 25

cleavers 42

compote, fruit 266

congee, rice 225

coriander (Chinese parsley) 25, *25*

corn oil 30

cornflour 26

country-style aubergine 192

crab 182-3
  with black bean sauce 184
  in egg custard 185
  steamed with ginger vinegar sauce 186
  sweetcorn soup with crabmeat *74*, 74-5

crispy 'seaweed' **v** 207

cucumber
  fans 51
  fried stuffed 209
  garlic chicken with 120
  stir-fried with hot spices **v** 208

curried
  chicken with peppers 121
  sweetcorn soup with chicken 64

deep frying 47-8

deep-fat fryers 42

desserts 252

dicing 45

dim sum 250, 252

dinner parties, suggested menus 55

dipping sauces and mixtures 38-9

doufu *see* beancurd

dried and cured meats 82

dried red chillies 22

drinks 54

drunken chicken 129

duck 118
  braised 145
  Cantonese roast 146
  crispy Sichuan 144
  Peking 142-3

dumplings
  potsticker 244-5
  steamed open 261

Dumplings, buns and pancakes 243-9

egg
  crab in egg custard 185

marbled tea eggs 258-9, *259*
  minced beef with scrambled 108
  noodles 29, *30*
  prawns stir-fried with 176
  tomato eggflower soup 62

egg white 26

eggplant *see* aubergines

Equipment 40-3

family meals, suggested menu 55

fan and *cai* 16, 218

fen rice noodles (sha he rice noodles) 30

fish
  balls with broccoli 166-7, *167*
  braised 161
  fried with garlic and spring onions 156
  fried with ginger 155
  in hot sauce 157
  in hot and sour sauce 158-9, *159*
  steamed with garlic, spring onions and
    ginger 160, *160*
  steamed salmon with black beans 164-5, *165*
  stir-fried with peas 162
  sweet and sour 163
  in wine sauce 168

Fish and shellfish 152-87

five-spice
  powder 26
  red-braised pigeons 148-9, *149*
  salt 38
  spareribs 95

flour 26, 243

flower peppers see Sichuan: peppercorns

fried rice 222-3
  with beef 229

fruit
  compote 266
  fresh 264

fryers, deep fat 42

frying 47-8

fungus *see* mushrooms

game birds 118

garlic 26
  chicken with cucumber 120
  fish fried with spring onions and 156
  fish steamed with spring onions, ginger
    and 160

stir-fried lamb with 109
stir-fried spinach with **v** 216
vinegar sauce 125
garnishes 50-1
ginger 27, *27, 129*
beef stir fried with 105
fish steamed with garlic, spring onions
and 160
fried fish with 156
sherry or rice wine 38
and spring onion sauce 39
steamed crab with ginger vinegar sauce 186
stir-fried ginger broccoli **v** 199
glutinous rice 31, 220
flour 26
goat 80
green beans *18*
deep-fried **v** 193, *193*
groundnut oil 30

ham 27
and bean sprout soup 68
and marrow soup 72
and pigeon steamed in soup 69
hoisin sauce 32
stir-fried broccoli with **v** 200
honey
glazed pork 93
syrup, peaches in 266
Hong Kong 8-9, 14-15, 250
hot pot, Mongolian *110,* 110-11
hot and sour
kidneys 114
sauce, fish in 158-9, *159*
soup 76

Ingredients 19-39

Jelly, almond with fresh oranges 264, *265*

kidney
and beancurd soup 70
hot and sour 114
stir-fried lambs' 113
stir-fried scallops with pigs' 172

lamb 82
Peking braised 112

stir-fried with garlic 109
stir-fried lambs' kidneys 113
leeks 27, *27*
chicken braised with 134
lemon chicken 127
lettuce leaves, rainbow beef in *100,* 100-1
lettuce with oyster sauce **v** 210
lily buds 28
lionhead pork meatball casserole 86
iver stir-fried in spicy sauce 115
long-grain rice 31, 220

maltose sugar 28
mangetout (snow peas) 28
stir-fried pepper beef with 106
stir-fried with water chestnuts **v** 210
mango
chicken 138-9, *139*
prawns 175
marbled tea eggs 258-9, *259*
marinating 46
cold marinated peanuts 253
marrow and ham soup 72
Meat 80-115
cuts of 82
dried and cured 82
Menus 52-5
and servings 54
suggested 55
milk, deep-fried **v** 217
mincing 45
Mongolian hot pot *110,* 110-11
monosodium glutamate 19
mushrooms 28-9, *211*
braised beancurd with **v** 194
and chicken soup 65
Chinese dried 28
Chinese wood ear fungus 29
spicy stir-fried **v** 211
straw 29
three mushroom braise **v** 213

noodles 29-30, 230
bean sauce 232-3, *233*
bean thread 30
beef noodle soup 234
chicken on crispy 236
chow mein 235

cold spicy 231
fen rice (sha he rice noodles) 30
fresh egg 231
hot bean thread noodles *240,* 240-1
Noodles 230-42
rice 30
Singapore 238-9
spicy Sichuan 242
stir-fried rice noodles with vegetables 237
wheat and egg 29, *30*

offal 82
see also kidney; liver stir-fried in spicy sauce
oils 30-1
okra, Chinese (silk squash) 35
oranges
almond jelly with fresh 264
stir-fried beef with 104
oyster sauce 33
beef in 103
braised cauliflower with **v** 201
lettuce with **v** 210
oysters
deep-fried 170-1, *171*
steamed fresh 169

pancakes, Chinese 248-9, *249*
paper-wrapped chicken 132-3, *133*
parsley, Chinese (coriander) 25
peaches in honey syrup 266
peanuts 31
cold marinated 253
peanut oil 30
spicy chicken with 122
pears, steamed 267
peas, fish stir-fried with 162
Peking
braised lamb 112
cabbage *see* Chinese leaves (Peking cabbage)
cold Peking pork 92
duck 142-3
prawns 180
peppers
cold, with black beans **v** 212
curried, chicken with 121
peppercorns, Sichuan 35
stuffed 262
pigeons

deep-fried 147

five-spice red-braised 148-9, *149*

and ham steamed in soup 69

poaching 46

pork 80, 82

with black bean sauce 83

braised with beancurd 94

braised pork belly 99

and cabbage soup 73

and chicken stock 60

chilli pork spareribs 96-7

cold Peking 92

crispy roast 90-1, *91*

five-spice spareribs 95

honey glazed 93

lionhead pork meatball casserole 86

steamed with spicy vegetables 98

stir-fried minced 84

stir-fried with spring onions 85

sweet and sour 88-9

twice-cooked 87

pots, sand or clay 43

potsticker dumplings 244-5

prawns 174

braised 177

mango 175

Peking 180

prawn crackers 253

sesame prawn toast 255

sizzling rice 181

stir-fried with egg 176

sweet and sour *178*, 178-9

quails, stir-fried *118*, *150*, 150-1

radish

Chinese white (mooli) 24, *25*

roses 50

rainbow

beef in lettuce leaves 100-1

rice 228

re-heating foods 49

red rice vinegar 37

rice 31

cake 224

chicken, sausage and rice casserole *226*, 226-7

congee 225

cookers 43

flour 26

fried 222-3

fried with beef 229

noodles 30

rainbow 228

sizzling rice prawns 181

steamed 221-2

stir-fried rice noodles with vegetables 237

washing 31, 220

wine 32, 38

Rice, noodles and doughs 218-42

roasted salt and pepper 39

roasting 49

roll cutting 45

salad, Chinese chicken 141

salmon, steamed with black beans 164-5, *165*

salt 32

five-spice 38

roasted salt and pepper 39

salt and pepper beancurd **v** 197

salted black beans *see* black beans

sand or clay pots 43

sauces and pastes 32-3

bean 232-3

black bean 83, 119, 184

chilli 22-3, 32, 38

chilli bean 32

cream 205

dipping sauces and mixtures 22-3, 38-9

garlic vinegar sauce 125

ginger and spring onion 39

ginger vinegar sauce 186

hoisin 32, 200

hot 157

hot and sour 158-9, *159*

oyster 33, 103, 201, 210

sesame paste 33

soy 33, 136, 206

sweet and sour 39

whole yellow bean 33

wine 168

sausages

chicken, sausage and rice casserole *226*, 226-7

Chinese 33, *33*

scallops

Sichuan-style 173

stir-fried with pigs' kidneys 172

scoring 46

'seaweed', crispy **v** 207

sesame

cold sesame broccoli **v** 200

oil 31

paste 33

prawn toast 255

seeds 34

shredded chicken with sesame seeds 128

shallots 34

shallow frying 48

Shaoxing rice wine 32, 54

sharks' fin 34

sherry 34

ginger 38

short-grain rice 31, 220

shredding 45

shrimps *35*

paste 35

Sichuan

crispy duck 144

peppercorns 35

preserved vegetables 35

Sichuan-style scallops 173

spicy noodles 242

silk squash (Chinese okra) 35

silken tofu 20

Singapore noodles 238-9

sizzling rice prawns 181

slicing 44-5

slow simmering and steeping 48

Snacks and sweets 250-70

snow peas *see* mangetout (snow peas)

Soups 56-79

asparagus and minced chicken soup 78-9, *79*

beancurd spinach soup 71

beef noodle 234

cabbage and pork soup 73

chicken and mushroom soup 65

chicken and spinach soup 61

chicken stock 58-9

Chinese cabbage soup 77

curried sweetcorn soup with chicken 64

ham and bean sprout soup 68

ham and marrow soup 72

ham and pigeon steamed in soup 69

hot and sour soup 76
kidney and beancurd soup 70
pork and chicken stock 60
sweetcorn with crabmeat *74*, 74-5
tomato eggflower soup 62
watercress soup 63
wonton soup 66-*7*, *67*
soy sauce 33
chicken 136
Chinese leaves in **v** 206
spareribs
chilli pork 96-7, *97*
five-spice 95
steamed with black beans 254
special dinner or banquet, suggested menu 55
spiced chinese leaves **v** 204
spinach 36
and beancurd soup 71
and chicken soup 61
with fermented beancurd **v** 216
stir-fried with garlic **v** 216
spring onion
brushes 50
fish fried with garlic and 156
fish steamed with garlic, ginger and 160
and ginger sauce 39
stir-fried pork with 85
spring rolls 256-7
skins 36
squid, stir-fried with vegetables 187
star anise 36
steamed
beef meatballs 107
buns 246-7
crab with ginger vinegar sauce 186
fish with garlic, spring onions and ginger 160
fresh oysters 169
open dumplings 261
pears 267
pork with spicy vegetables 98
rice 221-2
salmon with black beans 164-5, *165*
spareribs with black beans 254
steamers 42
steaming 48-9
steeped chicken 137
stir-frying 47
stock 56

chicken 58-9
pork and chicken 60
straw mushrooms 29
stuffed
cucumbers, fried 209
peppers 262
sugar 36, *36*
maltose 28
summer dinner parties, suggested menus 55
sweet and sour
cold Chinese leaves **v** *190*, 202-*3*
fish 163
pork 88, 89
prawns *178*, 178-9
sauce 39
sweetcorn
curried sweetcorn soup with chicken 64
soup with crabmeat *74*, 74-5

table setting 53
tea 54
Chinese black 36
marbled tea eggs 258-9, *259*
Techniques 44-51
thickening 46
toffee apples and bananas 268-9, *269*
tofu *see* beancurd
tomato
eggflower soup 62
roses 51
twice-cooked
chicken 135
pork 87
twice-cooking 49

vegetable oils 30-1
Vegetables 188-217
beancurd with **v** 195
cooking techniques 190
Sichuan preserved 35
steamed pork with spicy 98
stir-fried rice noodles with 237
stir-fried squid with 187
vegetarianism 16, 188
velveting 46
vinegar 37

walnuts

biscuits 270
caramel 263
walnut chicken 126
water chestnuts 37
stir-fried mangetout with **v** 210
watercress soup 63
white rice vinegar 37
whole yellow bean sauce 33
wine
fish in wine sauce 168
Shaoxing rice 32, 34, 54
winter dinner parties, suggested menus 55
wok 17, 40-1
accessories 41-2
steaming 48-9
wonton
fried 260
skins 37
soup 66-7

yard-long beans 24
yellow bean sauce 33
Yin Yang theory, food 15-16